AF505968

Studies in Russia and East Europe

This series includes books on general, political, historical, economic and cultural themes relating to Russia and East Europe written or edited by members of the School of Slavonic and East European Studies, University College London, or by authors working in association with the School.

Titles include:

Roger Bartlett and Karen Schönwälder (*editors*)
THE GERMAN LANDS AND EASTERN EUROPE

John Channon (*editor*)
POLITICS, SOCIETY AND STALINISM IN THE USSR

Stanislaw Eile
LITERATURE AND NATIONALISM IN PARTITIONED POLAND, 1795–1918

Rebecca Haynes
ROMANIAN POLICY TOWARDS GERMANY, 1936–40

Geoffrey Hosking and Robert Service (*editors*)
RUSSIAN NATIONALISM, PAST AND PRESENT

Lindsey Hughes (*editor*)
PETER THE GREAT AND THE WEST
New Perspectives

Krystyna Iglicka and Keith Sword (*editors*)
THE CHALLENGE OF EAST–WEST MIGRATION FOR POLAND

Andres Kasekamp
THE RADICAL RIGHT IN INTERWAR ESTONIA

Stephen Lovell
THE RUSSIAN READING REVOLUTION

Marja Nissinen
LATVIA'S TRANSITION TO A MARKET ECONOMY

Danuta Paszyn
THE SOVIET ATTITUDE TO POLITICAL AND SOCIAL CHANGE IN CENTRAL
AMERICA, 1979–90

Vesna Popovski
NATIONAL MINORITIES AND CITIZENSHIP RIGHTS IN LITHUANIA, 1988–93

Alan Smith
THE RETURN TO EUROPE
The Reintegration of Eastern Europe into the European Economy

Jeremy Smith
THE BOLSHEVIKS AND THE NATIONAL QUESTION, 1917–23

Jeanne Sutherland
SCHOOLING IN THE NEW RUSSIA

Studies in Russia and East Europe
Series Standing Order ISBN 0–333–71018-5
(*outside North America only*)

You can receive future titles in this series as they are published by placing a standing order.
Please contact your bookseller or, in case of difficulty, write to us at the address below with
your name and address, the title of the series and the ISBN quoted above.

Customer Services Department, Macmillan Distribution Ltd, Houndmills, Basingstoke,
Hampshire RG21 6XS, England

National Minorities and Citizenship Rights in Lithuania, 1988–93

Vesna Popovski
Lecturer in the Politics of Ethnicity
School of Slavonic and East European Studies
University College London

in association with
School of Slavonic and East European Studies,
University College London

First published 2000 by
PALGRAVE
Houndmills, Basingstoke, Hampshire RG21 6XS and
175 Fifth Avenue, New York, N.Y. 10010
Companies and representatives throughout the world

PALGRAVE is the new global academic imprint of
St. Martin's Press LLC Scholarly and Reference Division and
Palgrave Publishers Ltd (formerly Macmillan Press Ltd).

ISBN 0–333–79468–0

This book is printed on paper suitable for recycling and made from fully managed and sustained forest sources.

A catalogue record for this book is available from the British Library.

Library of Congress Cataloging-in-Publication Data
Popovski, Vesna.
    National minorities and citizenship rights in Lithuania : 1988–93 /
Vesna Popovski.
       p. cm. — (Studies in Russia and East Europe)
Includes bibliographical references and index.
ISBN 0–333–79468–0 (cloth)
    1. Lithuania—Social conditions. 2. Minorities—Lithuania. 3. Lithuania–
–Ethnic relations. 4. Minorities—Legal status, laws, etc.—Lithuania. 5.
Nationalism—Lithuania—History—20th century. I. Title. II. Series.
    HN539.9.A8 P66 2000
    305.8'0094793—dc21
                                                        00–033297

10   9   8   7   6   5   4   3   2   1
09 08 07 06 05 04 03 02 01 00

Printed and bound in Great Britain by
Antony Rowe Ltd, Chippenham, Wiltshire

To my late father and my mother

Contents

List of Maps and Figures   x

Acknowledgements   xi

Note on Transliteration   xii

Part I

1 **Conceptual and Methodological Issues Concerning
   Citizenship Rights of National Minorities**   3
   Introduction   3
   Why are citizenship rights important?   5
   Democracy and civil society   9
   Nationalism and national movements   12
   Methodological issues   15
   Structure of the book   18

2 **National Minorities Issues between the Two World Wars**   20
   Introduction   20
   Minority treaties and declarations   21
   Lithuanian legislation on national minorities and Jewish
     national autonomy   26
   Anti-Semitism   31
   The first Soviet occupation   35
   The Holocaust   37
   Conclusion   39

3 **Opposition Movements and the Birth of the Lithuanian
   National Movement**   43
   Introduction   43
   The birth of opposition movements   44
   The birth of *Sajudis* and the 'new' Communist Party   51
   Conclusion   58

4 **The Issue of Citizenship in Lithuania: Legislation and
   the Ways it was Perceived**   60
   Introduction   60
   Lithuanian legislation on citizenship   61

Lithuanian politicians and the way they perceived their
    minority legislation   70
Conclusion   73

Part II

5   **Introduction to Part II**   77

6   **Russian Responses**   81
    Introduction   81
    We label them Russians but who are they?   83
    Russian responses to citizenship issues   89
    Russian organisations   95
    Migration   104
    Conclusion   107

7   **Polish Demands**   109
    Introduction   109
    How much do the Poles differ among themselves?   111
    Polish perception of their citizenship rights   118
    The Union of Poles   122
    Polish passivity   125
    'Here everything is about history': the Vilnius question 127
    Territorial autonomy   129
    Conclusion   134

8   **Jewish Answers**   137
    Introduction   137
    Different Jews and the Holocaust   138
    The Holocaust in contemporary Lithuania – a formula
      of symmetry   145
    Rehabilitation of Lithuanians who took part in
      the Holocaust   148
    Jewish emigration   151
    Conclusion   152

9   **Postscript**   156
    Concluding remarks on events until 1993   156
    1993 to the present   159

    Appendixes   164
    Demographic data   164
    Education   176

Mass media 180
Questionnaire 182
Leaflet 182

Notes 183

Bibliography 235

Index 252

List of Maps and Figures

Maps
2.1   Lithuania in 1945   23
6.1   Russians in Lithuania, 1989   82
7.1   Poles in Lithuania, 1989   110
8.1   Jews in Lithuania, 1989   139

Figures
2.1   Population of Lithuania by nationality as percentage
       of total population, 1857–1923   21
3.1   Total population of Lithuania by nationality, 1959–89   44

Acknowledgements

Being able to write these acknowledgements makes me happy not only because I have finished this book but also because I clearly remember the process of writing and re-writing it. If it was not for all my friends who have supported me throughout all these years it would all have been much more difficult. Therefore my love and gratitude goes to (in alphabetical order) Pari Baumann, Marta Bruno, Tanya Burrows, Ian Eames, Anjali Mody, Clive Oppenheimer, Rathin Roy, Vicky Saporta, Asad Sayeed, Nik Sekhran, Dan Vadnjal, Edmund Waite, Liz Watson, Sallie Westwood, Neil Wilston and Rachel Wood. Furthermore, I would like to thank my colleagues at the School of Slavonic and East European Studies for allowing me to spend time at home and for their kind words of support. I would like in particular to mention Ian Agnew, Department of Geography, University of Cambridge for his cartographic artistry, as well as the staff of the Official Publications of the University Library in Cambridge.

I feel privileged that I was able to undertake research on Lithuania and I would like to thank my late PhD supervisor, Dr Graham Smith, for his help and for introducing me to the Baltic States. My special thanks go to people in Lithuania who generously gave their time and discussed the issues which I was interested in. They taught me a lot and without their contribution I would not be able to write this book. In the hours of doubt I always remembered them and felt that I had to carry on. I would also like to thank people who generously gave their time and commented on this book: Edmund Waite, Judy Batt, John Hiden, Sallie Westwood, Anjali Mody, Dan Vadnjal, Jonathan Steinberg, Barbara Metzger, Pari Baumann and Julia Waite.

I doubt that I would be able to cope with finishing this book if it was not for the love, support and help from Edmund. I would like to thank him for his thoughtful criticism and patience with my overinvolvement with the book. However, this book is dedicated to my mother and my late father without whose love and support it would have been difficult to carry on with my research. I would like to thank them, most of all, for teaching me to love people for who they are, not what they are.

London

Note on Transliteration

Works cited in this book are transliterated according to the *Cambridge University Library Reader's Handbook* except when I was given a different transliteration of first and second names as well as of work titles by people whom I interviewed.

Part I

1
Conceptual and Methodological Issues Concerning Citizenship Rights of National Minorities

Introduction

The last decade of this millennium will be remembered not only as a time when nationalism once again asserted itself on the stage of history but also for the issue of national minorities. In their quest for freedom and statehood, national majorities in the post-communist world have not always been ready to accept minority groups as equal partners and treat them fairly. Therefore, intrinsically, the study of nationalism has involved the question of the treatment of national minorities.

My research began with the hypothesis that citizenship rights of national minorities in Lithuania are the litmus test of Lithuania's orientation towards democracy. Therefore, it was important to examine the emergence of nationalism in Lithuania, specifically the Lithuanian national movement, known as *Sajudis*,[1] and its approach towards the citizenship rights of national minorities. The study concentrates on the period between 1988 and 1993 when the national majority and minorities began forming and debating citizenship rights.

The question of national minorities and citizenship rights is not ordinarily viewed as a problem with regard to Lithuania. This is primarily because Lithuania was able to adopt an inclusive policy towards citizenship, pointing out that its national communities were numerically smaller than in the other two Baltic states.[2] This inclusive principle is seen as complying with international laws dealing with the citizenship rights and national minorities. There was therefore an assumption by the international community that Lithuania had been 'doing better' than the other two Baltic states (Estonia and Latvia). This has meant that Lithuania has received little attention by scholars in comparison with her Baltic neighbours. My aim is to address this neglect, and test such assumptions, by exploring how the situation in Lithuania actually was. In particular, I felt that it was important not only to judge the Lithuanian situation according to the letter of the law but also to investigate how these laws were implemented and how both the majority and the minorities responded to them.

Despite its relative ethnic homogeneity, Lithuania contains sizeable minorities, Poles and Russians being the largest. In 1989 Poles and Russians made up 7 per cent and 9.4 per cent of the population respectively. As a result, in Lithuania there is not only the 'Russian question' but also the 'Polish one'. The former receives the attention of the world community, while the latter gets more attention in Lithuania itself. Furthermore, there is nowadays a very small Jewish community (0.3 per cent of the Lithuanian population), but before the Second World War the Jews were the largest national minority in Lithuania.[3]

I chose to study the 'children's years' because at that time different arguments were put on the agenda with an open enthusiasm and a wish to continue the struggle.[4] It was a period of trying to understand what had been happening. It was a period of surprise, trauma and delight, a period of (re)forming one's own opinion, learning to live with it and struggle for it. It was a lively and traumatic period in which every person was pushed to define him/herself and his/her place, within the newly independent state. Furthermore, it was a period in which the demand for sovereignty and the reclaiming of the right to continue its democratic past was made. This demand meant that issues like citizenship rights of national minorities were tackled in an atmosphere of national awakening and the rise of national feelings.

Lithuania has highlighted the fact that, until the Second World War, its treatment of national minorities compared favourably with those of Poland and the Ukraine. The newly independent Lithuania provided an inclusive legal framework for the citizenship rights of its minorities. Citizens of Soviet Lithuania were invited into citizenship of independent Lithuania, with a few exceptions as analysed in Chapter 4. However, *Sajudis* also highlighted the significance of language as an ethnic marker which was interpreted by national minorities as a barrier which could potentially exclude their members from participating in affairs of Lithuanian state and society.[5]

Both citizenship and nationalism are based on the concept of membership in a community. As such, citizenship and nationalism vary according to the inclusive or exclusive nature of the membership. In the newly independent Lithuania there emerged an increasing tension between citizenship and nationalism. Whereas citizenship was defined in inclusive terms, nationalism became increasingly exclusive. *Sajudis* based its identity on the struggle for independence and on a claim of restoring the 'democratic tradition of the inter-war period'. Its struggle for an independent democratic Lithuania was shaped by the affirmation of Lithuanian national identity. This was interpreted by some Lithuanians, Russians, Poles and Jews not only as against developing their own national identities but also as exclusion from the possibility of exercising citizenship rights which they were given according to the letter of the law. The analysis will be focused on the comprehension of citizenship rights in terms of how citizenship rights were translated into practice and were perceived by its citizens and residents. In other words, citizenship should not only be seen in relation to the state but also at the local level which gives it depth and vitality.[6] An analysis of citizenship rights approached within a democratic framework does not consist only of legal mechanisms but also of a political culture which respects (if not celebrates) diversity between *us* and *them.*

After the Second World War it was argued by the international community, primarily the United Nations, that the rights given to individuals were a sufficient guarantee, so collective rights did not need to be developed. This point has been questioned after 1989 by the same international community, starting especially in relation to Bosnia and Herzegovina. Two approaches have been developed by those who have undertaken research on collective rights. First, collective rights promote disunity as opposed to the common good for all citizens. Second, it is important to withdraw from the larger society to be able to integrate within it. The issue of collective rights was raised in Lithuania especially by the Polish community and ranged from a demand for cultural autonomy to a demand for political autonomy.

Why are citizenship rights important?

Citizenship has been a struggle from below. According to Sidney Tarrow, historically 'Citizenship emerged through a rough dialectic between movements – actual and feared – and the national state.'[7] Our present experience teaches us that this is still very much applicable. Citizenship is not a static notion, it is a relationship between individuals, social groups, civil society and the state. It can also be seen as an attempt to change the existing power relations. Therefore, it should be interpreted as an important category which provides seeds for a (new type of) democracy. National movements, nowadays, also subscribe to democracy by often couching citizenship in national terms. But could citizenship be comfortable wearing ethnic clothes?

During the communist period citizenship rights existed only as social rights, the right to education, health care and work. Political and civil rights did not exist because the nature of the communist system did not make provisions for them. Political rights could not be exercised in a one-party system because people did not have the possibility to choose between different political parties, but were only able to vote for an approved list. As the only official ideology, communism did not leave sufficient scope for the expression of individual opinion, personal autonomy and freedom of speech. The system tried, often sucessfully, to base its legitimacy in defining and delivering social rights.[8]

Although the primary interest of this book is citizenship rights, it is important to point out that an analysis of citizenship does not only include rights.[9] Social scientists have been mostly concerned with civil, political and social rights and entitlements as well as with duties and obligations. This needs to be broadened to include the involvement of individuals and groups in addressing as well as structuring the citizenship agenda. This issue is usually understood as active and passive citizenship. It is also important to look at citizenship from the perspective of institutions and the way they function. Citizenship is a dynamic concept which depends on social change and its consequences on different levels of socio-political context. Furthemore, it clearly points out that there is a difference between the letter of the law and the reality of everyday life. Although it is important to analyse and become familiar with the letter of the law, it is even more important to analyse how the letter of the law is implemented and how it affects different social groups, such as national minorities.

Citizenship rights are enjoyed only if people/members are able to benefit from them comprehensively. The argument that highlights that citizenship rights are enjoyed only if people/members are able to benefit from them comprehensively is important for an analysis of citizenship not only as individual rights but also as collective rights. The issue is whether the members of a community should be defined purely in terms of individuals or whether they should also be recognised as members of a group. Furthermore, collective rights as the only way to protect some ethnic groups has recently been put on the agenda, especially in the former Yugoslavia. This issue has great relevance to the situation of the Poles, who are mostly concentrated in the south-east of Lithuania, and who demanded various forms of collective rights.

Citizenship rights raise the issue of the treatment of different minority groups, among them national minorities. Is it enough to guarantee equal rights to an individual, or is it also important to guarantee additional rights to groups?

Iris Marion Young is concerned with disadvantaged groups (primarily women and black Americans) and their lack of capacity to assert their rights. She raises the question of how one can improve the means of expressing their rights. The answer is through establishing procedures to ensure additional representation of all disadvantaged groups. Full participation of different groups is only possible through recognising rights for these different groups.[10] 'Attending to group-specific needs and providing for group representation both promotes … social equality and provides recognition that undermines cultural imperialism.'[11]

Will Kymlicka argues that collective rights should be understood as the right to protect ethnic groups from the impact of the economic and political decisions of larger societies. This should be done as an attempt to promote fairness between majority and minority/ies because smaller groups are more vulnerable. Collective rights have three different forms: 'self-government rights' which means granting some form of political autonomy to the ethnic group, 'polyethnic rights' understood as legal protection and financial support for cultural and educational purposes, and 'special representation rights' which guarantee a certain number of seats to ethnic groups.[12]

Minorities are often more vulnerable and, therefore, are prone to face unfair disadvantage more frequently. Consequently, Kymlicka argues it is not sufficient to ensure that each single individual has a right to challenge any disadvantage, but the state has to recognise that it has a particular bias towards the majority culture. The state therefore has a duty to protect minority cultures, as well as the majority.

National minorities, together with Lithuanians, have been learning the importance of exercising their rights as individuals. In the early 1990s they started to realise that individual rights alone were not sufficient; it was also necessary to acquire collective rights.[13]

In the case of Lithuania, as analysed in Chapter 7, a group of Poles put forward the claim for territorial autonomy which was opposed not only by Lithuanians but also by other national minorities, including other sectors of the Polish community. Lithuanians claimed that Poles were already given sufficient rights in the form of cultural autonomy that acknowledged the right of each individual belonging to national minorities to be educated in their own language and provided state support for their educational, cultural and religious organisations.[14] Those Poles who opposed territorial autonomy perceived it in terms of siding with the communists and, therefore, with the USSR. Their battle was lost on ideological grounds. However, the Lithuanian national movement did not want to concede any political control over Lithuanian territory, especially in light of the Polish occupation of the Vilnius region between the two World Wars. (The issue of the Polish occupation of the Vilnius region will be discussed in Chapter 2.) The major problem with this type of collective right is that it does not build bridges between the communities.[15] It excludes a national minority from the larger community, and therefore does not allow for the possibility of belonging to different communities. It does not promote the co-existence of differences. However, one has to bear in mind that the rejection of self-government rights might possibly lead towards a movement for secession.

According to the International Covenant of Civil and Political Rights, 'polyethnic rights' are not defined as collective rights because they can be achieved through respect for individual rights.[16] Following this line of argument, the Lithuanian Constitution guarantees national minorities the right to education in their own language, to organise their cultural institutions and to follow their own religion. The state claims that it is also ready to support all these different institutions through its funds for culture and education. Some members of the national minorities claimed that a problem lay in the fact that the state supported the majority culture, and they therefore wanted a state guarantee that they would have the opportunity to maintain their culture. In other words, they did not want state support to depend on such factors as the number of people attending schools in a native language. They wanted their differences to be acknowledged through differential treatment.[17] Therefore, they saw 'polyethnic rights' as a collective right which could not be fulfilled through individual rights.

In Lithuania two issues were raised when 'special representation rights' were discussed. First, there was a proposal to define borders of electoral units along ethnic lines. Second, some members of the Polish community argued that it was important not to introduce a threshold for any political party that specifically represented Poles in the Parliament.[18] In relation to the first issue, Lani Guinier points out, analysing representation rights of black Americans, that these rights are not a guarantee that the needs of black Americans will be addressed in policy decisions because their representatives could be easily out-voted at the state level.[19]

Collective rights should be seen as a step towards a more tolerant society which would no longer need this type of rights. Therefore, from the point of view of political pragmatism, there is a rationale for them to be introduced. However, they are not compatible with the political aim of national movements and (newly-)independent states which is that of the political control of the whole territory.

As Chantal Mouffe pointed out, we have to view collective rights as a 'new type of articulation between the universal and particular'.[20] It is important to bear in mind that differences need to be acknowledged, but not in the same way as postmodernists do when they argue that 'pluralism understood as the valorisation of all differences should be total'.[21] Where should one draw the line? From the point of view of organising life in a community, acknowledging all the differences can lead towards a void where everything goes and where the community ceases to function effectively. A much worse scenario is a struggle between different groups in the name of difference. Here, it is important to stress that difference does not mean that there are no shared attributes. It is precisely this point that enables David Harvey to claim that similarities are important, on the one hand, in defining differences and, on the other, as a basis for political alliances and solidarity.[22]

Democracy and civil society

In the contemporary period, democracy became 'more or less universally popular'.[23] I would argue that democracy in the contemporary period cannot be simply seen in terms of government by means of party competition, majority rule and the rule of law, as is usually the case, especially in Eastern Europe. John Keane rightly points out that a new concept of democracy is not simply representative democracy, but it represents a striving to be open-minded, uncompromisingly pluralist, cosmopolitan and historically informed. For Keane, a democracy is 'A pluralistic system of power wherein decisions of concern to collectivities of various sizes within civil society and the state, are made directly or indirectly by all their members'.[24] Alberto Melucci points out that 'It would be illusory to think that democracy consists merely in the competition for access to governmental resources. Democracy in complex societies requires conditions which enable individuals and social groups to affirm themselves and to be recognised for what they are or wish to be.'[25]

Our understanding of citizenship as a dynamic principle highlights the importance of seeing it as a place of struggle for rights. That struggle takes place not only in state institutions but also involves non-state institutions. Civil society is related to democracy and it is a place of pluralism, a place which allows different types of non-state activities to blossom. Furthermore, civil society has to evaluate the transparency and accountability of the state, the market and their institutions. Finally, the functioning of a civil society should not prevent the state from fulfilling its role.[26] In the case of Lithuania, national minorities were guaranteed rights as individuals. As argued in the second part of this book, they were not satisfied with some of their rights. Therefore, they started to form different types of organisations to be able to challenge the Lithuanian legislation. They needed an independent space to learn to formulate their needs and the state had to learn to guarantee that space. In the case of Lithuania, the power relations influenced Lithuanian civil society and as a result the national agenda dominated this space.

The understanding of the state in Eastern European societies can be best described by a logic based on George Konrad's analysis of the totalitarian state; to live with the totalitarian state was possible only if one ignored it. In Eastern Europe the very idea of civil society meant exclusion from the state influence. This type of 'relationship' based on animosity enables civil society to develop parallel institutions, such as cultural, environmental and religious movements.[27] Zbigniew Rau goes a step further and claims that this approach to civil society enabled most of the 'Easterners' to argue that civil society was founded upon national consciousness.[28] They saw nationalism as encouraging the existence of all different types of social movements ranging from environmentalist to homosexuals, from human rights activists to rock-music fans.

Two issues are of interest to us. One is connected with the statement that civil society was founded upon national consciousness and the other discusses democracy as the only viable solution for Eastern Europe. Civil society did not exist in the former Soviet Union because, as an intrinsic aspect of the system, the state could not guarantee an independent and public space.[29] However, private space was of major importance in opposing the 'real-existing socialism'. Opposition groups challenged the existing order but their opinions were silenced by the government. However, the public was aware of their existence, not least because of government reports about 'enemies within our own people'. Even if we cannot acknowledge the existence of civil society we still have to take into account that elements for its existence were there; people who were prepared to challenge the state and society in which they lived.

Glasnost (a policy introduced from above) entailed the opportunity to go a step further and allow for the possibility of forming a space in which social movements would be able to exist. However, it has to be recognised that *glasnost* did not financially support social movements. Furthermore, the Communist Party supported socialist views which did not undermine the existence of communism. Therefore, it created conditions for a possibility of 'movement surrogacy'.[30] In Lithuania, for example, the anti-nuclear movement worded its opposition to the nuclear power station Ignalina, in ecological terms as well as in terms of nationhood. Environmental activists called the Lithuanian population to protect Lithuanian soil and nature which symbolise the Lithuanian nation. 'Though the *Zemyna* club continued to exist and participate in anti-nuclear activities, most of its active members shifted their attention to *Sajudis*, and it was *Sajudis* that organised future mass actions against the Ignalina station.'[31] This should not be interpreted in terms of there being a lack of genuine interest in the environment. As already stated, the environment was seen in natural terms as well as in national terms. Ideas around nationhood and statehood infused movements which were given, though not guaranteed, a space to challenge the state on non-political issues. *Glasnost* therefore strengthened the agenda of civil society but, at the same time, nationalised it. As a result civil society which, in theory, should be open to each individual was shaped by anti-Soviet and Lithuanian national ideologies. Nijole Lomaniene argues that social reality turned into a highly ritualised space.[32]

The second issue involves statehood understood as a demand for a democratic as well as independent state. Within Lithuanian society, there was considerable interest in events in Western Europe and the USA whose governments celebrated their own liberal democracies and proclaimed the 'end of history'. In the West there has been a constant dialogue between political scientists who defend and those who oppose liberal democracy. Even those who oppose this system argue that 'We must admit, following Bobbio, that only a liberal state can guarantee the basic rights without which the democratic game cannot take place. We should also agree with Bobbio that the struggle for democracy is the struggle against autocratic power in all forms.'[33] The major problem with the liberal tradition is that it sees the citizen as an abstract individual and no account is taken of sex, race, ethnicity, etc.

I see democracy as a political system which acknowledges the following principles: plurality, difference and heterogeneity. If the state is based upon these principles this means that it is ready to acknowledge differences in everyday life, in our case differences among national minorities and the majority, as well as differences within the majority and national minorities. This also means that the state is able to guarantee an independent space in which civil society can function.

This space is important because it allows for collective action to be developed, for different political projects to be put on the agenda and debated openly, according to democratic rules. Democracy is the only political system which is able to face up to conflicts. Civil society is also important because of its influence on the state and its institutions as well as on the market and its institutions. Influence is the critical tool of civil society. Civil society does not have any formal power, although its influence can change power relations. Formal power lies mostly with the state. Civil society should also be seen as a mechanism outside the official channels, which can evaluate the transparency and accountability of state and market institutions. I would agree with Jean Cohen, that it is important to highlight that civil society should be seen not only in relation to the state but also to the economy.[34] The western neo-liberal system clearly pointed out that the free-market economy can represent a danger to solidarity, social justice and autonomy. That model, in its different variations, was implemented in Eastern Europe and also in Lithuania. In Lithuania it definitely did not encourage solidarity, social justice and autonomy. In conjunction with nationalism, sponsored by the state, it fuelled hatred, especially against Russians. I would often hear the following sentence, 'Whilst we fought for independence, Russians withdrew into the economic sphere and now run our economy.' Needless to say there was no solidarity with Russian workers when the large-scale factories were closed down and Russians were made redundant.

Therefore, it is important to analyse how a national movement relates to proposals for equal citizenship, political democratisation, social justice, respect towards different types of groups, including national minorities.

Nationalism and national movements

Different theories of nationalism share an understanding of the importance of self-governance or independence. In Eastern Europe this claim for independence is based upon understanding that each single nation shares: '(i) a "memory" of some common past, treated as a "destiny" of the group – or at least of its core constituents; (ii) a density of linguistic or cultural ties enabling a higher degree of social communication within the group beyond it; (iii) a conception of equality of all members of the group organised as a civil society'.[35] The issues of memory, language and equality have been vital issues in Eastern Europe. Memory is oriented towards the past but its main purpose is to enter into the present and future. Language (of the majority nation within a state) is a vital ethnic marker which distinguishes *us* from *them*. Equality is a civic marker and the result of the commitment to democracy. However, this commitment (like the other two issues) can have boundaries. As a result one's remembering is selective and chooses only certain events from the past or certain interpretations of these events. Language is often defined in relation to the language of the *other* or *others*. Equality relates to respecting an individual as a member of a community but the community could be defined in ethnic terms. Even when it is legally defined in civic terms the lack of democratic political culture can hinder the implementation of the letter of the law.

Alan Touraine argues that national movements are characterised by the feature of 'setting an alternative agenda of historical action'.[36] Their aim is to reorganise the state structure and gain control over a certain territory to be able to fulfil their agenda. For a national movement to be successful, the following processes should take place: a crisis of legitimacy linked to social, moral and cultural strains, vertical social mobility among a non-dominant ethnic group, a high level of social communication including literacy, schooling and market relations and nationally relevant conflict of interests.[37]

I understand national movements as a challenge to the existing order, even when they do not define themselves in political terms of secession and independence. To understand national movements, organisational structures have to be analysed – the leadership and the core members, the larger segment of sympathisers, the movement-produced organisations, and the organisations and institutions externally supporting the movement and/or pursuing related goals.[38] It could be argued that *Sajudis* was an umbrella organisation which was founded by the Lithuanian intelligentsia. It attracted people and movements with different agendas who were ready to give up their immediate concerns in the struggle for Lithuanian independence. Therefore, for the purposes of our analysis, I would argue that there are two important issues. First, the relationship of ethnic groups towards the state and, second, their effort to reorganise that state. Ethnic groups see themselves as being culturally distinct from other groups within the same state. They also argue that their distinctiveness is not acknowledged. Therefore, they demand that the state needs to be reorganised along the lines of cultural autonomy which could lead towards federation, confederation and even towards secession, in the case where ethnic groups live in a compact territory. In the case of Lithuania, *Sajudis* claimed that

Lithuanian identity was suppressed during the Soviet era. This led them to demand sovereignty for Lithuania in 1988 and was responsible for the *Sajudis'* willingness to let the Lithuanian Freedom League challenge the Soviet Lithuania with a demand for independence. The movement looked for the support of the national minorities of Lithuania, and was indeed given support by some members of these communities. In Eastern Europe the aim of the majority of nationalist movements was a nation-state. Nation-state is not only a territorial organisation (with defined and fixed boundaries) but it is also a membership organisation.[39] National movements define this membership in ethnic or civic terms.

As is analysed in Chapters 3 and 4, citizens of the Soviet Socialist Republic of Lithuania were invited 'onto the stage of history' by the Lithuanian national movement, *Sajudis*, but the movement turned nationalistic after its Second Congress in April 1990, and as a result the praxis of citizenship was not encouraged. Individuals saw themselves or were forced to see themselves as Lithuanian, Polish, Russian, etc. Citizenship is, in the last instance, a result of a political decision and that decision in Lithuania was based on the 'zero-option' or on the inclusive principle. Citizens of Lithuania were guaranteed equal rights but citizenship is not only, as argued above, about rights. While important to begin with, citizenship is a dynamic principle that should entail learning to live with differences and provide for them. Citizenship needs institutional support which teaches tolerance towards different cultures. This institutional support did not always exist in Lithuania.[40]

The study of national movements and citizenship rights is very important because of their impact on the evolution of both state and society in Eastern Europe. Citizenship became the most important political issue with the re-establishment of state independence. Citizenship is based on the individual but that individual is a member of different communities, and it is sometimes only as a member of the community that the individual is able to claim and exercise his/her rights. It is seen as an aim which could be best reached through collective action, action in which all members of society, whatever their nationality, have to take part. Citizenship is politically determined because the state decides who may or may not be a citizen. However, this decision does not always have a democratic base and excludes people according to their race, ethnicity, religion, etc. I am primarily interested in this tension between citizenship as an inclusive principle and nationalism as an exclusive one. Citizenship needs democratic institutions in order to function effectively. Nationalism does not need to deny it.

Methodological issues

My methodology was very much coloured by the acknowledgement of the importance of the intelligentsia in the forging of national consciousness. Miroslav Hroch points out that the intelligentsia played a vital role in the nineteenth century during the period of national awakening, an important part of which was the struggle against Polonisation and Russification. After the Second World War, the Lithuanian intelligentsia highlighted the importance of belonging to a national community as a means of combating the policies of Russification and Sovietisation. Hroch points out that in the contemporary period, the Baltic region is once again a place where 'a local intelligentsia confronts a nomenclature elite of another ethnic origin, which refuses to learn the local language'.[41] As regards the national minorities, the Poles lost their intelligentsia after the Second World War through emigration and the Jews through the Holocaust. The majority of Russians came to Lithuania after the Second World War through the policies of industrialisation. They were encouraged by the State to migrate, in keeping with the ideal of the merging (*sliianie*) of Soviet nations. The events of 1988 came as a surprise to the majority of Russians and forced them to consider who they were. The intelligentsia of all three minorities were engaged in a process of defining what it meant to be a Russian, a Pole and a Jew. Furthermore, my interviews tended to focus on the intelligentsia in light of their significance in contributing to the debates over minority rights. Their answers were complex and varied in accordance to their perception of the present situation and future prospects for their community in Lithuania.

I first visited Lithuania in October 1992 and then again in May 1993. I was, therefore, able to interview some respondents twice and also had a chance to meet new respondents. I was in Vilnius in October 1992 when the Lithuanian Democratic Labour Party (*Lietuvos democratine darbo partija*, LDDP) won the elections. The mass media and politicians claimed that national minorities voted for the LDDP. According to my interviews, national minorities were divided on the issue of whether the LDDP would engage in minority issues. Therefore, when I returned in May 1993 it was important to discuss policies which the new government had introduced towards national minorities. It proved valuable interviewing some people twice because they were able to analyse their experience of how the new government had dealt with minority issues.[42]

As already pointed out, the intelligentsia has played a major role in forging national identity in Central and Eastern Europe. This factor had a vital influence on my decision to focus on the intelligentsia in my sample.[43] In targeting one strata in the population, I therefore opted for a non-probability sample. 'The statistical accuracy of probability sampling is less important than the criterion of "fit for purpose".'[44] Among these samples I used purposive and snowball samplings. The first type of sample, the purposive sample, is used in a situation where a selection of people who are to be interviewed is made according to a known characteristic. In my case it enabled me to target specific groups who were policy-makers and policy-takers. Because I went to Lithuania for the first time in October 1992 and had minimal pre-existing contacts, I also had to rely on the snowball method as a means of meeting people to interview them. Both these methods, purposive and snowball, helped me to meet more of the people who belonged to the intelligentsia. I wanted primarily to interview people who influenced and shaped policies on national minorities, which involved interviewing a wide range of people; from actors and poets to politicians both in government and opposition. The main problem with a purposive sample is that it targets a very specific group whose views may not be representative. This sample is usually defended with the 'fit for purpose' argument. The main problem with the snowball sample is that it may lead a researcher to collect data which belong to a particular perspective.[45] I tried to counteract this by interviewing people who belonged to different political parties, cultural and religious groups and also those not affiliated to any party or group.

In October 1992 I visited the Department of National Minorities in Vilnius where I was given the names of different organisations formed by national minorities. I was immediately warned that there was no up-to-date address book of all organisations because they were formed, and sometimes disappeared, very quickly. I visited the majority of them and talked to those members who were willing either to express their opinion or discuss issues concerning their ethnic group. I tried especially to meet members of national minorities through their various organisations such as, for example, at an exhibition at the Russian Cultural Centre or during the interval of the performance of *Majstor i Margarita* in the Russian Theatre.

I also interviewed all the MPs belonging to minority groups except for one, Emanuelis Zingeris,[46] as well as politicians who were engaged in minority issues, and presidents or members of different committees in the period 1992 to 1996. Furthermore, I interviewed two people who were in charge of the Parliamentary Committee which dealt with the issue of Polish autonomy in the period 1990–2. Being in the Parliament in the first days after the October 1992 elections, I talked to but did not always interview many MPs to get their views on national minorities issues. Members of different political parties proved a valuable source of information and opinion not only about national minorities, but also about the history of the opposition movement in Lithuania as well as of *Sajudis*. It was also important to interview people who played a vital role in the period 1988 to 1990 but who had withdrawn from the public scene as for example the former members of *Sajudis*. They were of both Russian and Lithuanian origins. The majority of them did not withdraw exclusively because of the treatment of national minorities.

At the University of Vilnius I met social scientists, lawyers, historians who were not only a valuable source of information but also found time to discuss issues which were on my agenda. I was also invited to three conferences, two on the Russians and one on the Poles. There I met social scientists and historians from Belarus, Germany, Poland, Scandinavia and the three Baltic states who had been engaged in issues concerning national movements in the Baltic region as well as in the states of the former Soviet Union.

Although I targeted the intelligentsia (non-Lithuanians and Lithuanians) I was ready to talk to anyone who was prepared to talk to me. I wanted to hear as many different opinions as possible. They were not always different but they were important in getting to know the atmosphere in which national minorities lived, which issues they raised and those they did not and why. The interviews varied in length from one hour to six hours. They also took place in different places, from offices to restaurants or cafes, kitchens and park benches.[47] All interviews were recorded with permission of the interviewees, who knew my research agenda.

My interviews were organised around a semi-structured questionnaire.[48] My questions were purposely quite generally structured so I could respond to issues raised by my respondents. 'Qualitative information about the topic can then be recorded by the interviewer who can seek both *clarification* and *elaboration* on the answers given. This enables the interviewer to have more latitude to *probe* beyond the answers and thus enter into a dialogue with the interviewer.'[49] The main disadvantage of this type of interview is possible difficulties with standardisation and comparability. However, I would argue that this disadvantage does not apply to this field-work because clarification, elaboration and discussion helped me to gather information, to formulate different points of view as well as 'to check them and re-check them against each other'.[50] Furthermore, I was able to compare these data with research material gathered by other social scientists.[51]

I have learned a lot from my respondents and the information they gave me shaped interviews with other respondents. Therefore, I sometimes produced a situation in which two individuals, who were not always willing to talk to each other, 'communicated' quite happily or angrily. I followed newspapers in Russian, Polish, Lithuanian and English as well as radio and television programmes in Russian and Lithuanian. Finally, I kept a diary. It proved to be of enormous importance once I was writing the book. It helped me to recall certain events and conversations as well as my first impressions about them. It enabled me to relive my days in Lithuania.

Structure of the book

This book is divided in two parts. The first part (Chapters 1–4) addresses the historical background to the issue of national minorities and their rights in the independent Lithuania between the two World Wars. It continues with an analysis of the rise of Lithuanian nationalism during the Soviet era and the Lithuanian national movement, *Sajudis*. It finishes with an analysis of the Lithuanian legislation concerning national minorities. The second part (Chapters 5–9) of the book is an analysis of the case study which took place in autumn and winter 1992 and spring and summer 1993.

In Chapter 1, I raise theoretical questions in relation to the more general literature, concerning citizenship rights, nationalism and national minorities. This enables me to explore more generally the tension between citizenship as an inclusive principle and nationalism as an exclusive principle, and its consequences for national minorities. It argues that democracy means learning to live with plurality, heterogeneity and difference.

Chapter 2 addresses the issues regarding the changing position of national minorities in Lithuania between the two World Wars (1918–40). The chapter concentrates, first, on the legacy of the Peace Conference (1919–20), primarily with regard to minority treaties. Then I analyse the Jews as the largest national minority in the political, social and economic context of Lithuania. The Jews are analysed as an example of the treatment of Lithuanian national minorities in this period. This is an important issue because inter-war Lithuania is viewed by contemporary Lithuanians as providing a fund of democratic traditions from which the contemporary state can draw.

Chapter 3 analyses the rise of the Lithuanian contemporary dissident and national movements. The chapter begins with an analysis of dissent in the Soviet period, especially during the leadership of Khrushchev and Brezhnev. In the second part, the focus moves to the rise of *Sajudis* and the split within the Communist Party of the Soviet Socialist Republic of Lithuania. This chapter briefly introduces the differences within respective national minorities in relation to the agenda put forward by the Lithuanian national movement.

Chapter 4 examines Lithuania's laws concerning national minorities between 1989 and 1993. It explores the approaches of national minorities to the legislation and highlights the issues which the national minorities considered to be vital for the evolution of democracy. A concluding section also considers the opinions of Lithuanian politicians towards this legislation.

Chapter 5 is an introduction to the second part of the book which highlights how citizenship issues have been intervowen with a search for national identity.

Chapters 6 to 8 focus on national minorities in the post-1990 state, the way they perceived the new state and their rights, and also how their rights compared to the late 1980s. First, the situation of Russians is explored taking account of their paradoxical position as being the largest nationality in the Soviet Union, and now a minority in independent Lithuania. Their responses towards issues raised by the Lithuanian national movement are further analysed. Russians, at the beginning of the 1980s, were oriented towards their own community. Only a minority of them tried to promote Russian cultural organisations within the Lithuanian context. In comparison with the Poles, the majority of Russians had not been keen to set up a Russian political party. The Poles as an indigenous population in the South-East, started immediately after independence to put demands to the new Lithuanian Parliament. They had been especially concerned with issues concerning land reform and local government in the South-East. For the Jews the Holocaust was the most important issue, as already pointed out, and proved to be vital in their decision to stay or leave Lithuania.

A postscript summarises and analyses my research findings, and briefly explores developments concerning national minorities since August 1993.

2
National Minorities Issues between the Two World Wars

Introduction

The focus on the inter-war period is important for two reasons. First, the newly independent Lithuania claims to be continuing the democratic tradition from the inter-war period. We need to evaluate this alleged democratic tradition in terms of its approach towards national minorities. Second, we need to understand the important role which not only democratic tradition but also national rhetoric had in influencing what happened in Lithuania in the inter-war period. These objectives are particularly important because the inter-war period has great emotional significance in contemporary Lithuania and plays a crucial part in national history. Memory of this period does not only entail perceiving it as a golden age but also has its territorial dimension of where the boundaries of a Lithuanian state are.

In this chapter it is argued that the League of Nations and the Minority Declaration played an important role in the political life of Lithuania in this period. The acknowledgement of Lithuanian independence was tied up with the Minority Declaration of the League of Nations. Although the Lithuanian Jewish community, who at that time were the largest minority in Lithuania, established national autonomy (or put into practice 'self-governing rights'), according to the Provisional Constitution from 1918, the League of Nations decided that the Provisional Constitution was not a sufficient guarantee that minority rights would be respected, so it asked Lithuania to sign the Minority Declaration. Lithuania agreed to implement the Minority Declaration in the hope that it would help her to regain the Vilnius region. The 1922 Constitution, the first Lithuanian constitution, did not address national autonomy. After the seizure of Klaipeda the government

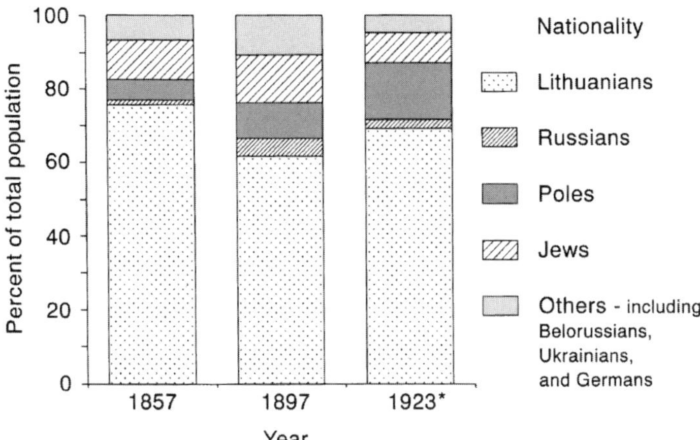

Source: *Lietuvos respublikos gyventoju demografine staistika.*
Vilnius: Tautybiu departamentas prie Lietuvos respublikos vyriausybes, 1992, p.6.
* Lithuanians for 1923, this data includes the data for Klaipeda region from 1925
and Vilnius region from 1931.

Figure 2.1   Population of Lithuania by nationality as percentage of total population, 1857–1923

started to abolish laws connected with the Jewish community, who were the largest minority in independent Lithuania (see Figure 2.1).[1] Furthermore, national rhetoric, together with the rise of the Lithuanian middle class, acquired nationalistic overtones which entailed discrimination against national minorities.[2] This rhetoric, together with the rise of fascism, proved to be of crucial importance in the development of anti-Semitism. This chapter finishes with an analysis of the 'first Soviet occupation' (1940–1) and the Holocaust. The memory of the Holocaust is the most important marker for the Lithuanian Jewish community and the most contentious issue between the community and the Lithuanian state.

Minority treaties and declarations[3]

The birth of national movements in the nineteenth century, through such processes as national awakening, liberation and consolidation threatened the existing empires. The basis of this threat had a democratic background. It was based upon the rights of peoples, primarily the right of self-determination. Before the USA entered the First World

War, Woodrow Wilson argued that 'Every people has the right to choose the sovereignty under which they shall live'. With the collapse of empires during the First World War and following the discussions around the Peace Treaties, self-determination was no longer understood in terms of the free will to decide in which state to live but was instead identified with nationality.

One important feature of this process was that boundaries were drawn without fully acknowledging that state and ethnic boundaries do not necessarily coincide. 'The result was that those peoples to whom states were not conceded, no matter whether they were official minorities or nationalities, considered the Treaties an arbitrary game which handed out rule to some and servitude to others.'[4] The main rationale behind these treaties was that minorities should be treated as groups rather than as individuals and, consequently, they were given collective rights.

The independence of Lithuania was won by the people of Lithuania, but her borders with both Poland and Germany were decided by the Allied and Associated Powers, in both cases by force. The Supreme Council of the League of Nations first laid down a border with Poland (on 8 December 1919) which followed ethnographic lines as closely as possible, the so-called Curzon line. However, this was later revised when Polish forces, under the leadership of General Zeligowski, seized disputed territory, the centre of which was Vilnius, on 9 October 1920 (see Map 2.1). The League came to accept this *coup de main* and recognised Polish possession of the territory. With regard to the German–Lithuanian frontier, the Peace Conference (1919–20) forced Germany to renounce her sovereignty over a strip on the right bank of the Niemen, including the port of Memel-Klaipeda (see Map 2.1). The motivation for this decision was mainly economic, as Lithuania would have found it difficult to exist without this port. It was also argued that although the town was in part German, the majority of the district's population was 'Lithuanian in origin and in speech', a statement which Germany contested in her reply. The Powers administered the port and the district themselves for some time. On 10 January 1923 Lithuania seized Memel by a *coup de main* and the Powers eventually assigned the district to Lithuanian sovereignty, but as an autonomous area with a statute guaranteed by the Principal Allied and Associated Powers.[5] The border with Latvia was settled by the British arbitrators.

In respect of the border with the Soviet Union, in December 1918 the Soviet Union had proclaimed the Lithuanian Soviet Socialist Republic with hardly any support in Lithuania itself. Fighting continued

Map 2.1   Lithuania in 1945

throughout 1919 and the first part of 1920. On 12 July 1920 the Soviet regime recognised the independence of Lithuania and on the same day the Treaty of Moscow was signed which settled the Lithuanian–Soviet border.

During the First World War the issue of national minorities was over-shadowed by the question of national self-determination. At the time there was a bitter discussion taking place about a draft of the Covenant of the League of Nations. In the original draft there was no mention whatsoever of national minorities. Mainly under the pressure of the American Jewish lobby, a Japanese proposal was accepted which argued for 'Equal and just treatment in every respect, making no distinction, either in law or fact, on account of their nationality'.[6]

As P. de Azcarate argued, the minority treaties had a political not a humanitarian aim, 'To avoid the many inter-state frictions and conflicts which had occurred in the past, as a result of the frequent ill-treatment or oppression of national minorities'.[7] He points out that the treaties could only establish and guarantee the minorities in respect of the majority 'equality before the law' and 'equality of treatment'.[8] The Peace Treaties acknowledged nation-states as states in which nation and citizen were clearly identified, but left Eastern Europe with nearly one-third of its people under international protection. It was implicit that the minorities should either assimilate or move to their national states. Hannah Arendt argued 'that the nationally frustrated population was firmly convinced, as was everybody else, that true freedom, true emancipation, and true popular sovereignty could be attained only with full national emancipation, that people without their own national government were deprived of human rights'.[9]

The Minority Treaty with Poland proved to be a blueprint for all other minority treaties and declarations to come. Before discussing this Treaty it should be noted that the Peace Treaties of Versailles, St Germain, Trianon and Neuilly included a clause which stated that each of the five countries (Poland, Czechoslovakia, Rumania, Yugoslavia and Greece) 'accepts and agrees to embody in a Treaty with the Principal Allied and Associated Powers such a provision as may be deemed necessary by the said Powers to protect the interests of inhabitants of Poland (or Czechoslovakia, etc.) who differ from the majority of the population in race, language, or religion'.[10] As a result negotiations started with the Council of the League of Nations.[11]

It is important to assess the Treaty with Poland and understand the circumstances of the negotiations in some detail, as they tell us about the power relations between the representatives of different countries. It is also of interest to us because of the dispute between Poland and Lithuania and consequently the way both states treated their respective minorities. Poland argued that it could not accept the protection of the League over its minorities because it would discourage 'their duties towards their own state'. Furthermore, asking for the consent of the Council of the League to change its own Constitutions meant 'infringing her sovereignty'. Poland could not agree with the religious tolerance clause because it 'might justify the Jews in refusing the military service'. It also argued that the School Article[12] and the two Jewish Articles[13] could not be a part of the fundamental laws which could only cover rights of all citizens and the general principles of liberty and equality. Poland objected to the proposed articles stressing especially the Jews' responsibility for strained relations within Poland. Paderewski, the Polish representative at the Conference, encapsulated the atmosphere and language of the Peace Conference. He said, 'It may be feared that the Great Powers may be preparing for themselves unwelcome surprises, for taking into consideration the migratory capacities of the Jewish population, which so readily transports itself from one State to another. It is certain that the Jews, basing themselves on precedent established, will claim elsewhere the national principles which they would enjoy in Poland.'[14]

Clemenceau, in his letter to the Polish government of 24 June 1919, explained that the Powers felt an inescapable obligation to secure 'the guarantees for certain essential rights' under any changes which could take place in the fundamental laws. He added that this was needed because 'The races had been estranged by long years of bitter hostility'.[15] He hoped that the knowledge that these guarantees existed would prevent any need to enforce them. He also pointed out that under the new system of international relations the guarantor was the League not the Powers. In the light of the Polish complaints about the first draft of the Treaty discussed above, the Polish government could not have been appeased by this letter although under pressure from the Powers, it signed the Treaty on 28 June 1919.

The Second Assembly of the League declared on 23 September 1921 that Lithuania (together with Latvia and Estonia) was ready to join the League which meant that it had enforced the principles of the Minority Treaty and was prepared to negotiate minority obligations with the Council. In regard to the Vilnius question, it has to be pointed out that the Lithuanian government had kept these two issues separate. Despite being dissatisfied with the way the League of Nations dealt with the Vilnius question, it went ahead with the Declaration on Minority Rights. It is possible that they hoped that a give-and-take strategy would prove fruitful, that not causing difficulties would be rewarded, or that once Lithuania was a member of the League it would be easier to lobby support for the return of Vilnius. Besides, one has to bear in mind that Poland continually raised the issue of the maltreatment of the Polish minority in Lithuania. However, Zeligowski's *coup de main* made their position vulnerable. There were no diplomatic relations with Poland and, therefore, 'There were no normative acts concerning the Polish minority'.[16] The Polish minority in Lithuania was also raising its voice.[17] Therefore, I would argue, the decision to agree with the obligations defined by the League was politically and strategically wise. It was easier to fight on the one front (the return of the Vilnius region).

Lithuania agreed to all the requirements placed before her and signed the Declaration on 12 May 1922.[18] It also agreed that the whole of the Declaration should be recognised as fundamental law. However, throughout the negotiations Lithuania kept pointing out that 'There had been adequate guarantees for the protection of minorities in Lithuania since the foundation of the new State.'[19]

As Macartney, Secretary of the Minorities Committee of the League of Nations from 1928, pointed out, 'I think that it is fairly safe to say that on balance the Treaties have been of some benefit to the minorities concerned … The effective results of the League's work to date have proved disappointing; it is useless to blink the fact. Moreover, they have been particularly disappointing in the cases of those minorities who had no friend at court (i.e. on the Council). The chief cases where the League has acted with any real effect have been where pressure has been put upon it by some power which could have championed the minority in question even without the League – a case which could not arise unless the question were one of "international concern".'[20]

Lithuanian legislation on national minorities and Jewish national autonomy

Lithuania declared already in 1919 that it was ready to provide a legal framework for the protection of the Jewish minority in the shape of national autonomy. This book is not primarily interested in the letter of the law but in its implementation and evaluation by national minorities. A declaration, however legally binding it is, is not enough to secure the implementation of a law. Therefore, we shall explore how the Jewish community understood national autonomy and, accordingly, organised its community life as well as the legal implementation of the Minority Declaration in Lithuanian Constitutions. Finally, the rise of Lithuanian nationalism together with a change in the aims of the Lithuanian foreign policy (after 1923) played an important role in the introduction of discrimination against its national minorities.

It is important to show that 'the Jewish minority succeeded, in 1919, in establishing a far-reaching autonomy based on communes (*Gemeinden*) and a National Jewish Council'. The National Jewish Council was given legislative powers as a result of the Peace Conference.[21] Pressure from the world-wide Jewish community was not the only reason for the extension of educational and religious rights to Jews.[22] We have to bear in mind the crucial influence that the gradually emerging awareness of minority issues raised by the world community at the Peace Conference had on the Minorities Treaties and Declarations and therefore their respective fundamental laws. According to the memorandums published in the League of Nations Journal, representatives of Lithuania did not perceive their own state as a nation-state but, as 'the state of different nationalities'.[23] For that reason a Zionist Conference held in Vilnius in December 1918 resolved to 'Greet the reconstruction of Lithuania as a free and democratic state based on full equality and national-personal autonomy for all peoples'.[24] That was precisely what the Jews longed for because they wanted to be able to continue developing their own heritage without being assimilated into the dominant culture, as was happening with the Jews in Russia or Poland.[25] However, there were Jews who were against any Jewish commitment to the Lithuanian state. The socialists around the *Bund* and the *Poale Zion*, saw Lithuania as a new bourgeois state and the Zionists thought that the Jews should be careful since it was still not clear if the Lithuanian military victory would be acknowledged by the world community and Lithuania accepted as an independent state.

Lithuania in the initial phase of independence needed the full support of its minorities, especially after October 1920. The Jews of Vilnius were loyal to the Kaunas government and did not take part in the plebiscite carried out by the Polish authorities after the annexation of Poland.[26] They also did not want to take part in the elections for a Diet on 8 January 1921 although 'The Polish government was anxious that they should participate, so that the decision arrived at, might impress the world as a faithful reflection of the wishes of the entire population'.[27] The Jewish representatives were invited to Warsaw to explain their reasons for not wanting to take part in the elections. It is reported that they 'stated their case fully and cogently. They regarded Vilna just as much a part of Lithuania as Kovno. They looked upon Lithuania not as the state of one nationality but as a state of various nationalities, in which all were entitled to equality. They were of the opinion that Vilna should belong to a Great Lithuania; but as the country was too small to exist independently and was closely connected with Poland historically, economically and culturally, they considered that the best solution would be that it should be federated with Poland.'[28]

The issue of national autonomy granted to minorities is interesting because it was to be put in practice for the first time in Lithuania. There was a rich Jewish cultural and institutional tradition in Lithuania.[29] This was important because it would enable the Jews to secure their autonomy and it suited the Lithuanian state which did not want its Jews being assimilated by the Russians as in the case of Latvia.

Furthermore, Jewish culture was an important element in neutralising the influences of Russian, Polish and German cultures with whom Lithuanians had a history of grievances.[30]

Jewish national autonomy can best be understood through the demands which the three Jewish ministers made to the Provisional Government in early 1919.[31] They 'demanded, in addition to the full rights of citizenship for the Jews in the spheres of politics, economics and languages, that representation in parliament, in administrative bodies, and the courts be based on the numerical proportion of the population. They also demanded that the autonomy in the cultural sphere be carried out through three institutions – the local *kehilla*,[32] a National Jewish Council, and a Ministry for Jewish Affairs.'[33]

Max Soloveichik, Minister without Portfolio for Jewish Affairs, proposed during the Conference on Jewish Autonomy (4–11 January 1920) that the autonomy should be built from the bottom upwards, starting with the *kehilla*. To continue the building of national autonomy the Jewish National Council was created.[34] Its aim was two-fold: 'The political struggle for Jewish rights and the distribution of aid for the economic and spiritual reconstruction of Lithuanian Jewry'.[35] The Jews who were originally in support of it, transformed the *kehilla* into a forum for their own arguments as well as endless discussions which did not produce any practical achievements.[36] With the exception of the schools and co-operative banks, set up to help the economic reconstruction of impoverished Lithuanian Jews, most forms of Jewish religious, social and cultural life occurred outside the official *kehilla*.

According to the Minority Declaration, 'racial, religious or linguistic minorities' were given 'the right to maintain, manage and control at their own expense, or to establish in the future, charitable, religious and social institutions, schools and other educational establishments, with the right to use their own language and to exercise their religion freely'.[37] First, national minorities were not mentioned *per se* because it was understood among the members of the Council of the league of Nations that 'racial' and 'ethnic' labels had the same meaning. Second, only Jews were guaranteed money for their schools (Article 7), in contrast to the case of other minorities where money was dependent on their 'considerable proportion' in towns and districts (Article 6). We do not know how this 'considerable proportion' was defined. Bearing in mind the issue of national autonomy, the Jews were guaranteed equal political and civil rights and minority schools. However, there was no mention of national autonomy. National autonomy was not universally supported by the Jews. The ultra-orthodox Jews as well as those of socialist orientation were strongly against it. It is important to point out that the Provisional Government of independent Lithuania was formed on 2 November 1918, under the auspices of the German occupation authorities who demanded the inclusion of the Jewish representatives in the transitional regime, to prevent pogroms and persecution of Jews. As a result three individuals were appointed to represent the Jews.[38] Besides, the *kehilla* was legally perceived as a form of local self-government but only according to the Provisional Constitution. It should also be noted that by the same law the *kehilla* was connected with the Ministry for Jewish Affairs not to the Jewish National Council.

As a result of the Minority Declaration the ethnic question was addressed in the First Constitution, adopted on 6 August 1922. This Constitution dealt with the issue of national minorities in two articles which were also included in the Constitution adopted on 25 May 1928.

Section 73. National minorities of citizens, which shall form an appreciable part of the citizenry, shall have the right, within the limits of the law, to administer autonomously the affairs of their national culture, public education, charity, mutual aid, and to elect necessary bodies to conduct these affairs in the manner prescribed by law. Section 74. The national minorities set forth in Section 73 shall have the right, in accordance with special laws for that purpose, to impose upon their members dues for needs of national culture, and they shall have the benefit of the proper portion of the sums set aside by the State and the local self-government for matters of education and charity, provided the sums allowed by the common State and self-government institutions shall not suffice for these needs.[39]

These articles were excluded from the third Constitution, adopted on 12 May 1938, which did not deal with the national minorities issues.[40]

It should be emphasised that the 1922 Constitution did not mention the institution of national autonomy. Macartney brilliantly summarised the issues concerning the Lithuanian Minority Declaration and its implementation saying

Lithuania, in her Constitution of 1922 and 1928, promised those of her national minorities which form a considerable proportion of the state population the right of cultural autonomy. These provisions have not, however, been carried through. ... It is true that the Polish

Treaty and the Lithuanian Declaration recognise the existence of the Jewish communities of Poland and Lithuania respectively, but do not allow these communities any right beyond that of appointing Educational Committees *locally* to whom, then certain scholastic duties are assigned. It will be noted that in each case the plural form 'communities' is used, so that it seems probable that the Treaties intended to recognise only local communities, and not national bodies.[41]

The Lithuanian government was not too keen on Jewish national autonomy.[42] The right-wing parties argued that the Minority Declaration should apply only if there were 10 per cent or more of citizens belonging to national minorities which would have meant that the Declaration was only a symbolic piece of paper.[43] In 1923 the government appointed as Minister for Jewish Affairs Bernard Friedman, 'a Russian assimilationist' who had to resign because of Jewish protest.[44] On 19 March 1923 the government removed the entire Ministry for Jewish Affairs from the cabinet budget. Jews were accused of prompting the need for new elections because their vote was seen as decisive in the no confidence vote against the government in March 1923. The right to deliver speeches in Yiddish in the Parliament was abolished in June 1923. On 15 July 1923 a decree was issued forbidding the display of Yiddish store-fronts and similar signs in streets. On 15 September 1923 the police prohibited the meeting of the National Jewish Council, because it was not registered as a private corporation. As pointed out above, the Council was never officially recognised by the Lithuanian government. After the 1923 elections the Christian Democratic Party returned to power.[45] One of its first acts (on 21 December 1923) was to confirm the abolition of the budget devoted to the salaries of employees of the Ministry of Jewish Affairs. When the new cabinet was appointed on 18 June 1924 there was no mention of the Ministry for Jewish Affairs. On 21 March 1925 a new law was adopted allowing several *kehillot* to exist in the same city.[46] On 8 March 1926 old *kehillot* were abolished. This meant that all three institutions of the national autonomy had ceased to exist. Nevertheless, 'Independent Lithuania afforded the Jews greater possibilities of providing their children with a good, nationally-oriented education. A Jewish press of high quality arose as an important cultural factor; the Jewish masses became more secular minded, more active socially and better organised.'[47]

Soon after independence the Jews were disillusioned with their political and economic situation in Lithuania. They were aware that they were as much to blame as the Lithuanian state for the fact that their national autonomy was never established. They were politically divided and, while losing their energy in ideological battles, did not have time for local issues.[48] However, the Lithuanian state did not abide by the minority legislation. It did not guarantee national autonomy to its minorities, although the state was ready to tolerate it. According to two Constitutions, cultural autonomy was acknowledged. Furthermore, it began to discriminate against its Jewish minority from 1923 onwards. After seizing Klaipeda the Lithuanian government knew that it could not expect to get the Vilnius region back. So it did not need the support of its national minorities on the same scale as after General Zeligowski seized the Vilnius region on 9 October 1920. The Jews hoped that the new state would allow them to develop their autonomy and continue developing and cherishing their culture and that in Lithuania they would strengthen their national existence, especially in the context of its lack of anti-Semitic tradition. But anti-Semitism started to emerge in the new state in the 1920s. It is important to analyse it because it has coloured the life of the Lithuanian and Jewish communities up to, and including, the contemporary context.

Anti-Semitism

Before we attempt to explain the rise of anti-Semitism it should be stressed that Lithuania had not had a tradition of anti-Semitism. One plausible explanation lies in the lack of the fully developed national movement and consciousness (national awakening was confined to a 'thin stratum of intellectuals') as well as 'the fact that there was no Lithuanian middle class'.[49] As soon as national awakening started it became coloured in nationalistic terms which insisted on an *us* and *them* dichotomy, which was sometimes understood in ethical terms of good and bad. At the same time we can see the rise of anti-Semitism supported by newly aspiring professionals who were competing with the Jews for the same positions.[50] The treatment of national minorities in the independent Lithuania and the experience of the Jewish and Lithuanian peoples living next to each other, not with each other, are of vital importance. Anti-Semitism should be analysed in economic terms, through the heritage of national cultures, and the rise of fascism in Europe.

This was not the first time in history that chauvinistic hostility has been displayed towards a national group perceived as being economically successful. Here the role of the state is again of vital importance together with institutions it supported like co-operatives and social processes it promoted, such as the formation of the Lithuanian bourgeoisie. The so-called Sunday blue/rest laws were adopted,[51] together with a law prohibiting business records in Yiddish, a law abolishing the privileges for trade co-operatives and a law introducing tax and credit discrimination.[52] After the war there was a tendency to concentrate trade and industry in the hands of the government or co-operatives. The Jews were affected the most because they were traditionally in trade and industry.[53] It should be added that trade and industry had higher taxes which again affected the Jews.[54] The Lithuanian government also initiated a campaign against Jewish employees, especially artisans.[55] In 1934 a law was introduced which required qualifying examinations for artisans, bookkeepers, domestic servants, chauffeurs and dancing instructors. The exam consisted not only of a thorough knowledge of the trade but also proficiency in Lithuanian language and history, etc.[56] As a result of these anti-Semitic policies the Jews began to lose their income and some of them decided to emigrate, mostly to Palestine and South Africa.[57] Therefore, Oscar Janowsky argues that 'the emigrant from east-central Europe bears silent testimony to the fact that the policy of elimination, the "cold pogrom", has proved effective'.[58] The most anti-Semitic organisation in Lithuania was the 'Lithuanian Businessmen's Association of "Lithuanian stock"', *Verslininkaj*, which called for a boycott of Jewish businesses.[59] Its slogans were 'Lithuania for the Lithuanians' and 'The Cities must be Lithuanian' and its president was secretary-general of the Nationalist Union.[60]

Discrimination against the Jews has to be seen in relation to two factors: the Lithuanian population gaining education and entering the labour market and the economic depression of 1929. Lithuanians, who at the turn of the century lived mostly in rural areas and were barely educated, were encouraged after independence to move to the towns and gain an education. The Lithuanian Student Corps demanded that Jews and Lithuanians should sit separately in the lecture halls and that a *numerus clausus* should be introduced, while ultimately hoping for the complete expulsion of Jews from the University.[61] As a result, the *numerus clausus* was introduced and the number of Jewish students halved in the period 1928 to 1933 and continued to fall thereafter.[62] Furthermore, the Jews were forced out of their traditional professions, law and medicine, and were not appointed to the civil service, and those who had jobs were made redundant.[63] This new urban population also changed the employment structure in industry.[64] By the middle of the 1930s around 50 per cent of Lithuanians lived in urban settlements in comparison with 11.5 per cent in 1897.[65] Anatol Lieven argued that the change was on such a scale that it could be called a 'social revolution'.

Discrimination against the Jews in the economic sphere also has to be seen in relation to the international context, where the 1929 economic depression had a particularly severe impact on Lithuanian agriculture. Britain and Germany, who were Lithuania's trading partners, were no longer ready to import agricultural products, which were a vital part of the Lithuanian economy.[66] The depression could be seen as a factor which made Lithuanian people move to urban centres.

In the 1926 election the Populist-Social Democratic coalition came to power with the support of national minorities. It stayed in power less than half a year, and in December 1926, with the help of the Army, the Nationalist Union (*Tautininkai*) came to power. The Nationalist Union was a party which openly sympathised with fascism. However, its leader, Antanas Smetona showed support for the Jewish population in Lithuania and had Jewish friends.[67] In 1929 he dismissed his Prime Minister, Augustinas Voldemaras, who had been influenced by fascism and who founded the paramilitary force *Gelezinis Vilkas* (The Iron Wolf). In 1934 Smetona imprisoned Voldemaras after repeated coup attempts staged by his force.[68]

According to my interviews, even when Jews assess this period as totalitarianism or authoritarianism, all of them point out that Smetona protected them and that he should be distinguished from his more anti-Semitic supporters.[69] Often they draw a parallel between Smetona and Vytautas Landsbergis, pointing out that Landsbergis is not anti-Semitic and that his parents sheltered their Jewish friends, despite his father having been a member of the Lithuanian Provisional government under German rule in 1941.[70] Many Jews in contemporary Lithuania argued that it is possible to draw another parallel between what can be termed 'a provincial culture of Kaunas' and a 'cosmopolitan culture of Vilnius'. They pointed out that Vilnius has been a cosmopolitan city founded by Lithuanians (the Grand Duke Gediminas) but built by the Jews and Poles[71] in which these cultures coexisted with the Russian cultural heritage. The culture of Kaunas has always been more inward looking, towards an exclusively Lithuanian cultural tradition which is mostly based on peasant folklore and which despises the cosmopolitanism of Vilnius. To put Kaunas in perspective, one has to bear in mind that Lithuania's gaining of independence gave rise to an understandable degree of national pride. To Lithuanian intellectuals, it was obvious that peasant folklore could not be compared with the Jewish, Polish or Russian cultural heritage. The Jews themselves pointed out that, although after independence Lithuania's 'first enemy' were the Poles, Lithuanians also had some animosity towards Jews. In the opinion of Lithuanians, Jews were doing much better in the Lithuanian state. Jews were preceived as professionals living in the towns while Lithuanians were still poorly educated peasants. Research on anti-Semitism has shown that the production of ethnic stereotypes has far more to do with the complex needs of the creators of these stereotypes than it has to do with any empirical reality.[72]

One has to bear in mind that the Catholic tradition was, to say the least, not always kind to Jews as well as to the other religions. The Devil is often perceived as a foreign person but 'close at hand'.[73] However, because of its pagan tradition devils were seen as morally neutral, often portrayed as clowns or a stupid person who thinks that he is clever. Czeslaw Milosz captured this tradition in his novel *The Issa Valley*.[74] Among the displays at the Devil's Museum in Kaunas, collected mostly from churches and people's homes, one can see many Jewish faces.[75] Jews were definitely not known to Lithuanians; they were foreign. They lived in towns, spoke different language/s, prayed to a different God. Lithuanian and Jewish cultural traditions hardly had any contact. 'The Jews of Lithuania were characterised by a strong national consciousness and by resistance to assimilation. According to an often quoted statistic, in 1937, 98 percent of the Jews declared their nationality as Jewish. Lithuanian Jewry possessed a very proud heritage as the intellectual centre of East European Jewry.'[76] Lithuanians were also not known to Lithuanian Jews before independence. They lived in the Russian Empire and did not think of Lithuanians as a fully-fledged nation although they were aware of their national movement. They did not know their culture and did not speak their language.[77]

For the first time in the independent Lithuania, the Jews were faced with the Lithuanians as a nation, a nation proud of its language, a nation which fought fiercely for its independence and was as proud of its own state, as much as it was disappointed (one cannot say furious because of ethnic stereotypes about Lithuanians) by the loss of its capital.[78]

The rise of anti-Semitism can only partly be explained by the specific national heritage of Lithuania, as well as social and economic developments within Lithuania. It also has to be seen in a broader European context. In particular one has to take into account the spread of fascist influence throughout Europe. 'Smetona's authoritarianism was essentially an antidote to the earlier experiment with parliamentary democracy. The nationalist regime persisted in its efforts to discredit that type of democracy and crystallise its own political principles. In the end, these principles acquired a certain psychological and political affinity with those of fascism.'[79] Smetona was addressed as Leader of the Nation[80] and the Nationalist Union was organised around the Leader-Principle. Smetona adopted the role, supported by the intelligentsia, of 'treasuring', but not defining,[81] national culture. This was shaped by his belief that 'a nation without consciousness is no nation, and that a nation without leaders is no nation: both are necessary'.[82] According to these views, the army command should not only educate but also 'indoctrinate', the teachers should make an effort to develop a 'monolithic national body and a collective soul' and artists should concentrate on developing 'a national orientation'. Smetona's aim was to create an organic state which would provide for the needs and security of its citizens. As a result, there would be no need for 'formal rights'. However, historians of that period agree that in political practice Smetona's regime was not as brutal as those of Hitler or Mussolini and the party members often argued that he allowed 'a good deal of freedom' although they themselves did not support this principle. Members of his party also did not support his occasional statements about religious tolerance in Lithuania.[83] In practice, both educational institutions and courts retained a real measure of independence, although the regime was not liberal. Smetona wanted to distance himself from the foreign ideas not only of democracy, but also of fascism, perceiving his regime as authoritarian.[84] Smetona wrote: 'It is not a secret that the Nationalist Union sympathises with the present political rule in Italy…But…Lithuanians must form a particular system of national power such as flows from the circumstances of their existence. Lithuanians must necessarily reform their own society in order to get rid of out-of-date traditions of liberalism and stand on their own basis.'[85]

The first Soviet occupation

When the Red Army entered Lithuania in 1940 and proclaimed the Soviet Republic of Lithuania, the Jews accepted this new authority. How was that possible? One has to see that acceptance in the light of the events in Germany since Hitler's rise to power and his wish to establish a *Juden frei Deutcshland* (a Germany free of Jews) as well as the *Juden frei* Third Reich. Furthermore, the relationship between the Jews and Lithuanians had been getting worse from year to year in the independent Lithuania as analysed above. When Vilnius was returned to Lithuania in October 1939 there were riots against the Jews which resulted in about 200 casualties. In several towns the windows of Jewish homes were smashed and some houses were even set on fire.[86] According to my research, it is possible to conclude that there was an ethnic stereotype developing, perceiving Jews as rich and not allowing the Lithuanian people to start their own businesses.

The support for the Soviet regime was also reflected in the number of Jews who became members of the Communist Party. It was very often acknowledged in my interviews that a considerable number of Jews joined the Communist Party and followed the communist ideology.[87]

In contrast with the Jews, the majority of Lithuanians were terrified of the reality of being a Soviet Socialist Republic. They had fought so hard to keep their independence during the First World War that they could not accept or even imagine the possibility of losing it, especially to those who had, in a different guise, been their former rulers. While some Lithuanians welcomed Soviet rule and sang 'Shiroka strana moia rodina' (This large country is my homeland) the vast majority were against the occupation.[88]

This differing response to the Soviet occupation led to an even deeper tension between the Lithuanian and Jewish communities. The Lithuanians were so eager to retain their hard-earned independence that they tended to perceive the Jewish acceptance of Soviet control as active support. The Jews were therefore seen as traitors. Lithuanians were not always willing to try to understand the Jewish fear of the Third Reich.

One also has to bear in mind that Lithuanians saw the Germans as a lesser evil than the Soviets, whereas for Jews the opposite was the case. When the Germans occupied Lithuania in June 1941, Lithuanians entered into a marriage of convenience with the Germans. However, this relationship did not live up to Lithuanian expectations since it materialised into being a case of the Germans ruling over rather than sharing Lithuania.[89]

The first Soviet occupation of Lithuania (as it is usually referred to by Lithuanians to differentiate it from the second period of occupation in 1945) was usually remembered for the deportation of Lithuanians who were not citizens of Lithuania in mid-June 1941. It has to be recognised that the deportation claimed the Lithuanian cultural and political elite as well as workers and peasants, but it also included Jews. In 1990, in the first issue of the journal *Pergola*, an article by Dov Levin was published/re-printed, 'Arrests and Deportations of Lithuanian Jews to

Remote Areas of the Soviet Union, 1940–1941' which was originally published in 1984 in Israel.[90] In this context it is of interest to point out that, in relative numbers, Jews were the largest community to be deported. Seven thousand Jews, making up 3 per cent of the Jewish population, were deported and they made up 20 per cent of the total number of people deported.[91] This was a result of the Soviet nationalisation of commerce and industry which affected the Jews more severely than any other group, labelling them as 'bourgeois elements'.[92] The majority of Jews who were arrested and deported belonged to the Jewish 'political, cultural and communal elite, as well as … large numbers of young people of draft age'.[93] Furthermore, religious, social and national organisations were suppressed as well as political movements. 'Hebrew schools have been dissolved and the Jewish press has been suppressed.'[94] Only the Zionist youth movement later consolidated and continued its activity in a covert manner.[95] This can possibly be understood in the light of the Soviet system being perceived as a lesser evil than the German Reich. There was, therefore, possibly a reluctance to organise a struggle against a system which, while taking away their wealth and freedom, did not endanger their lives (as happened in Germany). 'The Jewish people felt very free. This was not too bad. No impoliteness was allowed; this was true for the Russians, Jews and Lithuanians. No one could call us names or insult us because if they did they would be sent to jail for six months. Every Jew held his head high.'[96] The Jews were also invited to join governmental offices which they accepted. Furthermore, among the Jews there were supporters of the communist ideology. However, that ideology and regime also had its supporters (though not many) among the left-wing Lithuanians and Lithuanian workers and peasants.[97]

The Holocaust

The Holocaust was of major importance for every Jewish individual. For this reason this episode has to be dealt with in some depth. When the German Army captured Lithuania in June 1941 (in two or three days) only 15 000 Jews succeeded in leaving Lithuania and 8000 were killed trying to leave the country.[98] The majority of Lithuanian Jews stayed in the country and within six months 180 000 (out of roughly 220 000) were killed by Lithuanians and Germans.[99] Out of the remaining 40 000 the majority were sent to the ghettos of Vilnius, Kaunas,[100] Siauliai and Svencionys from which the Jews were sent to concentration or labour camps. However, within the ghettos and camps there were underground organisations whose ultimate aim was to save as many Jewish lives as possible. These underground organisations assisted 1500 Jews to escape. Another 650 escaped on their own. Most of them joined the resistance movement or partisan movement in Lithuania and also Belorussia.

In the summer of 1941, the Lithuanian Activist Front (LAF), an underground national organisation, issued the following proclamation: 'Lithuanian brothers and sisters: The time has come to make a final accounting with the Jews. ...The ancient right of refuge for Jews in Lithuania granted in the time of Vytautas the Great is hereby abolished. Every Lithuanian Jew, with no exception whatsoever, is hereby warned to leave the soil of Lithuania immediately.' In another proclamation, those Lithuanians who took part in the Soviet regime were given the opportunity for an amnesty 'if they could prove that they have killed at least one Jew'. The same proclamation ends with a call to Lithuanians: 'At the designated time, seize their (the Jews') property so nothing is lost.'[101]

How can one explain that so many Jews were killed in Lithuania during the Second World War? The following quotation casts light on the matter.

> The Lithuanians are divided on the Jewish question. There are three main views: according to the most extreme, all the Jews in Lithuania must be exterminated; a more moderate view demands setting up a concentration camp where Jews will atone with blood and sweat for their crimes against the Lithuanian people. As for the third view? I am a practising Roman Catholic; I – and other believers like me – believe that man cannot take the life of another human being...but during the period of the Soviet rule I and my friend have realised that we do not have a common path with the Jews and never shall. In our view, you must be separated from us and the sooner the better. For that purpose, the Ghetto is essential. There you will be separated and no longer able to harm us. This is a Christian position.[102]

From this answer it is obvious that there were only believed to be two solutions to the Jewish question; to kill the Jews or to enclose them. In both cases they were to be concealed from society. Why did the Lithuanians opt for the first solution?

This question still remains. One has to bear in mind the development of anti-Semitism in inter-war Lithuania. Furthermore, during the Second World War the Nazis conducted 'research'[103] on Jewish involvement in the atrocities committed against the Lithuanians during the Soviet period. The result was published in 1942 in Kaunas in a four-volume series *Lietuviu Archyvas* which claimed Jewish responsibility for these atrocities. The Nazi propaganda claimed that 'Judeo-Communism' was destroying the world and this propaganda fed the prejudice of the masses. It did not matter that the Jews were also deported (as was pointed out above, the number of the Jews deported to the Soviet Union was higher in relative terms than the number of Lithuanians). This fact has not been considered at all among the older generation of Lithuanian historians. One can possibly suggest two reasons for this. First, the historical archives were not always available and they doubted the scientific credibility of the Jewish scholars which was, to start with, mostly based on personal documents and experience. Second, their country's loss of independence pushed them towards reinventing their national myth which made the Jews, as a nation, even more prone to prejudices which are 'not so much dependent upon the nature of the object as upon the subject's own psychological wants and needs'.[104] However, Bishop Vincentas Brizgys[105] discussed Jewish behaviour in the period of the first Soviet occupation. 'In the mass killings carried out by the Russians at the beginning of the war, Jews were also among the victims. While it is true that in many cases Jews were actively involved in carrying out these murders, it cannot be denied that Lithuanians also participated, except that the Lithuanian masses did not recognise them as Lithuanians'.[106]

The Jews whom I interviewed argued that Lithuanians did not want to discuss the Holocaust[107] and some of them were even prepared to justify it.[108] Lithuanians whom I interviewed were divided on the issue of the Holocaust; some accepted Lithuanian responsibility for it, the others claimed that the Nazis did it. I have not met anybody who justified it. The majority of Lithuanians tired to explain the Lithuanian involvement in the Holocaust with the support which the Jews showed for the Soviet Union and the communist ideology. Jews were also hurt by statements of the Lithuanian authorities that the Nazis annihilated the Jews. My interviews with the LDDP politicians showed that they were ready to address this issue, as is argued in Chapter 8.

Conclusion

In relation to minority rights, two issues have to be raised which are not only applicable to the inter-war period, but are also relevant in the newly independent Lithuania and will be analysed in the following chapters. First, we have to analyse the understanding of the need and the respect for minority legislation within Lithuania. It should be recognised that the Jews were vocal during the Peace Conference and successfully put forward a draft for the Polish Minority Treaty which served as a blueprint for other Treaties and Declarations. Being vocal was interpreted as being influential and consequently the Lithuanians wanted them as their allies. I would argue that both these issues were important in influencing the proposal of two articles which extended the Jewish educational and religious rights. The Jews were allowed to form Education Committees, though only on the local level, as Macartney pointed out. Their existing National Council survived only until 1923 with hardly any support from the Lithuanian government. The Lithuanian minority legislation was created by the world community. Lithuania accepted this legislation because it faced a diplomatic struggle with Poland to regain the Vilnius region, for which it needed the support of the world community as well as the Jewish community. In the period of national awakening, however, the Lithuanian political elite did not favour this legislation. As was previously pointed out, right-wing nationalistic groups were openly against it.

Second, Lithuanian national awakening did not create sufficient space for the acceptance of minority legislation as well as the accommodation of different peoples and cultures. Legislation, which was seen by the League of Nations as a protection of minorities, was qualified as a privilege by Lithuanians. The newly formed Lithuanian middle class was in competition with the minorities for educational resources and jobs. The middle class did not want to be treated equally with other citizens but instead wanted privileges because Lithuania had 'finally' established its own state. That is the reason why the slogan 'Lithuania for the Lithuanians' was launched and supported.

Polish people and culture belonged not only to the occupying forces of that time but throughout Lithuanian history they were seen as the main denationalising force. The border was militarily drawn and Vilnius was a part of Poland while Klaipeda (Memel) was a part of Lithuania. It was gradually acknowledged that Vilnius would stay within Poland and that, despite the guarantees granted to minorities according to the Polish Minority Treaty, the Lithuanian schools would be closed in Poland. On the other side of the border Lithuania made provisions for its national minorities. According to Artur Ploksto, 'the rights of the Polish people in Lithuania were dependent on state relations. Therefore, it does not come as a surprise that Poles left Lithuania. In the inter-war period they were not able to exercise their rights.'[109] After the coup in

1926, 48 Polish schools were closed in Lithuania.[110] In 1937 in Kaunas there was only one Polish secondary school, one German, one Russian and six Jewish secondary schools.[111] Poles saw this as another example of discrimination, given the fact that after the Jews they were the largest national minority in Lithuania. Regina Zepkaite pointed out that in 1939, when the Lithuanian Army took over Vilnius, 'Some Poles were made redundant and the rest were obliged to learn Lithuanian. The first deadline for this was half a year and then it was prolonged to a year.'[112] She argued that this, together with other measures,[113] was a very 'drastic change for Poles but it was the only way forward'.

Russian people and culture belonged to former political rulers, with the exception of the Old Believers who faced religious community discrimination in Czarist Russia until 1905. In the independent Lithuania they opened their own schools and different cultural institutions which had 'enlightenment purposes'.[114] But Russians who moved to Lithuania to escape the Red Army were mostly White Army officers and their families.[115] According to Nikolai Medvedev, their main problem was 'psychological'. They lost not only their money but also their fatherland. However, they were left with their education and their church. 'They did not have anyone to turn to except the Orthodox Church.' They came to the country which was Catholic and as 'orthodox people did not feel comfortable although Lithuania took care of them'.[116] As a result, in 1922 Russian refugees in South-East Lithuania formed their own religious community, the Mikniskes (Michnovo) Orthodox Community.[117]

The two issues analysed above lead us to the following conclusion. The Minority Treaties and Declarations clearly point out that the protection of minority rights could not be successfully guaranteed by an international body. Leaving minority protection to such a body puts minorities in a vulnerable position in their country of residence where they are perceived as privileged and overprotected at the expense of the majority. Having rights is very much interconnected with achieving national sovereignty which equates state and nation and, therefore, gives minorities two possibilities – to assimilate or to leave the country. The irony is that this was understood and supported by the creators of the Treaties[118] but the Minority Treaties and Declarations were still seen as the only way to prevent another world war.

As was pointed out at the beginning of this chapter, this period is looked upon favourably by the contemporary Lithuanian state. It is valued in terms of Lithuanian independence and it is seen as providing a Lithuanian democratic tradition. I would argue that contemporary Lithuanians somewhat overidealised the inter-war period and overlooked the fact that increasing restrictions had been placed on national minorities. Officially, national autonomy existed until the 1938 Constitution but in the reality of everyday life the rights of minorities began to be curtailed in the early days of independence. The praxis of citizenship was defined by the interests of the state. The rise of Lithuanian nationalism did not provide for the coexistence of Lithuanians and its minorities. Minority communities were also not always open to the Lithuanians. The nationalism was of an exclusive nature and wanted its own state primarily for its own nationals. This conflicting impetus of citizenship and nationalism, though mediated by the post-communist establishment of democracy, is also characteristic of the contemporary period.

3
Opposition Movements and the Birth of the Lithuanian National Movement

Introduction

Vladimir Efremov, a Russian actor from Vilnius, quoted a line from a well-known song, 'Our address is the Soviet Union' (as opposed to a specific republic or province).[1] Returning to Lithuania in autumn 1988, after a stage tour in Russia, he was completely taken aback by the pro-independence events of that summer. Justinas Marcinkevicius, a Lithuanian poet who symbolised national reawakening in 1988, said that for him national reawakening started in 1964, not in 1988, when he realised that to be Lithuanian meant to be against the Soviet Empire.[2] These two statements can be seen as very much characteristic of their national groups. The majority of Russians tended to see Lithuania as a part of the Soviet Union at a time when Lithuanians had striven for independence.

This book is concerned with both the rights which minorities have been given, as well as rights they have been struggling for. This requires an examination of how Soviet nationality policies and the Lithuanian national movement dealt with the question of national identity, and also with how they shaped the understanding of citizenship and more specifically citizenship rights. Citizenship is defined by the state and it needs institutional support in order to be effectively exercised. These institutions play an important role in promoting tolerance towards different cultures. Therefore, it is important to trace the political development of the Lithuanian national movement.

This chapter will concentrate on the events between the end of the Second World War and the gaining of independence. I shall briefly analyse responses to the nationality policy of the former Soviet Union. This policy has drawn the attention of quite a large number of social

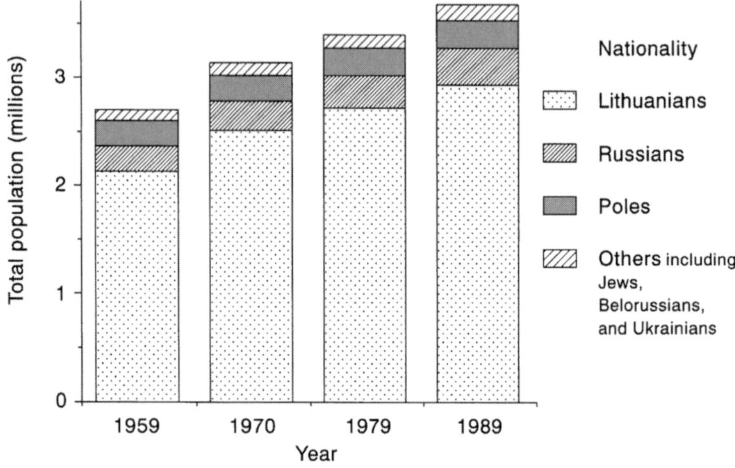

Source: Lietuvos respublikos pagrindiniu tautybiu gyventojai.
Vilnius: Statistikos departmentas prie Lietuvos respublikos vyriausybes, 1991, p.1.

Figure 3.1 Total population of Lithuania by nationality, 1959–89

scientists, but the way in which it was understood by Lithuanians, implemented and fought against, has been studied by far fewer.[3] Next, I shall discuss the birth of *Sajudis* and the split in the Communist Party of Lithuania, with an emphasis on their impact on the national minorities. This chapter will provide the backdrop for an understanding of why some Russians, Poles and Jews joined the Lithuanian national movement, *Sajudis*, and some others joined the movement in support of the Soviet Union, *Edinstvo*, while the rest were not politically involved at all and the small minority opted for involvement in cultural and religious organisations.

The birth of opposition movements

The secret speech, delivered by Khrushchev in 1956 to the 20th Congress of the Communist Party of the Soviet Union, together with the events in Hungary in 1956, played a very important role in the rebirth of Lithuanian nationalism in the 1960s.

Khrushchev supported the 'flourishing' (*rascvetanie*) of the Soviet nations but, at the same time, hoped for their 'merging' (*sliianie*) as he hoped that federal borders would soon lose significance.[4] In the period 1958–61 he purged the 'national communists' as he described them.[5] In comparison with Khrushchev, Brezhnev pursued more decentralised nationality policies, which, while not amounting to Lenin's *korenizat-siia* (indigenity),[6] nonetheless allowed for culture, education and cadre policy to be under the control of the republics.

This was a period in which Lithuanians, like the Estonians and Latvians, more openly addressed their national history, mostly through cultural means of expression, especially literature and poetry.[7] As Marcinkevicius himself pointed out, the themes of homeland, language and culture were the main topics of his poetry because they rekindled, and made him more conscious of, his Lithuanian origins. They were therefore of crucial importance in shaping his national identity. Poetry was his own national awakening, his personal *Sajudis*.[8] This cultural renaissance was also vital in giving rise to opposition movements which challenged the political reality.

The invocation of a personal *Sajudis* has its roots in the memory of independence, of the Forest Brothers movement and of exile in Siberia.[9] This stream of national sentiment was also based upon the dissidents who were encouraged by Khrushchev's and especially Brezhnev's coming to power as well as the 1975 Helsinki Agreement, and the communists who supported movements with a national orientation.

Furthermore, the Soviet federation was built on a paradox because, 'while it did not define the state or citizenry as a *whole* in national terms, it did define component *parts* of the state and the citizenry in national terms'.[10] The union republics were territorial units, according to the letter of the law, but in practice they corresponded to titular nationalities after which they were named. In 1989 only 140 000 or 4.5 per cent of Lithuanians lived outside Lithuania, which was the smallest such percentage in the Soviet Union.[11] *De jure* union republics were given a right to self-determination but *de facto* they were not allowed to raise the issue of secession.

The leadership of the union republics were able to champion the interests of their republics but under the scrutiny of the centre. This was possible because of the policy of *korenizatsiia* which legitimised the preferential treatment of the titular nation, especially in relation to education and employment. Although this policy was introduced in the 1920s and actively promoted until the early 1930s, it continued to be tolerated throughout the Soviet period.

My analysis will concentrate on the last two groups, dissidents and communists, and their importance for the birth of the Lithuanian national movement. They are vital in understanding how and why *Sajudis* was born. They are also important because they clearly highlight that a national idea, understood either as a 'political principle' in Ernest Gellner's terms or as a flourishing of the Lithuanian language and culture, was on the agenda.

These two groups (dissidents and communists) played a crucial role in defining and shaping civil society. Civil society was not acknowledged by the state; on the contrary, it was permanently invaded and, therefore, to paraphrase George Konrad, 'it turned its back towards the state'. One can argue that in a closed society there was a closed space which performed civil society activities. That closed space produced activities which were issue-oriented such as religion, culture and environment. All these issues had and still have a national dimension which brought their supporters together in the form of the Popular Front movement, in opposition to a common enemy of the Soviet Union.[12]

The post-Stalin Soviet leaders believed that the nationality question had been solved politically and ideologically although they acknowledged that there were still national problems. This belief was based on an underestimation of the national question and on an inadequate knowledge of the facts involved, which resulted in a hope that the national question could be solved only if national differences were eliminated.[13] The post-Stalin Soviet leaders hoped that the Soviet federation together with policies of Sovietization, Russification, *korenizatsiia* and inter-republic migration, would create both the flourishing and coming together of different Soviet nations. They believed that Soviet patriotism would overshadow national interests. However, all the above policies paved the way for the disintegration of the Soviet Union and highlighted the importance of the national issue.[14]

In the 1960s Khrushchev introduced the doctrine of the Soviet people (*Sovetskii narod*) and Soviet culture. The common Soviet culture is understood as 'a synthesis to which the nationality culture may contribute a part of its original culture, thereby preserving certain of its own features in the newly formed general socialist Soviet culture'.[15] The party leaders during the Brezhnev period argued for a depoliticised cultural ethnicity. They believed in internationalist and patriotic ritual,[16] because the main values of that culture were: collectivism, discipline, love of work, patriotism, internationalism and atheism.[17] These were building blocks towards the ultimate goal to create a '*Homo Sovieticus*'. New rituals to bolster the policy of national integration were introduced in the late 1950s.[18] As the sociologist

Iurii Arutiunian argues, the highly organised rituals had minimal effect.[19] They were seen as an 'organised show'.[20] This led to dualistic behaviour which enabled people to coexist with the authorities. The ultimate result seems to have been a *Homo Duplex*. However, Gorbachev still believed 'that there is such an entity as the Soviet citizen who would rise above the citizen of the republics and ethnic communities'.[21]

Religious and national dissent

Lithuanian dissidents wanted to protect Lithuanian identity and save their homeland (*tevyne*) from the influence of Soviet culture. They put forward a religious and national agenda and they had an emotional bond to their homeland. Research undertaken by Theresa Smith and Thomas Oleszczuk found that dissidents[22] in the Soviet Union in the period 1965–81 were concentrated in four areas: the Baltic republics, Armenia, the Ukraine and Moldova.[23] Lithuanian dissidents were very careful when it came to organising or joining a particular group.[24] Even under these conditions, Lithuania had by far the highest number of dissidents in relation to its population.[25] Smith and Oleszczuk also pointed out that the nationalities activists, as a group, were disproportionately well educated and white collar.[26] All the data show that the Baltic republics suffered the least repression in the former Soviet Union, despite having the highest number of dissidents.[27] One reason for this, I would argue, was that Soviet State officials were aware of national tendencies in the Baltic republics and did not want to use too much pressure which could lead towards wider support for secession movements. Another reason was that the Baltic republics had a very important economic role within the Soviet Union. They acted as a crucial shop-window for the West. As a result, a more mixed approach was adopted, sometimes drawing upon conciliatory measures more widely than in the case of other nationalities in the Soviet Union.

In the case of Lithuania, Oleszczuk argued that we should distinguish between religious discontent, nationalism and human rights.[28] Nevertheless Oleszczuk held that different types of dissent were closely related in reality because all of them were 'simply aspects of the same set of problems' and have 'common bases of recruitment'.[29]

A practical consequence for the opposition movements in Lithuania was the awareness that, in the reality of everyday oppositional activity, these movements were influenced by each other, and therefore worked closely together.[30] In Lithuania, religion and nationality have been synonymous for more than one hundred years.[31] The Catholic Church has seen itself as a guardian of national identity, and the Lithuanian State has been, and still continues to be, supportive of the Church.

An analysis of the Roman Catholic Church in Lithuania reveals two noticeable characteristics. First, during Czarist times, the clergy provided not only ecclesiastical but also secular leaders in Lithuania because those with secular higher education had to leave the country. The result of the Russification policy introduced by the government of Czar Nikolai I was not the withering of the Lithuanian nation and religion, but a convergence of nationality and Catholicism. Furthermore, the religious and educational policies of Bishop Motiejus Valancius of Kaunas, which forged the 'Catholic Lithuanian nation' played an important role.[32] Second, the clergy openly fought the incorporation of Lithuania into the USSR in 1940 and 1944–5. As a result, three out of four bishops were arrested as well as a third of Lithuanian priests.[33] Throughout the Soviet era, the Lithuanian Catholic Church struggled for religious as well as national rights.[34]

As a result of the conference in Helsinki in 1975, whose final agreement was also signed by the Soviet Union, human rights groups mushroomed all over Eastern Europe and the former Soviet Union.[35] In Lithuania several publications with a national perspective joined the *Chronicle of the Lithuanian Catholic Church*.[36] In November 1976 the Lithuanian Helsinki Watch Group was established. The founders of that group made a public announcement about their membership and the issues about which they were concerned. This was a significant factor in distinguishing them from other opposition movements, which carefully protected the identity of their members. Unlike the other opposition movements in Lithuania, the Lithuanian Helsinki Watch Group was concerned with the human rights record of the Soviet Union in general. Their report dealt with people with different religious, ethnic and political orientations who had been persecuted in the Soviet Union. They worked closely with other Helsinki Watch Groups in the former Soviet Union. In practice this meant signing petitions on issues like the Soviet invasion of Afghanistan, the banishment of Andrei Sakharov, the 1939 Nazi–Soviet pact, the persecution of Russian Baptists, etc. Nevertheless, the issues raised by the Lithuanian group itself were mostly connected with religious rights and the banishment of bishops and priests. As Oleszczuk himself admits, 'only one percent of dissidents (six cases) were solely human rights activists'.[37]

Lithuanian communists

Although Catholic dissent played the most important role during the Soviet era, it was not responsible for the collapse of the Soviet regime. Nor was Landsbergis responsible for the collapse of the Soviet Union, although he liked to claim that this was the case.[38] Nevertheless, *Sajudis* played the most important role in national reawakening, carefully distancing itself from the existing dissident movement. Among the people who were active in this movement were the members of the Communist Party of Lithuania. Aleksandras Shtromas argues that 'the first and most outspoken Baltic dissidents were former communist idealists'.[39]

Shtromas highlights the role which Lithuanian communists played in the Soviet period. 'By the first half of the 1950s there were no more indigenous Baltic people who continued to support the Soviet regime out of idealism or conviction. Nor did any of the indigenous Balts still believe in communism as represented and implemented by this regime.'[40] This sweeping generalisation allows us to conclude that there were three groups of people forming the new political elite; those who supported the regime for their own benefit, those who supported the regime in order to do something for Lithuania and finally genuine communists whose ideals were crushed by the Soviet reality.[41] The first group of people, then, made a primarily rational choice and for private reasons, ranging from fear to greed, blindly supported the regime. Defining himself as belonging to the second group, Gediminas Kirkilas pointed out, 'If Lithuania was occupied, the communists were occupied too. They could be called collaborators but somebody had to take that role. Because of their aim, more sovereignty for Lithuania, they were ready to collaborate with the regime which understood only top-down orders and showed unhesitating readiness to destroy any genuine local level initiatives. The intelligentsia realised that it is either *us* or the Russians.'[42] Some people were ready to obey the orders and to try to readjust them towards protecting their national culture. Juozas Karosas argued that the Communist Party members, including himself, made a 'moral compromise' with themselves and enrolled in the Party to 'save Lithuania'.[43] I would accept that the majority of the members of the Communist Party were not genuine communists. Most of them earned their money from the Soviet regime, but were not committed to it. They became members for various reasons, including the goal of fighting for an independent Lithuania as well as more pragmatic considerations, such as the wish to enrich themselves or 'buy' themselves a job, a flat, a passport, etc. They accepted the rules of the game and this influenced their value system and their behaviour. They stayed silent when it came to expressing their own opinion and were vocal in expressing the official one. Therefore, membership in the Communist Party meant being a part of a new political elite and engaging in the process of political and social mobility. This could be an explanation, on the one hand, for the stability of nationality relations and on the other hand, for the demand for more autonomy.[44]

In comparison with V. Stanley Vardys, Shtromas highlights the support which Russian dissidents gave to Lithuania.[45] Vardys argued in 1978 that only 'Future historians will be able to tell what actual influence the Russians had, or did not have, on the Lithuanian ideas.'[46]

The Lithuanian dissidents were much more involved in dissident movements of other Soviet republics that were striving for independence (for example, Georgia, Armenia and especially Ukraine) than in the Russian dissident movement. How far could this attitude be explained by identifying Russians with Soviets? When it comes to the main focus of the Lithuanian opposition movements, their attitude towards Russians in Lithuania is of crucial importance. The Russians, especially those who came after the Second World War and who made up the majority of Russians in Lithuania, were seen purely in terms of a community which symbolised the Kremlin and Soviet totalitarian rule.[47] They were often treated as a single category. From 1956 onwards, demonstrators would carry banners declaring, 'Freedom for Lithuania' and 'Russians out of Lithuania'.[48] The legitimisation of the regime was questioned because it came to power through the secret protocol of the Soviet–Nazi non-aggression pact of 1939.[49] Although the official view differed and Soviet politicians argued that the communist system was introduced at 'the request of the people of Lithuania' and by the Lithuanian Communist Party, they could not deny the active role that the Communist Party of the Soviet Union and the Red Army had played in these developments.[50]

This pact between the Soviet and Nazi regimes allowed for the policies of Russification and Sovietisation which were imposed on the Baltic people by the Kremlin.[51] According to the Lithuanian opposition movements, the most important role in their implementation was played by the Russians and 'a lot of different nationalities whom they invited here'.[52] No account was taken of the fact that all decisions in the Soviet Union were made by the political elite, and the Russians who were sent to the Baltic states were usually just obeying orders.[53] Nevertheless, they were still perceived as a symbol of the Kremlin and therefore there was 'a growing opposition to the settlements of

Russians in the Baltic region as well as to the Russianisation of political, economic, cultural institutions and social relations'.[54]

In 1988, prompted by the emergence of the Lithuanian national movement, an increasing number of people who had previously remained silent during the Soviet era joined *Sajudis*. They had stayed silent until this time because, although they could not accept the regime, they did not have the courage to challenge it. As I have pointed out, dissident groups were very suspicious and operated in a covert manner. They relied on a small number of people and well trusted friends. This very much resembled the first organisations within the Communist Party, usually called cells, consisting of only a small number of people in the knowledge that a larger group would entail higher chances of infiltration by an agent provocateur. It is no surprise, therefore, that quite a number of people acted individually and struggled against the regime in their own particular way.[55] Romualdas Ozolas remembers this period as the time 'after 1968 when it was obvious that socialism was dead. After the Tashkent Conference people were furious and they decided that something had to be done. ... *My* way of fighting the Soviet regime was through editing classical translations, not Marxist texts.'[56]

The birth of *Sajudis* and the 'new' Communist Party

Sajudis was not formed as an opposition movement.[57] The very name of the movement (meaning restructuring) suggests that it was in tune with Gorbachev's *perestroika*. Initially, *perestroika* was understood as the economic project of 'acceleration' whose aim was to transform the Soviet economy.[58] The experiment was supposed to take place in the Baltic republics because they were industrially the most developed parts of the Soviet Union. In the republics themselves, there was a lot of support for economic restructuring, both among the party members and the wider population, especially the intelligentsia. The intelligentsia interpreted it not simply as economic restructuring, but as a vehicle towards economic independence. This interpretation was based on the fact that the process of acceleration also entailed increased economic responsibility. It meant not only learning and developing responsibility for both managers and workers, but it also questioned the very nature of the Soviet economic system. In the centrally planned economy, there were no incentives either for workers or managers to work harder. Both their jobs and salaries were guaranteed. In this period of reform, there was space to ask questions about whether economic deterioration was the result of economic stagnation under Brezhnev, or whether the whole idea behind the system should be rethought. The Baltic intelligentsia supported the re-thinking of the idea behind the system.[59]

In the Political Programme of *Sajudis*, which was presented at the constituent congress in October 1988 under the category General Principles, it was argued that one of the main goals of *Sajudis* was the 'revival of the political, economic and cultural sovereignty of the Lithuanian SSR'.[60] This represented a new vocabulary in the public realm of the Soviet Union.

> In 1988 it was possible to talk in terms of sovereignty, democratisation, openness etc. mostly as a result of *glasnost*… Although, *glasnost* is usually translated as 'openness', it did not only mean, as in the Khrushchev period, the airing of certain forbidden themes.[61]

Etymologically, *glasnost* derives from the Russian word *glas*, which is a medieval version of the modern word *golos* meaning 'voice'.[62] Therefore, for the intelligentsia[63] in the Soviet Union *glasnost* also meant expressing and hearing different opinions.[64] However, Gorbachev still emphasised 'socialist' voices. For the majority of the population, it was very difficult to understand the meaning of yet another socialism, although they were aware that the meaning was still decided by the Party leadership (as in the preceding decades).

In the Soviet Union, in 1988, 'democratic' opposition was expected to be expressed within the socialist ideology.[65] However, in Lithuania the Party was challenged by, and had to respond to, the Lithuanian intelligentsia and the people. This response was embodied not only in a new leader but also in new policies. Algirdas Brazauskas was seen as a reformer and as somebody who could sense and understand the popular mood. His election was welcomed by *Sajudis*. He attended the *Sajudis* Constituent Congress which was held on 22 and 23 October 1988, two days after his election,[66] and he played a very important role in the discussion about its Political Programme. On Brazauskas' initiative, 'the right to secede' was dropped from the Programme. 'Once *Sajudis* was founded, it attempted to marshal its forces. In turn, the Communist Party of Lithuania attempted to contain *Sajudis*'s influence.'[67]

However, Brazauskas was not the only member of the Communist Party of Lithuania who attended the Congress.[68] When the National Council of *Sajudis* was elected, 15 out of 35 members were members of the Communist Party. Throughout the Soviet era, the Party became increasingly indigenous.[69] It should be noted that 'there had been no cohort of Lithuanian emigrants in the Soviet Union who could return and become Moscow's local representatives'.[70] It had long been argued that the Communist Party of Lithuania had been protecting Lithuanian national interests.[71] According to a Lithuanian *samizdat* author who was personally familiar with Antanas Snieckus, who led Lithuania with a strong hand, Snieckus 'changed beyond recognition' in the late 1940s and the beginning of 1950s.[72] He increasingly sought to protect Lithuanian national interests while, at the same time, staying in 'Moscow's good books'.[73] Snieckus is viewed as one of 'The "realistically minded" native apparatchiks who learned how to avoid risks and continued to serve the regime obediently [and] were perhaps more bitter about the situation in which they found themselves than anybody else.'[74]

Bearing in mind the already mentioned paradox of Soviet federalism, I argue that a 'territorial bureaucracy' model[75] is partly able to explain how it was possible for an 'autonomist' nationalist or 'national' communist to remain in power for so long.

> For in a territorial bureaucracy, to the gap between horizontal strata is added the distance between the place where rules are formulated and the place where they are implemented. To the lack of communication between strata is added the partial independence that territorial agents enjoy because the bulk of their actions are hidden from their superiors. And to the resentment of lower-level bureaucrats at the irrelevance of the impersonal rules they administer is added their social and personal affinity to the local population. Thus, the sharp edge of central policies is softened by the peripheral agent of the state in his contacts with grassroots public.[76]

The phenomenon of territorial bureaucracy results in a very pronounced psychology of 'enclaving' in the ethnoregional territorial bureaucracy. Rank-and-file members felt that within their republics they should be the decisive group. 'In an authoritarian system, the politics of policy implementation (assumes) at least equal importance with the politics of policy formation.'[77] As a result, the Moscow policies were imprinted with a national stamp. Everything related to the distribution of power between centre and periphery, and Russians and non-Russians.[78] The Lithuanian Communist Party had an increasingly large component of the indigenous population in its rank and file (as previously pointed out). If we accept Shtromas's distinction between different groups of people forming a new political elite, then we can argue that 'enclaving' was possible because of a willingness to have loyalty towards both the official and the national ideology. One must also take into account the importance of the territorial unit within the Soviet federal system. In the Soviet Union 'educational and occupational advantages accrue to members of ethnic groups residing in their own republics: the composition of elites and professional cadres is governed largely by the principle of territorial representation'.[79]

In the context of power relations between centre and periphery, it would be useful to understand the distribution of power between centre and periphery according to the sociological theories of conflict. We should take into account authors like Ralph Dahrendorf,[80] who highlights the coercive aspect, or Lewis Coser,[81] who emphasises the integrative functions of social conflict, drawing upon Parsons. In other words, these theorists discuss groups within a society who are either in conflict because of 'the dichotomous distribution of authority' which involves 'conflicting interests' in relation to power, values or scarce resources, or who are ready to become 'flexible' so their 'pragmatic interests' serve 'defensive purposes' and prevent disintegration. These theories also highlight the importance of acknowledging that there are multiple interests and that different interests are of equal importance in shaping the political climate in a particular republic (as was pointed out in the analysis of the behaviour of Lithuanians during the Soviet era). Central government in Moscow lacked moral authority and therefore shared its power with the local leadership who also wanted to preserve the existing structure. The Lithuanian leadership believed that they had found the best formula to protect national interests and keep the regime going, while at the same time providing themselves with a secure living and associated perks. In the words of Tomas Venclova,

> The mandarins conformed to the system, half-submerged in the morass of reciprocal flattery, intrigue, and personal conflict, deprived of the critical attitude towards the society and themselves, but at the same time convinced that they were the bearers of culture and the champions of Lithuanian identity – beliefs fostered by the fact that the regime would lightly reprimand them once in a while.[82]

When opposition groups were able to implement their interests to challenge the existing system, conflict appeared because the system was too rigid to change.

Drawing upon the territorial model and conflict analyses, allows us to understand why the Party, under Brazauskas, agreed to actively collaborate with the Lithuanian national movement. I would argue that the

Party realised the 'reality of life' (the phrase Brazauskas loved to use) in acknowledging that *Sajudis* was the 'decisive group' within the republic. This entailed the realisation that the Communist Party did not have its ideological ally in the Communist Party of the Soviet Union but 'at home' and that it had to respond to the issues which were already put on the agenda by *Sajudis*. In this period, *Sajudis* came out with a recommendation that the Day of Soviet Constitution should not be celebrated because 'not a single Soviet Constitution, respected its own words/what it said'.[83] How did the Communist Party of Lithuania respond? Given the extent to which being Lithuanian and being Catholic were identified, it comes as no surprise that there was a liberalisation of the restrictions on religious life.[84] If we also remember the importance of language in Lithuanian nation-building, then it is also no surprise that the Lithuanian language was officially legalised as the state language. The national flag and anthem were legalised, reflecting the vital role of national symbols.[85] Furthermore, some political prisoners were released.[86] The Communist Party of Lithuania responded to the demands of *Sajudis*, rather than actually initiating policies themselves. They played the role which they knew quite well; the role given to them, and consequently remained an indecisive group.

Those members of the Communist Party who were also members or supporters of *Sajudis* realised that the only way for the Party to survive was to change its status *vis-à-vis* the Communist Party of the Soviet Union and the State as a whole. When the Supreme Soviet of the Soviet Union admitted the existence the Soviet–Nazi Pact in August 1989, the legitimation of Soviet rule was destroyed. On 23 September 1989, the Supreme Soviet of Lithuania declared that the Soviet law which had accepted Lithuania into the Soviet Union was illegal. Another factor in the Party's decision to change its status in 1989 was the fact that the 2nd Congress of the USSR People's Deputies was supposed to take place in Moscow on 23 December 1989 and adopt the Constitutional Compliance Law. The Baltic republics were against this law because 'It could become an "instrument for the recarving" of the republican constitutions on the plea of bringing them into line with the all-Union fundamental law.'[87] This argument was the rationale behind a decision of the 20th Congress of the Lithuanian Communist Party, held on 20 December 1989, to declare the Party an independent political organisation with its own programme and statute.[88]

In the course of my interviews, no one questioned the need for the Party to survive. An explanation for the survival of the Party in 1989 would certainly have differed from one in 1992, when the LDDP and *Sajudis* subscribed to different positions. I would argue that the

Party reasoning could be connected with their pride in the way they had cherished national culture during the Soviet era. However, neither their efforts at preserving national culture, nor the implementation of Party reform prevented Lithuanian communists from losing the first multiparty elections.[89] It was a sweeping victory for the candidates supported by *Sajudis*, among whom were the members of the independent Communist Party. When the new legislature met on 10 March 1990, *Sajudis* had a quorum of two-thirds needed for a constitutional action and on 11 March Lithuania was declared independent. The right-wing section in *Sajudis* were keen to gain independence and although quite a few people whom I interviewed argued that they were surprised by the speed of events they felt they could not, and should not, alter the course of these events. Their political instinct told them to slow down the process of declaring independence and to negotiate with Gorbachev (to prevent hard-liners in Moscow from being given an excuse to clamp down on Lithuania). However, emotionally, they supported independence.

Sajudis was, at the beginning, a movement which united Kaunas nationalists, Vilnius liberal intellectuals and reform communists.[90] Its aim was Lithuanian independence, although it used the language of sovereignty.[91] Therefore, it behaved like an umbrella organisation, embracing all those who were in support of their main goal. This goal was achieved just a month before the Second Congress of *Sajudis* in April 1990. According to the official documents, this congress is remembered for a decision to separate *Sajudis* deputies in the Supreme Soviet from the *Sajudis* movement.[92] This was in contradiction to the claim that *Sajudis* wanted to remain a movement rather than being turned into a party.[93] Transformation into a party was perceived as the desire to transform *Sajudis* into a 'state party which is very much a socialist approach'.[94] Nikolai Medvedev saw it as the re-introduction of totalitarian thinking although its rhetoric was anti-communist.[95] According to the participants, the atmosphere in the congress corridors began to be increasingly nationalistic. *Sajudis* had created a conflict around the question: who is a real, proper Lithuanian? Furthermore, it claimed that it knew the answer, which consisted of uniting under the national flag for the sake of a 'brighter' future. This congress made a considerable number of Vilnius liberal intellectuals and reform communists leave the movement.[96] They felt uncomfortable with policies that divided the population into 'patriots' and 'communists'. This meant that *Sajudis* was now made up predominantly of right-wing Kaunas nationalists.[97] Their rhetoric turned more and more nationalistic.

This shift towards a nationalistic attitude had major implications for the communists and national minorities.[98] In relation to national minorities, *Sajudis* argued that the Poles in the South-East of Lithuania were manipulated by the Communist Party of the Soviet Union, and it was this that lay behind their demand for autonomy in September 1989. This demand was interpreted as an attempt to secede and join the Soviet Union in May 1990. *Sajudis* argued that the Soviet blockade, which was enforced in April 1990, showed that the communists were prepared to reverse the pace of change and negotiate with Gorbachev.[99] Kazimiera Prunskiene, the Prime Minister, was prepared to talk to Gorbachev and persuaded Landsbergis to implement a moratorium on independence on 23 June 1990.

The moratorium again fuelled the right-wing section in *Sajudis* to maintain their distinction between *us* and *them*, 'patriots' who are for independence and 'communists' who are ready to negotiate with Moscow. Prunskiene was 'charged' with having connections with the KGB during the Soviet era. In autumn 1990 there was a reshuffle in the Soviet government which brought hard-liners to power. This fuelled nationalistic rhetoric even further. People whom I interviewed even referred to this in terms of 'hysteria'. On 11 January 1991 Gorbachev ordered the Soviet troops to take over Lithuania. In the second part of January, Lithuania was united, but only temporarily. Prunskiene and Arvydas Juozaitis joined forces and formed the Future Forum in April 1991, together with quite a few former members of *Sajudis* and members of the LDDP, such as Gediminas Kirkilas. This was an attempt to generate an opposition to Landsbergis and *Sajudis*. Its meetings were attacked not only verbally but also with petrol bombs and stones. The failed August 1991 coup brought international recognition to Lithuania but the nationalistic attitude stayed. It was regenerated by the opening of the KGB archives, which occurred in spite of the fact that the leader of the right-wing section of *Sajudis*, Virgilijus Cepaitis, was the first individual to be found 'guilty'.[100]

In the months before the Third Congress, held in December 1991, all the attention was turned towards Landsbergis.[101] He saw himself as the 'Father of the Nation', a title that had been used by Antanas Smetona. Present was oriented towards past and the past was turned into a myth highlighting the importance of one man, who was seen as father of the Lithuanian Nation and State. Landsbergis was always surrounded with Lithuanian national symbols and this symbolism reached its peak during the Congress. The Third Congress of *Sajudis* is officially remembered as being Landsbergis's attempt at restitution of the presidency.[102]

Juozaitis argued that 'great *Sajudis* turned into a pioneer organisation of the old Soviet times'.[103] This Congress is also remembered for Landsbergis's refusal to outline a programme. 'Stressing certain priorities will be similar to a programme. These should be honest work, family and native land.'[104] Again when it came to congress corridors and the backstage, there was a constant attack on the former communists and, in relation to this, national minorities.[105] Anti-Soviet attitudes began to evolve into anti-Russian and anti-Polish attitudes, as analysed in Chapters 6 and 7. The De-Sovietisation Law was discussed with the aim of driving all former communists out of power. It was especially aimed against Brazauskas. The 'hysteria' against communism and the Commonwealth of Independent States (CIS) reached its peak at this time. Foreign relations with CIS were non-existent. 'If *Sajudis'* first phase was academic anti-communism, this was the phase of militant anti-communism.'[106] Juozaitis called the last phase 'national socialism'.[107] If *Sajudis'* three congresses were seen as three steps backward by the LDDP Vice-President, the 20th Communist Party Congress was seen not as a step forward but as a step out of the entrenched circle defined by the Soviet communist ideology.[108]

Despite losing the 1990 elections and, in the period 1990–2, 33 out of 40 MPs,[109] the LDDP consolidated itself and began to oppose the *Sajudis* policies of conflict and differentiation. As a result, it won the 1992 elections. According to Ozolas, one explanation for the LDDP popularity and the 1992 election victory was the widely felt need to avoid conflicts.[110] National minorities differed in their approach to the LDDP victory.[111] Some of them were happy to see the demise of *Sajudis* and argued that the current situation could not get any worse. Others were ready to wait and see what the LDDP would do for Lithuanian national minorities. The minorities' responses to the *Sajudis* and LDDP attitudes will be analysed in Chapters 6–8.

Conclusion

This chapter has pointed out that the Lithuanian national movement has its origins in Soviet nationality policies as they were interpreted in Lithuania, as well as in the history of the Lithuanian dissident movement. The Soviet policies kept the national issue alive and the dissident movement bolstered the national agenda through its constant re-invention of Lithuanian history, highlighting its glorious past which needed to be reawakened. *Sajudis* was responsible for facilitating this revival. Initially, *Sajudis* was open towards national minorities, as long as they were in support of Lithuanian sovereignty and later independence. However, when the goal of independence was achieved *Sajudis* changed its rhetoric from being anti-Soviet to anti-Russian and anti-Polish. National minorities were viewed as political opponents. *Sajudis* and Landsbergis's thirst for power were expressed in nationalistic, as opposed to national, rhetoric.[112] All the above mentioned issues are crucial to our analysis of the role which national minorities played in the period of national reawakening or, more precisely, in the period before and after the independence (1988–93). We analyse how the issues that were raised by the Lithuanian national movement influenced their understanding of themselves and their national group. Given the importance of the cultural dimensions in nation-building, as well as of the 'political principle', we are dealing with issues of 'who I am' and 'where I belong'. This book concentrates primarily on issues of citizenship and how they galvanised national minorities to define themselves and their place in the independent Lithuania. Therefore, in the next chapter (Chapter 4) we shall analyse Lithuanian legislation on citizenship and the responses of minorities, which were mostly critical. As will be analysed in the second part of the book, this emergence of a nationalistic attitude was to have major implications for the citizenship of national minorities in independent Lithuania. To use Brubaker's terminology, one can define *Sajudis'* perception of Lithuania in this stage as a 'nationalising state', a nation-state which was insufficiently national, a state which had to push for the promotion of its own language and culture.[113]

4
The Issue of Citizenship in Lithuania: Legislation and the Ways it was Perceived

Introduction

This chapter analyses Lithuanian legislation on citizenship in the period from 1988 to 1993, as well as responses of national minorities and politicians. The question of how national minorities – the Poles, Russians and Jews – perceived the citizenship issue was a vital element in their acceptance of the new political surroundings and political boundaries. There are a few questions which should be considered. Were people familiar with the existing laws, and if so, how did they become aware? How did people interpret these laws? What did they feel about the ways in which the laws were implemented, and how did they perceive the relationship between the letter of the law and the reality of the implementation of the law? This last issue is critical to my research because the way in which national minorities and Lithuanian politicians interpreted the laws, raised particular issues and specific demands concerning citizenship rights. To interpret the letter of the law one has to bear in mind the political context in which the letter of the law exists. This context influences the understanding of the letter of the law very much. Additionally, we shall consider the laws concerning the citizenship issue in the context of international law and how these were understood by national minorities (in Chapters 6–8) and Lithuanian politicians. The opinion of Lithuanian politicians is crucial because they were the policy-makers and played a key role in debates and negotiations in the early stages of the evolution of minority laws.

The principal concern of this discussion is citizenship rights which fall into the area of human rights. Human rights are mainly the rights of individual human beings against their infringement by the state.

The rules of international law, framed in terms of the protection of human rights against state interference, are largely a post-1945 phenomenon.[1] Before this period, international law emphasised rights stemming from the membership of a nation rather than an individual's rights.[2] There are four principles which fall under the broad notion of human rights, and they are well established in the International Bill of Human Rights:[3] (1) The human right of people to political self-determination and of minorities to conditions that facilitate the preservation of their culture; (2) The inviolability of existing borders and the integrity of states; (3) The human right to citizenship; and (4) Constraints on forced or discrimination-induced population transfers across international borders.[4]

The way in which newly independent states treat their minorities is a strong indication of their attitude towards democracy. In literature on the Baltics, the citizenship issue is primarily raised in relation to the treatment of national minorities. In assessing the treatment of minorities, various factors of potential discrimination need to be taken into account. First, the region has had a history of animosity between different national groups. Second, there has been a tendency among majorities to value their own national group and territory as something special. Third, democracy was poorly developed due to the dictatorship that existed before the Second World War and the communist regime that came after the war.

Lithuanian legislation on citizenship

The evolution of Lithuanian citizenship legislation must be understood, more generally, in the context of the rise of the Lithuanian national movement as described in the previous chapter. However, it should also be seen in the context of one of the central issues of Lithuanian foreign policy in the late 1980s and early 1990s; the withdrawal of Russian military forces from the territory of the Republic of Lithuania.[5] Until the Russian military forces left their country on 31 August 1993, Lithuanians did not feel that they were a sovereign and independent country.[6] Furthermore, the pressure from members of the national minorities as well as Lithuanians played an important role in shaping the Lithuanian legislation on citizenship.

In order to understand citizenship issues in Lithuania, it is necessary to analyse the following laws: the Law on Citizenship, the Law on National Minorities, the Decree on Language, the Law on the Legal

Status of Foreigners in the Republic of Lithuania and the Law on Immigration.[7]

The Provisional Basic Law and the Lithuanian Constitution

Before analysing these laws, I shall briefly summarise the Provisional Basic Law of the Republic of Lithuania of 11 March 1991 and the 1992 Constitution.

According to Article 14 of the Provisional Basic Law, all Lithuanian citizens 'shall be equal before the law'.[8] Furthermore, because citizens of Lithuania 'have equal rights', discrimination on the basis of nationality 'shall be prosecuted by law'.[9] However, when it comes to the right to be educated in one's mother tongue there is 'the possibility to receive instructions at schools in one's native language'.[10] Only citizens have the right to organise political parties and social organisations.[11] The issue of property was not defined by this Law but it was left to the other 'laws of Lithuania and inter-state agreements'.[12]

The 1992 Constitution guarantees equal rights to 'all people'.[13] The Constitution uses the terms: individual, person and people interchangeably. National minorities are mentioned for the first time in Article 37 which guarantees 'the right to foster their language, culture and customs'.[14] In comparison with the Provisional Basic Law, this Constitution guarantees cultural autonomy to its national minorities. 'Ethnic communities of citizens shall independently administer the affairs of their ethnic culture, education, organisations, charity, and mutual assistance. The State shall support ethnic communities.'[15]

The Constitution was criticised both by foreign observers and liberal Lithuanians because it underlined the importance of family and nation over the individual.[16] National identity was very often perceived in biological terms, 'Something that gives authenticity to human beings'.[17] Virgilijus Cepaitis argued that 'it is one of the first feelings of a human being. The other one relates to the family. Family and nation are bringing people together, tying them up.'[18] The Constitution also highlights the importance of morals or morality without defining them. For example, religious organisations can be forbidden if they 'contradict morality or the law'.[19] Furthermore, citizens can be refused the right to organise a peaceful meeting if it is judged 'necessary to protect the security of the State or the community, public order, people's health or morals, or the rights and freedoms of other people'.[20]

Laws on citizenship

The current law on citizenship, passed by the *Seimas* (Lithuanian Parliament) on 5 December 1991, replaced the Citizenship Law of 3 November 1989.

The 1991 Citizenship Law grants automatic citizenship in the Republic of Lithuania to:

1. Persons who were citizens of the Republic of Lithuania prior to 15 June 1940, and their children and grandchildren provided they have not acquired citizenship of another state;
2. Persons who were permanent residents in the territory of the Republic of Lithuania from the period 9 January 1919 to 15 June 1940, as well as their children and grandchildren, provided that on the day of entry into force of this Law they have been permanent residents in Lithuania, and are not citizens of another state;
3. Persons who acquired citizenship of the Republic of Lithuania or had it restored to them prior to 4 November 1991 under the Law on Citizenship which had been in force before the enactment of this Law;[21]
4. Persons who have implemented the right to citizenship of the Republic of Lithuania, or had citizenship of the Republic of Lithuania restored to them under this Law; and
5. Other persons who have acquired citizenship of the Republic of Lithuania under this Law.[22]

Citizenship may also be granted (upon his or her request) to a person who meets the following conditions:

1. Has passed the examination in the Lithuanian language (can speak and read Lithuanian);
2. For the last ten years has had a permanent place of residence on the territory of the Republic of Lithuania;
3. Has a permanent place of employment or a continuous legal source of support in the territory of the Republic of Lithuania;
4. Has passed the examination in the basic provisions of the Constitution of the Republic of Lithuania; and
5. Is a person without citizenship, or is a citizen of a state under the laws of which he or she loses citizenship of said state upon acquiring citizenship of the Republic of Lithuania, or if the person notifies in writing of his or her decision to refuse citizenship

of another state upon being granted citizenship of the Republic of Lithuania.[23]

On the question of Lithuanian citizenship these two Laws (November 1989 and December 1991) differ on one main issue. The 1991 Law did not grant automatic citizenship for permanent residents 'while those who were citizens of Lithuania before 1940 were still granted citizenship without naturalisation'.[24] Article 12, paragraph 2 indirectly stated that Lithuania does not consider citizenship of the Soviet Union legally valid. The 1991 Citizenship Law addresses two additional issues. First, the 1991 Law allows the possibility that 'Citizenship of the Republic of Lithuania may be granted to foreign nationals who have been of merit to the Republic of Lithuania without applying to them conditions of granting citizenship specified in Article 12 of this Law.'[25] Second, the 1991 Law was more elaborate on the issues which can preclude the granting of citizenship.[26]

The revised Law on Citizenship is regarded as meeting international standards. As Bernhardt and Schermers reveal,

> We have been told that an overwhelming majority of the members of the minority (more than 90 percent[27]) have opted for Lithuanian citizenship, and we have not heard any complaints about the applicable rules and their implementation. This does not exclude that in individual cases hardship and injustice may result from the rules in practice. But we do not find any indication that the rules in general do not meet international standards.[28]

As will be seen later (Chapters 6–8), I would argue that there were in fact quite a few individual cases of injustice both according to my interviews and reports in newspapers.[29]

First, though, I would like to address the issue of the laws themselves and suggest that there are five potential problems in these laws; three mentioned in the report quoted above and two which still need to be addressed. The first problem is the issue of dual citizenship which was particularly drawn to my attention in various interviews with Russians. Bernhardt and Schermers are less concerned with Russians' complaints than with the extent to which the letter of the law is 'in conformity with international and especially European standards'.[30] The problem was the wording in the Provisional Basic Law of Article 13 which starts, '*As a rule*, a citizen of Lithuania may not be concurrently a citizen of another country…' (my emphasis). This clumsy definition allowed

Kazys Bobelis, who had American citizenship, to be given Lithuanian citizenship so he could take part in the 1992 Lithuanian parliamentary elections.[31] However, according to Article 18 of the Citizenship Law (adopted in April 1991), it was explicitly stated that there was no possibility of having dual citizenship. Dual citizenship was not addressed in the 1989 law and, therefore, one could argue, implicitly existed.[32] Nevertheless, according to Article 16 one could get Lithuanian citizenship if one was of 'merit to the Republic of Lithuania'. The 'Russians of Lithuania', especially, felt that they should be treated differently because they had been living in Lithuania for a very long period of time and wished to remain there.[33] The Labour government claimed that 'each state should primarily take care of its own nationals'. However, this proposal was disputed not only by national minorities, but also by the Department of National Minorities, which pointed out that it violated the Lithuanian Constitution.[34] Nevertheless, in December 1993 an amendment to the Citizenship Law was passed which granted dual citizenship to a larger number of émigrés.[35] This was a direct infringement of human rights, because it favoured one ethnic community over others, of which the Lithuanian government was aware.[36]

The second problem arises from the issue of loyalty to the Lithuanian state, which is required from Lithuanian citizens (Law on Citizenship, Article 3). While the law itself did not define what it meant by loyalty, the representatives of the Council were told that it 'means for all citizens that they must respect and abide by the law'.[37] The third problem was connected with the possibility that an individual may be deprived of Lithuanian citizenship by a decision of the Presidium or if s/he has committed grave offences against the Republic or humanity (Article 20). It can be argued that the deprivation of citizenship should be a legal issue and not a political one. Furthermore, the UN Convention on the Reduction of Statelessness (1961) in Article 7 clearly states that 'such a renunciation shall not result in the loss of nationality unless the person concerned possesses or acquires another nationality'.[38] The fourth problem is the lack of clarity as to what will happen to the people who were permanent residents of Lithuania between 15 June 1940 and 3 November 1991 if they had not applied for Lithuanian citizenship before 3 November 1991 (as required by the 1989 Law).[39] The fifth problem relates to the treatment of the officers of the Soviet Army. It seems that the Law on Citizenship is ambiguous. In the Resolution on the Procedure for Implementing the Republic of Lithuania Law on Citizenship, in Article 5 it is not clear whether or not Soviet Army Officers can apply because they 'may not be considered as permanently residing or employed in Lithuania'.[40] What does 'may not' mean? This could possibly be seen as a loophole in the law which gives the state the power to decide each case individually. I came across several cases where people would raise the question as to how the officers of the Soviet Army managed to get passports.

Law on National Minorities

The Law on National Minorities in Lithuania respects international treaties, particularly after the amendments of 29 January 1991.[41] The Law is inspired by universally accepted norms regarding the status of national minorities.[42] The language is regarded as the most important element of a national culture and, therefore, everybody has the right to be educated in their native tongue. National minorities are entitled to publish newspapers, and broadcast radio and TV programmes in their native language. Minority groups have the right to practise their own religions and should be allowed to develop all forms and types of cultural organisation.[43] The centrality of language within national culture is demonstrated very clearly in the various amendments that have been added to the Law. They are all connected with the right to use the native language. The amendment to Article 2, for example, guarantees the right of an individual to be educated in his/her native language. Articles 4, 5 and 7 are completely new and address the use of native language in areas with a 'substantial minority group',[44] arguing that the minority language should be used in addition to the official language of the state. Information signs in these areas should be written in both languages; and the state should support the educational and cultural institutions of minorities. 'In practice, however, the amendment works only where the minority is in fact a local majority. Thus in Vilnius and Klaipeda, while Russians represent over a quarter and over a third of the population respectively, this has not prevented the banishing of Russian from street signs, official name-plaques, and many official documents.'[45]

Decree on Language

All of the above mentioned issues are connected with the Decree on Language which became law on 25 January 1989. Lithuania (then still a Soviet Socialist Republic) was the first of the Baltic states to amend its Republican Constitution and make Lithuanian the official state language on 19 November 1988. While some provisions for the minority languages were made in the Decree on Language, the primary objective was the protection and propagation of the Lithuanian language. Article 1 states:

> That the Lithuanian language shall be the official language, that is the principal means of official communication for the people of the Republic. Lithuanian shall be used in carrying out the business of state and social bodies, in all spheres of public education, culture, science, industry, public services, communications and other areas of social life, and in all enterprises, institutions, and organisations of the Lithuanian SSR, irrespective of their institutional chain of command (with the exception of the armed forces).[46]

However, it allowed institutions (Article 2) whose business was until that time conducted in Russian to have a transition period of two or possibly three years. In accordance with the preamble it is stated in Article 8:

> That persons whose native language is a language other than Lithuanian shall be provided with appropriate facilities for organising pre-school education, classes, elementary and secondary education, for training teachers, for publishing books and newspapers in their native language, and for establishing societies of language and culture, clubs, museums, theatres, musical groups, etc. In pre-school educational institutions, elementary and secondary schools, and cultural organisations established for persons whose native language is other than Lithuanian, correspondence and other business may be conducted in the appropriate language.[47]

On 29 January 1991 the Parliament extended the learning period until 1 January 1995 to accommodate the national minorities in the republic.[48] In connection with the Law on National Minorities, however, the Parliament voted to allow state employees in areas with non-Lithuanian majorities (primarily South-East Lithuania which is predominantly inhabited by Poles) to use the language of national minorities in addition to the state language. This vote did not have any legal significance because the negative vote would have violated the amended Law on National Minorities. However, it differed from the Decree on Language which in Article 5 states: 'That seals, business forms, signs and plaques used in offices and in public places, as well as destinations on goods produced in the Republic and their description, shall be in the Lithuanian language.'[49] There are various explanations as to how it became possible for Parliament to vote on the issues already dealt with in the legislation. One possible explanation is, as we shall discuss later, the lack of adequate juristic knowledge.[50] In the previous chapter we pointed out that in the period of national reawakening so many events occurred simultaneously that people were not able to adequately follow them or register them. It could be argued that the parliamentary vote was a political gesture from MPs, the *Seimas* trying to gain credibility in the eyes of the minorities and the world community. After all, politics and ethics have been in many cases separated if not divorced.

Law on Immigration

Vytautas Landsbergis argued in 1990 that 'No migration control regulations have been worked out as yet. It is evident, however, that the economic sovereignty of the Republic and the law on Lithuanian citizenship should be a guarantee of limiting migration to Lithuania.'[51] Article 6 of the Law on Immigration states that an 'immigration quota shall be established by the Supreme Council of the Republic of Lithuania on the recommendation of the Government of the Republic of Lithuania'.[52] While this quota was discussed it is clear from existing evidence that it was never established. The lack of clarity on this issue is reflected in what Everistas Raisuotis had to say: 'I am not very familiar with the Law on Immigration. However, I think there must be some problem there too because there is a quota of how many people can move from the East to Lithuania. I cannot remember the number.'[53] Nevertheless, one has to bear in mind that this was a period when Lithuania had a negative net migration.[54] This may explain why the quota was never established in Lithuania.[55] One might also suggest that the quota was not implemented because the number of national minorities did not make up as substantial a proportion of the population as they did in Latvia and Estonia where there has been a worry that they could outnumber the native population.

Law on the Legal Status of Foreigners

The legal status and rights of people who apply for permanent residence and are already in the country is defined by the Law on the Legal Status of the Foreigners in the Republic of Lithuania, which was ratified on the same day as the Law on Immigration (4 September 1991). According to Article 17 of this law, 'Foreigners, who are permanently residing in the Republic of Lithuania and have a legal job, shall enjoy the same economic and social rights as citizens of the Republic of

Lithuania.' It is interesting that in connection with the issue of 'legal jobs' Lithuania introduced a system of fines for enterprises which imported workers but they have been rarely implemented. The Law of the Employment of the Population applies, except for the citizens of the Republic, only 'to foreign citizens and stateless persons according to the general procedure, with the exception of cases regulated by other laws or international agreements'.[56] However, Article 23 adds, 'Foreigners staying in the Republic of Lithuania shall enjoy the same rights to cultural properties as citizens of the Republic of Lithuania. Foreigners shall be guaranteed the right to use their native language, to protect and foster their culture and traditions.'[57] The problem with this article is that the mechanisms, especially financial, which will enable the implementation of the guarantees are not defined. Bernhardt and Schermers pointed out that 'Enumerations of specific rights suggest that foreigners have only a limited amount of fundamental human rights, excluding for instance, the freedom of expression.'[58] They are especially worried about Article 3 which, on the one hand, argues that foreigners 'shall enjoy the same rights and freedoms as the citizens of the Republic of Lithuania' and immediately adds that these rights could be restricted if the foreigners 'carry out activities detrimental to the interests of the Republic of Lithuania'. They also pointed out that Article 4 which states, 'The provisions of this law shall be applied with regard to citizens of foreign states upon a basis of reciprocity', is in clear conflict with Article 1 of the European Convention on Human Rights which states, 'It is unacceptable that the violations of human rights committed abroad against Lithuanians are retaliated against by violations of human rights against (usually innocent) citizens of a foreign state.'[59]

The response of the European Union to Lithuanian legislation on citizenship

This brief analysis of Lithuanian legislation shows that Lithuania is following the universally accepted norms regarding the status of national minorities.[60] This was confirmed in the report prepared for the Council of Europe.

A global answer to the question as to whether the legal order of the Republic of Lithuania meets the human rights standards, as enshrined in the Statute of the Council of Europe and the European Convention of Human Rights can be given in the affirmative; there can be no doubt according to the available information, that a democracy based on the rule of law has been founded and is in a process of further reform in order to eliminate still existing deficiencies. ... There are good reasons to assume that the law is not always adequately implemented. An independent and competent judiciary is necessary to overcome shortcomings. Law reform and adequate implementation of the law are equally needed.[61]

In connection with the analysis which follows it is important to quote Bernhardt and Schermers who in their report also tackled the issue of people's knowledge of human rights. Their observations confirm my own. 'In general, people have only vague ideas what human rights are. Often human rights are seen as the right to a good life. Any bad situation is therefore considered as an infringement of human rights.'[62]

Taking into account the above quoted report and his visit to Lithuania (21–23 January 1993), Max van der Stoel, CSCE High Commissioner on National Minorities, declared,

> I am pleased to note that the problem of citizenship for members of the Russian and Polish minorities has been virtually resolved. The relationship between the various population groups seems on the whole to be harmonious, even though a number of desiderata remain unfulfilled. I did register complaints of the Polish minority concerning registration procedures for regional elections. In this connection, I take the liberty to recommend to you the creation of the office of an Ombudsman, which could have as its main task to address in a non-judicial way complaints concerning administrative decisions and practices.[63]

It is interesting that Algirdas Brazauskas in February 1993, outlining policy priorities, stated, 'We are particularly worried about our bureaucracy, which sometimes gives people of different nationalities grounds for voicing grievances.'[64] This clearly indicates the fact that Lithuania was eager to show that it complied with the suggestions of the European Community. As a result on 14 May 1993 it became a State member of the Council of Europe.

Lithuanian politicians and the way they perceived their minority legislation

The opinions of the politicians on the legislation and its implementation differed according to the political party to which they belonged. It is difficult to talk in terms of left-wing and right-wing political parties, but one can use these concepts based on the opinion of the politicians themselves. However, according to my interviews, an important difference between right-wing and left-wing parties was their attitude towards communism. Right-wing parties were anti-communist while left-wing parties were post-communist. The right-wing parties concentrated primarily on condemning communist ideology, whereas the left-wing parties argued that the communist legacy should be taken into account while concentrating on developing a programme for the Lithuanian democratic future.

V. Stanley Vardys and Judith Sedaitis argued that one of the fundamental deficiencies in the political life of Lithuania was the 'underdevelopment of political platforms and party ideologies'.[65] My experience in autumn 1992 supports this statement. Before the general elections in October 1992 it was very difficult to obtain the political programmes of the different parties which took part in the elections. When it comes to our interest – national minorities – one could find hardly anything connected with that issue.

Those who, broadly speaking, perceived themselves as right-wing felt that Lithuania had very good laws in general and some of them could not understand why there were separate laws for national minorities.[66] The politicians who saw the need for minority laws argued that the laws were needed because 'in the most democratic state the minority rights could be easily violated'.[67] The second group indicated that all people should be treated equally and should not have special privileges. In the words of Romualdas Ozolas, 'I think our Law on Citizenship is liberal enough so we do not need a special Law on National Minorities.'[68] They viewed the Law on National Minorities as giving privileges to the minorities. They pointed out that its introduction reflected the Lithuanian orientation towards democracy and an understanding of the Soviet period which violated the rights of all nations and national minorities. 'During the Soviet years people were moved around with the aim of forgetting their own nationality in order to feel Soviet.'[69] Because of the years of violation of national rights, national minorities had to be given additional laws to feel comfortable. Lithuania was able to do that because, as Cepaitis argued, 'We were an important state and we know how to live with Slavs and other nations.' They proudly referred to the Grand Duchy and independent Lithuania. They argued that a part of the Lithuanian national identity was a 'feeling for statehood'. Their sense of pride was even more evident, once they compared themselves with the other two Baltic states 'which do not have a long tradition of statehood'. They would always add that they completely understood and supported the other two Baltic states for not being able to exercise the similar laws because of the large Russian minority.

It could be argued that this was a dangerous way of thinking because it viewed minority rights as being dependent upon historical circumstances and as a debt which needs to be payed due to the 'communist occupation'. Needless to say, the issue of collective rights was not seen as a real issue at all. These politicians did not see a lot of problems at the level of everyday life and, if problems existed, they were connected with a non-developed democratic culture, that is, underdeveloped as a result of being suppressed during the Soviet period. Their vision of democratic Lithuania did not involve a need to acknowledge differences among national groups. They were left to a private sphere, and accordingly, on the public stage an individual should not wear ethnic clothes.

Members of the so-called left-wing parties were also proud of the Lithuanian legislation.[70] They were ready to discuss the legislation, the implementation of laws and reality of everyday life. All these three levels were responsible for problems which national minorities faced. When it came to the level of legislation, they were ready to point out that hardly any changes should be made. However, the Poles particularly raised the issue of land reform and that of the Polish University.[71] Nearly all politicians addressed the issue of the language exam in Lithuanian. Mindaugas Stakvilevicius argued that when it came to 'old people' they should be exempt from the language exam in relation to job applications. 'This exam is very difficult to pass even for Lithuanians.'[72] He added that the language exam required for citizenship application is much easier and it should not cause any problems.

With regard to the second issue, the implementation of the laws, the majority of them acknowledged it as a problem. The issue which was most often raised, was the lack of books and teachers for teaching Lithuanian as a foreign language.[73] Nikolai Sokolov, Russian Vice-Ambassador, argued that there was also a psychological problem among some Russians who did not feel able to learn Lithuanian.[74] The first point made some politicians state that many mistakes had been made since the independence. They saw their own Parliament and government, under the influence of *Sajudis*, turning more and more nationalistic. The members of left-wing parties were ready to blame *Sajudis* because of its 'civil service' reshuffle.[75] They argued that when *Sajudis* came to power they made a number of able bureaucrats redundant just because they were employed by the Soviet regime.[76] Democratic culture was underdeveloped in Lithuania, not only because of the violation of rights during the Soviet period, but also because of the political behaviour of *Sajudis'* representatives who did not push for the development of a democratic culture that would include respect for the rights of national minorities. Therefore, national problems arose in the reality of everyday life.

The problems appeared on the street and in the shops, hospitals and public transport.[77] Nikolai Medvedev argued that the problem appeared because 'Lithuanians accuse Russians'.[78]

However, some politicians, especially those who belonged to the LDDP, thought that there was no need to have 'national policies'. 'Our laws and practise are good and therefore we do not need the Department of National Minorities. It would be enough to have a commission or a committee in Parliament. Otherwise our policy could be seen as national and as favouring national minorities.'[79] In their opinion, what Lithuania needed, and was developing, was 'democratic politics'. However, they thought that most of their ethnic problems had derived from poor economic performance or, at least, ethnic issues should be discussed within an economic framework. As a result, they argued that the economic situation had to be improved and that would sort out the majority of ethnic problems. Juozas Karosas argued, 'Ethnic relations are good…except within the large factories'.[80] These large factories employed mostly Russians and Poles. The factories underemployed people during the Soviet period and they were not economically viable. Therefore, redundancies were made on a large scale but the first to be made redundant were people who did not speak Lithuanian.[81]

Both political groups were not only satisfied but also proud of the Lithuanian legislation. However, they insisted on their different perspectives. The right-wing parties saw Lithuanian legislation as proof, not primarily of their democratic tradition and orientation, but as concessions which they have had to make because of their undemocratic Soviet past. The left-wing parties saw the legislation as proof that they were on the road towards democracy.

Conclusion

Sovereign states assume an international duty to safeguard the human rights of every individual under their jurisdiction. Needless to say, discrimination against people on grounds of national identity is outlawed. But since states are permitted to differentiate between citizens and other residents when it comes to their political, social and economic rights, equal protection is not safeguarded for persons who are not citizens of the state in which they live. There is, therefore, a major problem arising from combining state sovereignty and the role and authority of international bodies. As a result, one can claim that the role of human rights is important but limited, first, because many multi-ethnic states see their own ethnic group as something special and, second, because there is a long destructive history between different ethnic groups. Human rights do not, by themselves, provide multi-ethnic societies with unfailing guidance on how to cope with their particular inter-ethnic conflicts. Solutions must necessarily include compromises. No solution to any type of ethnic conflict can be resolved if the parties involved do not abide by the constraints on strategies, procedures and outcomes defined by universal human rights law. Whenever feasible, the policy choices and strategies of political actors in the former Soviet Union should promote the loyalty of the Russian diaspora towards the state where they are presently residing. Peace and the realisation of democracy and human rights in these societies depend, to a large extent, on the successful long-term integration of their new Russian, Polish, etc. diasporas.

Democratisation, by definition, means that citizens must be allowed to participate in spheres of civil society and affairs of the state. It refers to two things; first, to have rights and obligations and furthermore, to be able to exercise these rights, and, second, to support a division between civil society and state. In the case of Lithuania neither the state and its institutions nor civil society and its activities were fully developed in the period under investigation. People were still learning the language of human and citizenship rights and highlighted the importance of civil and political rights. Everybody identified citizenship rights with the right to vote and to free speech. Social rights were not often mentioned. This is connected with the communist legacy, which needed to be overcome, as well as with the official state approach and presentation of human rights. The state promoted a free market economy which curbed social rights. Nationalistic rhetoric argued that Lithuanians gained independence, for which it is worth putting up with social and economic difficulties. Even if everybody agrees that all people should be treated equally, and that nobody should be discriminated against, there is always room to curb rights or postpone their implementation because of 'specific circumstances'. Therefore, it is important to see how the perception of citizenship rights influenced national minorities in defining their place in the independent Lithuania.

Part II

5
Introduction to Part II

In the Introduction of Chapter 1, I argued, first, that national minorities were not a homogenous group and, second, that they were pushed to identify themselves primarily in ethnic terms. The first part of this book has documented the rise of nationalism in Lithuania and the establishment of citizenship as well as the tension between the two. The next three chapters focus on the responses of minorities to these developments. As it was argued, the Lithuanian legislation introduced an inclusive approach to citizenship while the Lithuanian national movement highlighted the importance of national identity. According to the legislation citizenship was defined in relation to an individual regardless of his/her religious, national or any other type of belonging. However, in the reality of everyday life national belonging was of importance. National belonging was not only defined in terms of *us* and *them* but also was seen as a single category which did not acknowledge differences among the members of the same ethnic group.

Before discussing identity choices, I would like to point out that it is universally the case that individuals are multi-dimentional beings. We all have different identities which may co-exist. We all belong to certain places, certain regions, certain country/ies, certain social groups, certain religion/s. 'The concept of a *single*, exclusive, and unchanging ethnic or cultural or other identity is a dangerous piece of brainwashing. ... The only people who face us with such either–or choices are those whose policies have led or could lead to genocide.'[1] If we recall the cases which insist on national homogeneity, as in the past in Germany or today in Serbia or Croatia or Rwanda, we can see that there are different layers of identity, connected with states or even regions within the same state. People are Germans, but they are either the Schwabens, the Saxons or the Franks. People in Baden-Wuerttemberg are Germans but either Badeners or Wuerttembergers and they do not like to be mistaken for each other. People are Croats but they are also Dalmatians, Istrians, from Zagorje and are keen to maintain this identity. Lithuanians, also, have different layers of identity ranging from towns, especially Klaipeda and Kaunas, to regions, Suvalkai, Zemaiciai, Dzukai and, finally, to Lithuania.[2] These identities are not discussed here, but instead I shall discuss identities which belong to different nation-states and how they are evaluated. The argument goes that ultimately there is a 'basic difference between *us* and *them*'. The question which follows from this is: Why do *we* think that when it comes to *us* and *them* nationality matters in a sense which makes it impossible for *us* and *them* to share the same country? This still leaves room for arguing that *they* are 'our Russians' or 'different Russians'. I often heard these two phrases in Lithuania. Their meaning was quite vague and varied from knowing the Lithuanian language, to being engaged in the struggle for independent Lithuania. It was also dependent upon the respondents' political point of view.

Following research carried out in the Baltic states, there is a need to acknowledge that Russian, Polish, Jewish and, I would add, Lithuanian national communities, are not homogenous categories. After the initial euphoria, different survey research centres[3] began to analyse results, no longer in pairs of titular nation and non-titular communities, but tried to distinguish between different ethnic communities. According to my interviews, research that might highlight the differences within the same ethnic community had not been carried out, even when there was an awareness that there are differences.[4] As Richard Rose points out:

> Divisions among each nationality occur for the greater majority of questions, a finding that is not surprising when one thinks of the importance of age, education and other social structure differences causing division in West European societies. More surprising (*sic*!) is the extent of similarity among Baltic and Russian nationalities in their replies to many questions. *Differences within ethnic communities are often greater than differences between ethnic communities.*[5]

This is confirmed by the research carried out by Aadne Aasland, who was struck by the strong diversity among the Russians in Latvia.[6]

To understand present identity choices, and speculate on future ones, we have to bear in mind, the size of the national minority group, when their members arrived in our case in Lithuania, and the compactness of their residence. It is also important to know whether they come

from mixed marriages, if they speak the native language, how culturally close and welcome they feel. The way legislation in connection
with national minorities is worded and also interpreted should also be
taken into account. Another important element is connected with the
ways the national minorities perceive the social, political and economic situation in our case in Russia, Poland, Israel and Lithuania.
Minorities have and cherish their own imagined understanding of
these countries but, at the same time, they judge them from their own
political standpoint and their perception of their own economic survival. It is also important to bear in mind the social structure in our
case of Lithuanian minorities, and especially their intelligentsia, since
it plays an important role in the formation of national identity.[7]

Furthermore, we have to take into account the way the national
majority has defined and preserved its identity. In Lithuania, national
minorities faced a group which was not only a majority in its own
republic, but also a group which cherished a memory of independence
and underlined its historic cultural differences from the Poles and from
the Russians, the latter being especially the case after the Second World
War.[8] Therefore, it is important to assess not only how a particular
national group uses these factors in defining its own identity, but also
how these factors enable national groups to define each others'
identities.

National movements treat homeland as a mythical entity.[9] However,
that mythical entity could be defined in different ways. Here we are
not primarily interested in how Lithuanians define(d) their homeland.
We saw, for example, that *Sajudis'* understanding was changing during
the struggle for independence, from seeing their homeland as a multicultural state to belonging primarily to the titular nation. For them
their homeland, *tevyne*, was Lithuania, and the Soviet Union was not
rodina but an occupying power. The majority of the population of
Lithuanian national minorities saw multicultural Lithuania as their
homeland. The *Sajudis'* identification of Lithuania with Lithuanians
made them feel at the very least uncomfortable. However, their
responses towards this identification differed in accordance with their
support for Lithuanian independence.

All the above mentioned issues are crucial to our analysis of the role
which national minorities played in the period of national reawakening or, more precisely, in the period before and after independence
(1988–93). We analyse how the issues that were raised by the
Lithuanian national movement influenced their understanding of
themselves and their national group. Given the importance of the

cultural dimension in the process of nation-building, as well as of the 'political principle', we are dealing with issues of 'who I am' and 'where I belong'. This book concentrates primarily on issues of citizenship and how they galvanised national minorities to define themselves and their place in the independent Lithuania. Chapters 6–8 will address the issue of how the Lithuanian national movement and the legislation on citizenship influenced the national minorities to confront the question of 'who I am' and 'where I belong'.

6
Russian Responses

Introduction

This chapter will focus on how the Russians defined their identity, or rather identities, and found their place in Lithuania. It is important to stress here that it was much more a case of the Russians being in a position of reacting to events rather than being in a position to shape these events.

It will be stressed that the Russians should not be seen as a homogenous group; while labelled as Russians they differed very much among themselves. Rogers Brubaker lists different responses to non-Russian nationalism in the former Soviet Union: assimilation, acculturation, collective mobilisation and migration.[1] All of these responses were potential strategies available for Russians in Lithuania. In this chapter it will be argued that assimilation was not an option for Russians. Moreover, I am uncomfortable with the use of the notion of acculturation because it means 'to assimilate the cultural traits of another group'.[2] I prefer the concept integration because it means preserving one's own identity in combination with acquiring new identities. I would argue that this process took place in Lithuania *via* two processes: searching for national identity and defining one's role in independent Lithuania. Collective mobilisation took place as well, particularly in the form of two organisations; one Russian (The Russian Cultural Centre) and one Soviet (*Edinstvo*). Migration was one response to the rise of nationalism and Lithuanian independence but, at the same time, it was a rational choice made 'in anticipation of impending political or economic conflict or hardship'.[3] I would also like to stress that I do not see these categories as mutually exclusive. I would argue that a person can opt for more than one category such as integration and collective mobilisation. For

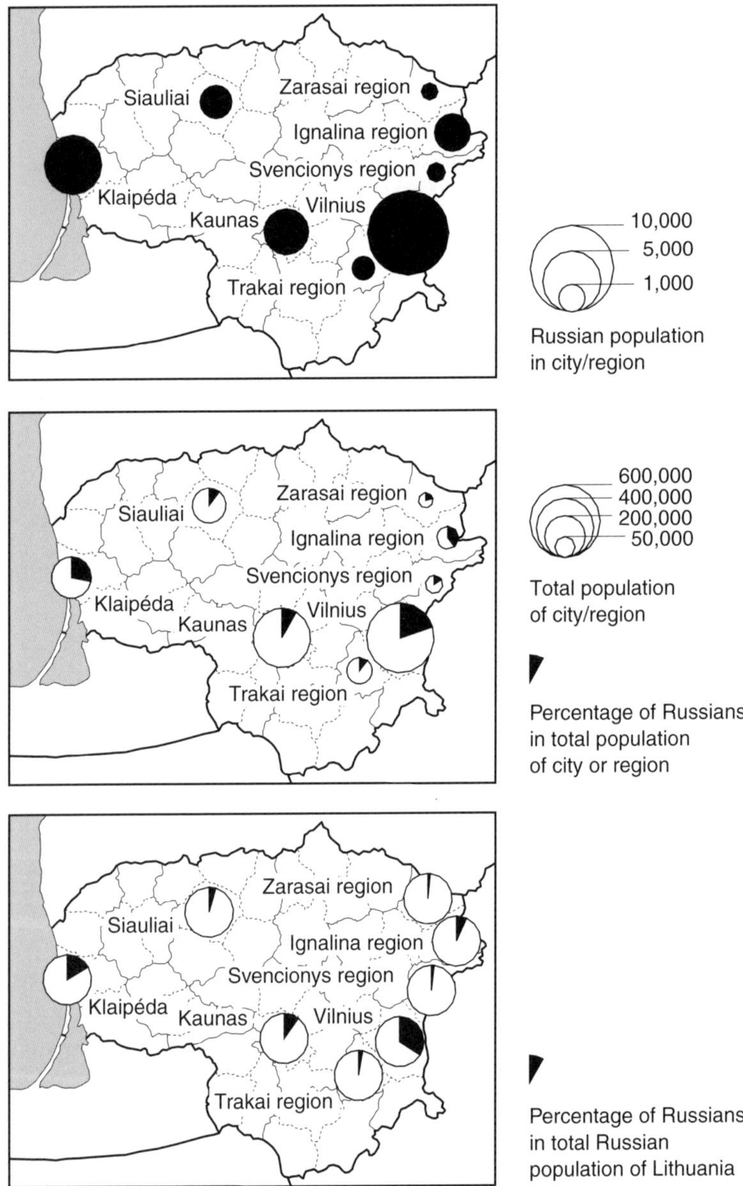

Map 6.1   Russians in Lithuania, 1989

example, some Russians in Lithuania felt integrated into Lithuanian society but they also organised themselves, in order to promote their rights.

The Russian community is the largest national minority in Lithuania and is heterogeneous in composition. Historically, Russian Old Believers came to this region in the seventeenth century because they were unable to practise their religion in the Russian Empire.[4] The second large influx was after the October Revolution and the First World War. The third and the final migration was after the Second World War, particularly in the 1960s, when many large factories were built. 'According to a survey by Richard Rose and William Maley in late 1993, 81 per cent of Lithuania's Russians have lived in Lithuania for 21 or more years. An additional 10 per cent have been resident for 11–20 years, with only 8 per cent of all Russians having lived in Lithuania for 10 or fewer years.'[5] Socially, they were a predominantly urban population, belonging mostly to the working class and technical intelligentsia.[6] A small number of Russian intelligentsia were very well known, if not always respected. Geographically, they were spread all over Lithuania, living mostly in large cities (see Map 6.1). These differences must all be taken into account when considering the Russian community. Therefore, it was difficult to account for all of their demands as one single unit.

We label them Russians but who are they?

Russians varied a great deal in accordance with how they judged independent Lithuania, politically, culturally and economically. Their attitude towards independent Lithuania and the Soviet Union, and later also towards Russia, was an indicator of their political beliefs.[7]

As regards cultural responses, Russians varied in terms of the emphasis they placed on Soviet culture, on the one hand, and influences of Lithuanian culture, on the other. Russians also varied in terms of how they interpreted the economic situation in Lithuania, particularly with regard to whether they saw the rise of unemployment among the Russian population as an ethnic or purely economic issue.

My interviews with Russians clearly showed that Russians were aware that they differed among themselves. (They would also acknowledge that there were differences within other national groups, including Lithuanians.) When they attempted to differentiate among their community, their distinctions were mostly connected with the time of their arrival in Lithuania which, in their opinion, often pointed towards the type of job they were engaged in and the political opinion they held. This point is important because it confirmed my thesis that, in general, Russians distinguished the population of Lithuania according to socio-economic and political categories rather than ethnic ones,[8] although they often used ethnic labels. The Lithuanian national movement made national identity the most important category of differentiation, especially in the period 1989–92. Along Benedict Anderson's lines, the Lithuanian nation was imagined as a territorially defined community of brothers. Russians and Poles within Lithuania were seen as the *other* against whom the Lithuanians had to protect its borders and sovereignty.

I am aware that the categories which I am outlining in this and the following two chapters are snapshots which cannot do complete justice to the varieties which exist in everyday life. They have analytical rationale. They also help us to analyse similarities and differences among different categories and enable us, as the saying goes, to see both the forest and the trees, national minorities and the majority as members of their respective ethnic groups as well as members of smaller groups within the same ethnic group. These categories are important because they are moving in the direction of acknowledging and studying differences. Furthermore, I would like to highlight, once again, that identities are both multi-layered and dynamic categories. The latter is especially true in times of transformation which, in our case, Lithuania embarked upon at the end of the 1980s. Bearing in mind both the multi-layered and dynamic character of identities I would also like to make clear that when I am quoting my respondents I am doing that without the intention of suggesting that they belonged to any of these categories.

'Lithuanian Russians'

As already argued, the Russians who declared themselves in support of an independent Lithuania (despite being surprised by the speed of events) called themselves 'Lithuanian Russians'.[9] They highlighted that they were Russians 'who are oriented towards Lithuania, not Moscow'.[10] As Vladimir Efremov said in relation to Vilnius: 'I hope that I carry in myself the characteristics of my town; that very special warmth, very special cultural atmosphere and multi-language ability.'[11] For this group being Russian was only important if it was seen as affiliated with Lithuania. One without the other did not make any sense because both cultures were mutually enriching. This point is important because it highlights that the identity of 'Lithuanian Russians' was seen as being definitely formed in Lithuania.

'Lithuanian Russians' supported the Lithuanian national movement from the very beginning because the Soviet Union 'destroyed language, architecture, landscape, historical memory, culture, everything that makes human identity'.[12] In their opinion, human dignity was connected with national identity. 'Lithuanian Russians' argued that they understood that it was important for Lithuanians to finally have a free space where they could express their own thoughts and feelings. They perceived Lithuanians as being much more repressed than themselves in the Soviet Union and they were ready to listen and to support them, and take an active role only when they were asked to do so.[13] Juozas Lakis argued that 'the most sensitive Russians are ashamed of everything that the Soviet Union did to Lithuania even if they themselves, as individuals, did not do anything wrong'.[14]

These people were culturally integrated into Lithuanian society, knew the native language and were familiar with Lithuanian culture.[15] These Russians were integrated, rather than assimilated into Lithuanian society.[16] First, 'Lithuanian Russians' demanded cultural autonomy: 'We would like to be educated in Russian and we should be able to receive education in Russian as long as we want.'[17] They saw their rights as those belonging to an individual, rather than as collective rights. Second, they also pointed out that Lithuanians would distinguish them as a separate national group, even when they called some of them 'our Russians'.[18]

According to my interviews, 'Lithuanian Russians' mostly belonged to the Russian community which came to Lithuania before and after the First World War. Here we should distinguish between three groups. The first group was made up of Old Believers who were in support of Lithuanian independence because Lithuania offered them 'a shelter three centuries ago', as one individual put it, and allowed them to maintain their own religion. Their identity was primarily shaped by their religion. While claiming to be Russian and Orthodox, they explained that they respected pre-reform Orthodox rites. In Lithuania they had always carefully maintained their own identity, especially in relation to Russians. Historically they went either to Lithuanian schools or, in most cases, were educated at home and thus remained poorly educated.[19] They avoided Russian schools because of religious differences that existed between them and other Russians. According to Vasilii Baranovskii, they had been integrated into Lithuanian society.[20] In the first independent republic, Old Believers made up the majority of the Russians in Lithuania, comprising 32 000 out of 50 000[21] and (according to Baranovskii) there are no more than 35 000 of them today in

Lithuania.[22] The second group was made up of descendants of people who came after 1795 (following the Third Partition of Poland, Lithuania was incorporated into the Russian Empire). The people who came after 1795 were mostly civil servants (who ruled the new *guberniia*) and land owners (who obtained land in the newly conquered province) as well as peasants and craftsmen.[23] The third group was made up of White Russians and their families who came to Lithuania after the October Revolution.[24]

According to research conducted by Natalija Kasatkina, these groups of Russians and their families were loyal to the inter-war independent Lithuania.[25] For example, Nikolai Medvedev argued that 'when Russia was in *gulag* (after the October Revolution) Lithuania took care of me'.[26] When Lithuania was occupied by the Soviet Union, he stayed loyal to the ideal of an independent Lithuania, and therefore joined *Sajudis*. Often these Russians came from a mixed marriage background (sometimes, but not always Lithuanian and Russian). However, some members of this group were also Russians who had arrived following the Second World War. According to my interviews, they usually belonged to the intelligentsia and were often married to Lithuanians.

'Russians of Lithuania'

'Russians of Lithuania' were taken by surprise by the events in the late 1980s and argued that 'everything happened too fast'.[27] They saw Lithuania in 1992 as their country. Until 1988, they did not question the issue of Lithuanian lost independence. This was a state of affairs which they did not (at least openly) question. It was much easier to question a Lithuanian quest for independence, especially in the light of being described as a people 'who carry their roots in suitcases';[28] as a people who do not have a national identity. Although they (as well as the rest of the Russians in Lithuania) were labelled as occupiers they had a strong identification with the land.[29] They saw themselves as hard-working people who 'built Lithuania' and who were disadvantaged in comparison with Lithuanians.[30] This group mainly consisted of working-class people but also included Russian technical experts and, to a lesser degree, humanistic intelligentsia.

This group argued that *perestroika* and Gorbachev were not given a chance.[31] They had an ambivalent relationship with the Soviet Union; 'they were loyal to it although they did not like it very much'.[32] In the light of this argument and the difficult economic situation in the Soviet Union, 'Russians of Lithuania' supported the Lithuanian demand for economic sovereignty but they did not support its struggle for political independence. For example, they openly opposed the statement of Kasatkina's (a member of the Russian Cultural Centre), during Gorbachev's visit in January 1990, that the Russians in Lithuania supported Lithuanian independence.

While the 'Russians of Lithuania' accepted that Lithuania was no longer a part of the Soviet Union, they argued that there was insufficient understanding for national minorities and their problems in the independence period. They felt neglected by the LDDP (Lithuanian Democratic Labour Party) which 'did not want to deal with the problems of national minorities'.[33] An LDDP official maintained that 'we have not got a developed programme on national minorities but also we have not got a programme on agriculture, industry, education etc.'[34] The LDDP's main priority was the economy. In my interviews with the members of the LDDP the majority of them argued that once the economic situation was improved, ethnic relations would be seen in a different perspective.

This group of Russians argued that the national minorities felt under pressure and claimed that it was futile to pretend that discrimination along national lines did not exist. While they felt that it was mainly their responsibility to develop their own culture, they stressed that no help was offered from the government or from their fellow citizens. Most of them argued that they needed a guarantee from the Lithuanian government that their culture would be supported. Therefore, 'Russians of Lithuania' asked for cultural autonomy which was understood as a collective right (as argued below).

From the viewpoint of the 'Russians of Lithuania', *Sajudis* and LDDP had concentrated on the problems of Lithuanian culture, while ignoring other cultures. First, 'Russians of Lithuania' felt they lived 'in a vacuum'.[35] Russian organisations were financially supported[36] but they were never asked to write a single report about Russian culture for the government.[37] This point led some 'Russians of Lithuania', together with the 'Lithuanian Russians', to argue that the government fulfilled its duty in front of the world community, but was not actually interested in their opinion. Juozas Lakis agreed that Russians faced a 'cultural vacuum', going on to explain that Russians had not been engaged in Lithuanian culture and 'today they are even less connected with Moscow than they were before'.[38]

Second, the 'Russians of Lithuania' particularly emphasised the issue of Russian schools in Lithuania which were of poor quality, even when teaching Russian. Irina Arefjeva argued that 'the Russian language introduced to Lithuania in the last 50 years was very poor'.[39] They argued that the Lithuanian state was not ready to invest in their schools, while Russia was also not prepared to help.[40]

'Russians of Lithuania' would compare Russia with Poland and stress that Poland helped the Poles in Lithuania. 'Even in the Polish Parliament the Polish question was discussed and a letter was sent to the Lithuanian Parliament. These two countries behaved as European countries. Russia does not do that. They are not aware that they should get in touch with the Russian Diaspora in Lithuania.'[41] In comparison with the 'Lithuanian Russians', who saw Russian culture as being integrated into Lithuanian culture, they put more emphasis on cultural influences coming from Russia.

'Soviet Russians'

According to my research, the 'Soviet Russians' were the smallest group of Russians but they were also very vocal. They were attached to the Communist Party of Lithuania (in support of the Soviet Union) and *Edinstvo*. The majority of them left Lithuania (although I do not want to suggest that all people who left were 'Soviet Russians').

'Soviet Russians' felt threatened by all the discussions and the outpouring of national sentiment as analysed in Chapter 3.[42] At the same time, 'Soviet Russians' felt uncomfortable about those Russians who supported *Sajudis*. They found it difficult to understand that there was Russian support for 'such a nationalistic organisation'. They also felt uncomfortable with the decision of the Lithuanian Communist Party to support *Sajudis*, which ended with a split within the Party.

The establishment of Lithuanian independence made 'Soviet Russians' feel estranged from their 'ideological land'.[43] First, this group was very much settled in the culture of the Soviet Communist Party which was considered international.[44] Their culture celebrated the Communist Party and its leaders who were the blueprint for *Homo Sovieticus*. An integral part of this culture involved paying respect to the Soviet Union, seen as a unique country in the world. This Soviet culture was seen as encouraging the blossoming of national cultures and friendship among different nationalities. Those people who did not accept this world-view 'fell out of history'.[45] Therefore, there was a lack of understanding for national cultures because 'we all share the same culture'. Consequently, they put no effort into learning Lithuanian because 'we all speak Russian'.[46] But there was also no wish to learn Lithuanian because there was no need to do so during the Soviet period. Second, in the 1990s they still tried to prevent territorial changes.[47]

'Soviet Russians' were very often referred to as the 'Russian-speaking population', especially by Russians who perceived themselves as 'Lithuanian Russians' and were eager to point out that this group of people only nominally shared the same language and culture. They were seen by 'Lithuanian Russians' as 'de-Russified'. As Medvedev argued, 'Their Russian is different in comparison to the Russian of Pushkin and Dostoevski, their language is full of abbreviations. Their culture is a synthetic culture imposed on all nations within the former Soviet Union.'[48] These were the people for whom being Soviet meant more than being simply Russian. 'Soviet Russians' considered themselves Russian only because they spoke Russian. They did not perceive their national identity as Russian because they felt that they had overcome it, outlived it. A minority of Lithuanians perceived them as Soviet people rather than Russians.[49] 'Soviet Russians' were only concerned about Soviet culture, without taking account of the long history of Russian culture in Lithuania.

The differences highlighted above are important in understanding issues raised further in this chapter which are concerned with how the above analysed groups of Russians found their place in Lithuania. As discussed in the previous two chapters, there existed a tension between Lithuanian citizenship legislation and the Lithuanian national movement. The lack of civil society and democratic institutions meant that national groups were the main collective actor. As is argued later, the majority of Russians remained passive. 'Lithuanian Russians' got involved in both Russian and Lithuanian organisations. 'Russians of Lithuania' oriented themselves towards Russian organisations with the aim of cherishing their culture and language. 'Soviet Russians' formed *Edinstvo* to prevent the breakup of the Soviet Union and when they did not succeed the majority of them decided to leave.

Russian responses to citizenship issues

It was interesting to note that the Russian organisations and individuals came up with a set of problems which were held in common. However, this agenda was approached from different points of view, which were in turn shaped by differing visions of an independent Lithuania and self-perceptions of Russian identity. During discussions, seven topics seemed to be connected with the Lithuanian citizenship legislation, and the way in which it affected their everyday life from the political, social, economic, cultural and psychological points of view.

1. In general, the majority of Russians that I interviewed, were satisfied with the Lithuanian legislation but felt that it could be improved.[50] They were especially concerned with the laws concerning language and citizenship. There was much discussion about the state language. The 'Russians of Lithuania' felt that under the existing conditions, they were not able to learn Lithuanian until 1 January 1995.[51] They argued that there were no textbooks or teachers who were able to teach the language, especially to adults.[52] This issue was raised not only by the Russians but it was also stressed by some Lithuanians and members of the LDDP government. Mindaugas Stakvilevicius, for example, argued, 'There are no teachers and textbooks for language exams. Nothing is organised.'[53] Even under such circumstances Eugenija Krukauskiene argued that 90 per cent of national minorities wanted to learn Lithuanian.[54]

   However, some 'Lithuanian Russians' and Lithuanians would point out that there was a lack of motivation among Russians to learn Lithuanian. The 'Lithuanian Russians' argued that 'Russians have to understand that they should learn Lithuanian'.[55] One indeed noticed that there was quite a strong psychological barrier,[56] and many Russians felt that they were unable to learn Lithuanian. A 16-year-old girl declared, 'It is not only the lack of facilities for learning Lithuanian but I am too old to learn it.'[57] The majority argued that it would be difficult to learn a language which substantially differed from their own, belonging as it does to a different linguistic family. In the course of my interviews, some Russians, especially 'Russians of Lithuania' were keen to emphasise the Russian tradition in Lithuania, especially in Vilnius.[58] Pride was also at stake – they felt that they had to swallow their pride and go to school to learn the language they had always considered not worth learning because it was not spoken by 'half of the world', like their own. Eugenij(us) Petrov(as) argued that Lithuanians were not always ready to 'encourage' Russians to learn their language. Being called 'occupiers' certainly did not help.

2. The Russians also expressed a concern about the citizenship of the officers of the Soviet Army. They referred to a statement of the Supreme Council, issued after the Act of Independence, which clearly asserted that members of the Soviet Army would not be able to apply for Lithuanian citizenship and would be expected to leave the country. 'Let us be friendly and polite: we will thus part on good terms.'[59]

   During my interviews, two questions were consistently raised. First, how should officers who had retired before and those after the Lithuanian independence act be treated? Second, is there any difference between Lithuanians who were/have been Soviet Army officers and other nationalities? The majority of retired officers will have to wait three years to apply for citizenship. According to the Law on Citizenship people who are married to a person with Lithuanian citizenship have to wait three years.[60] Stakvilevicius further argued that Lithuanian and Russian officers were treated the same, 'Some Lithuanians cannot obtain citizenship because they were members of the occupying forces and they have to wait another three years. We are talking roughly about one hundred people. Lithuanians who were members of the Soviet Army and joined the Lithuanian Army had already obtained Lithuanian citizenship.' Former officers as well as war veterans and invalids of the Soviet Army, were also concerned about military pensions which were much higher in Russia than in Lithuania. If they had obtained Lithuanian citizenship they would have had to give up their pensions.[61]

3. The other set of problems in the Citizenship Law was connected with dual citizenship. For Lithuanians this issue had economic and political dimensions. First, they did not feel comfortable with having Russians as foreign citizens because 'In Russia anything can happen. Eltsin can lose power to Zhirinovski.'[62]

   Second, the issue of dual citizenship was raised not because of the law *per se* but because of a Law on the Privatisation of Apartments which only allowed citizens the option to acquire investment cheques and buy property under relatively more favourable conditions.[63] As explained by Edvardas Gruzas, the Lithuanian government was concerned with '2000 Russians, Belorussians and Ukrainians who are giving up their Lithuanian citizenship, selling their apartments and buying new ones in Russia'.[64]

   However, there was also a group of people who genuinely had a bond with both states. They saw Lithuania as being their country. As one individual said, 'The graves of my families are here.'[65] Their family histories tied them to Lithuanian land as much as the Russian language tied them to Russian land. Some of them felt that with *Sajudis* becoming increasingly exclusive in its nationalism, there was an increased potential for discrimination along ethnic lines and they felt that Russian citizenship would bring them security.

4. The issue of property which belonged to Russian organisations was a contentious one. The Russian Community sent a letter to President Brazauskas demanding the return of the houses and apartments which belonged to different Russian organisations.[66] (These buildings

had been appropriated after the Second World War.) In its Statute the Russian Community promised to continue the tradition of those organisations which enabled them, according to their interpretation, to put their claim towards this property.[67] 'Yes, there is no law. But this is not our fault but our misfortune, also the misfortune of this state. Some time ago it was pointed out that the non-existence of this or that law meant lawlessness. In this case it also means no respect for the rights of national minorities and discrimination against them.'[68]

Another problem concerned Russian churches which had been given to other denominations instead of being returned to the Orthodox Church.[69] The Archbishop of the Orthodox Church in Lithuania argued, 'There are problems with local political authorities, especially in Vilnius, who are not ready to co-operate. We are entitled to some property, especially churches, which we cannot get back. On the one hand, the Lithuanian Parliament introduced property rights, on the other hand, it does not want to return our property. Some of our property is even used by the Mafia.'[70] The chairperson of the Vilnius Committee on National Minorities stated that the problem lay in the fact that some buildings had been occupied and property relations needed to be sorted out before they could be returned.[71] However, the Lithuanian government was very unhappy with all the claims that had been coming from the Poles and Russians, especially those that related to Vilnius. Between the two World Wars, there were hardly any Lithuanians in this area, and the property in the Old town belonged mostly to either Jews, Poles or Russians.[72] The Lithuanian government agreed that minorities should be given a certain space where they could organise their activities and they pointed towards the property which had already been returned to them[73] but also argued that more time was needed to sort out property relationships which often had a chain reaction, as in the case of the Russian theatre. 'To whom should it be returned? To the Poles who built it or to the Youth theatre which used it. Where to put the Russian theatre?'[74]

5. Some 'Russians of Lithuania' were primarily concerned with economic problems. They claimed that they were the first to be made redundant, and the last to be employed. 'A lot of my friends left Lithuania because they could not find a job. I do not have a job and shall not be able to find one.'[75] These impressions were particularly strong among those who worked in large factories. There were always many Russians, Belorussians, Ukrainians and other groups in these factories. A large number were closed down, but due to the

fact that there was no economic rationale behind them, rather than because most of their employees were Russian-speaking people. According to the Vilnius Labour Exchange (in a survey done on 10 November 1992), there was no significant difference between Lithuanians and non-Lithuanians in relation to being registered, looking for a job and finding employment. However, as Boguslavas Gruzevskis argued, 'Although research on the connection between employment and the knowledge of Lithuanian has not been done it seems that the language issue is vital'.[76] 'Lithuanian Russians' were particularly clear in indicating that one should not put too much stress on economic problems as they were common for all Lithuanian citizens.

6. All Russians were very keen to maintain education in their own language. This was connected with three sets of issues: (a) the quality of education in Russian schools, (b) educating teachers in Russian, and (c) integrating Russian schools into the state education system. The majority of Russians argued that they would like to integrate into Lithuanian society rather than assimilate and they wanted to preserve their national identity. As far as educational standards were concerned, everybody commented that the general educational level in Russian schools was much lower than in Lithuanian ones. Tat'iana Iasinskaia argued that this had consequences not only for Russians but also for other minorities who were educated in Russian. Furthermore, 'because we think that it is important to grow in one's own culture some are considering moving to Russia if the situation does not improve'.[77] Ana Shinkariova argued, 'There is a tendency to send our children to Lithuanian schools.'[78] It should be pointed out that, according to the official statistical data, the number of Russian primary and secondary schools and Russians as well as the number of pupils were growing after 1992.[79] However, the number of Russian children attending pre-school education was falling as well as the number of students studying in Russian.[80] With regard to the issue of kindergartens, it was argued that they were closed down because parents did not have enough money to pay the kindergarten fee.[81] A further problem were textbooks in Russian schools. During the school year 1992/3 only 16 out of 132 textbooks were published in Lithuania because they were expensive to publish and it was difficult to find authors to write them.[82] As a result Russian children in Lithuania were not introduced to specific Lithuanian issues but were 'only learning about Russian landscape, culture, etc'.[83]

With regard to the issue of educating teachers in Russian, the state did not have enough money to educate them.[84] Furthermore, we have to remember that the number of students who studied in Russian was constantly falling.[85] Two explanations were usually given. First, numbers were falling as a result of the closing down of departments that taught in Russian. Second, the Lithuanian authorities argued that people needed to be educated in Lithuanian so as to have better job opportunities.

Nina Makeeva argued that 'Russian schools should be integrated into the Lithuanian educational system but nobody knows how to do it. It is very good that this issue has finally started to be discussed.'[86] Petrov(as) suggested that 'Russian children should be taught in primary schools in Russian and then increasingly gain more education in Lithuanian as they progress through the system.'[87] In this way they could both preserve their Russian roots and integrate into the new society and state. Sergei Temchin hoped that because in those days hardly anybody studied Russian, the Russian Department at the University of Vilnius would have time to reorganise itself and re-think its curriculum not only in relation to Russian literature but also to literature written in Russian (including the Soviet) as well as to Lithuanian, Polish and European literature.[88]

7. The Russian population in Lithuania was very interested in developing closer relations between Russia and Lithuania; an issue that had been neglected by both countries. Lithuania had been oriented much more towards the West, neglecting the East. When the LDDP came to power it argued that Lithuania had to develop policies towards Russia and 'stop a *Sajudis* policy which was politics without diplomacy and compromise'.[89] Russia did not display much interest in developing relations with Lithuania. When Russia finally appointed its ambassador to Lithuania it was obvious that the Embassy was not briefed at all about the situation in Lithuania and that was noticed, with sadness or as a fact, by the whole of the Russian community. In an interview with Iasinskaia, Nikolai Obertishev openly stated that before coming to Lithuania, 'I was not given any specific instructions or duties. I do not think that one needs them. We follow the understanding that we and the Baltics have been developing together for the last fifty years. We have to collaborate, it is not a question of what we want or do not want.'[90] 'Russians of Lithuania' pointed out, during their first meeting with the representatives from the Embassy, that they were disappointed because Russia had not shown any interest in their problems and grievances in the period from 1988

until October 1992, when the LDDP came to power. However, this new Russia was not able to offer much help. It openly stated that it would take care only of Russian citizens in Lithuania and was not able to assist financially people who decided to move to Russia to look for accommodation there. Finally, Russia argued that it did not have sufficient financial resources to help Russian schools in Lithuania.[91]

These issues were vital for the Russian community in Lithuania. The majority of Russians who stayed in Lithuania wanted to continue living there.[92] They were becoming increasingly aware that it was their responsibility to find their place and role within the new Lithuanian state and civil society. In Kymlicka's terms, Russians wanted 'polyethnic rights' to be put into practice and respected.[93] However, there were differences between the 'Lithuanian Russians' and 'Russians of Lithuania' as to how these rights were interpreted. 'Lithuanian Russians' perceived them as individual rights. 'Russians of Lithuania', defining themselves as a disadvantaged group primarily because of the way the legislation was implemented, argued that only through a group would they be able to 'amplify their voices'.[94] This was made clear by a group of Russians from Visaginas who wanted 'their difference to be acknowledged'.[95] Neither group of Russians supported the other types of rights discussed by Kymlicka ('self-government rights' and 'special representation rights') because they argued that there was no need for them.

Russian organisations

Grievances caused by either the Lithuanian legislation and/or its implementation were only one factor in shaping a need to form Russian organisations. The search for one's own identity was represented in the need to form Russian organisations as well as in the need to withdraw from Lithuanian society. Nobody knew the exact number of organisations that were established. However, a certain number were valid only for a short period of time. Three issues are relevant in this regard: first, the majority of Russians did not become engaged in Russian organisations or in Lithuanian public life; second, Russian organisations did not represent the Russian community in Lithuania;[96] and third, there was no attempt to establish a Russian political party. The organisation issue is furthermore important because it addresses issues connected with being a national minority. All organisations were formed to protect Russian culture, in the context of being a minority population in a new state.

Why were the Russians passive?

The first issue addresses passivity. Passivity was a result of the breakdown of communication. First, according to my interviews, the majority of these Russians were 'Russians of Lithuania'. They were not able to communicate either their needs or their complaints to the Lithuanian authorities. This group felt that the new authorities were not willing to listen to them. They withdrew from public life which they perceived as having only one dimension: a national one. As some of them pointed out, they were afraid to speak Russian in public. They turned into a 'silent opposition' towards *Sajudis* because that movement shaped the political, cultural and economic present and future of Lithuania. They were also passive because they were surprised at the nationalistic rhetoric, as well as with the support among Lithuanians for this rhetoric. Second, they looked towards other Russians and they were surprised at the variety of different opinions.[97] All these events and situations made the majority of this group depend on their own families and friends, where they found the security that did not exist for them in the public sphere.

Furthermore, Archbishop Khrizostom argued that passivity should be seen as a result of years of 'moral and spiritual decline' during the Soviet period which made 'Russians politically passive, destroyed solidarity among them and made them self-centred without any wish to think about organising any Russian organisation'.[98] Passivity should be explained in connection with the Soviet era. In this era, Russians felt that the organisations effectively chose them.[99] These organisations were organised by the state for the Russian-speaking population and for other nationalities. They did not cater for national cultures because the destiny of Soviet nationalities was seen as merging. 'Russians did not have the experience of living together, how to make connections among themselves. What exists today is not done by them.'[100] Only a few organisations were organised by Russians, for example, associations which would organise poetry evenings or alternative theatre at the University of Vilnius. They were tolerated but they were not welcomed.[101] The authorities turned a blind eye, especially in the 1980s.

This factor of being organised by the state is important in relation to the mass media. In Lithuania there were newspapers and journals published *in* Russian for the Russian-speaking population.[102] However, they were not about Russians and their culture in Lithuania. There was no equivalent of *Znad Willie* or *Jeruzalem of Lithuania* which were published by the Poles and Jews respectively. Russians argued that there was a need for a newspaper or journal because the Russian language and culture needed to be introduced to the Lithuanian populations.[103] Russians claimed that *Vilnius* or *Lad* could not perform that role.[104] The Editor-in-Chief of *Vilnius*, Evaldas Matvekas, argued that articles he received about national minorities kept repeating themselves and as a result a section on national minorities did not have a *raison d'être*.[105] In the case of *Lad*, Pavel Lavrinec, a member of the editorial board, argued that the journal was not published on a regular basis because there were financial problems. However, these journals were popular only among a smaller group of Russians and they were viewed as Lithuanian journals in Russian. Russians had radio and TV programmes *in* Russian but again these were not about Russians and their culture in Lithuania.[106] They were also able to watch Russian television. The TV station *Ostankino* was popular among both the Russians and Lithuanians and when the Lithuanian authorities tried to stop broadcasting it there was a huge protest among all Lithuanian citizens.[107]

Russian organisations

When it comes to the issue that Russian organisations did not represent the Russian community, I would like to argue that there was no possibility of representing the whole community because, as argued above, Russians differed among themselves and most of them were passive. The Russian organisations mushroomed in number from the national reawakening period onwards.[108] According to my interviews, the majority catered for the needs and interests of individuals not groups. Iasinskaia argued that there were more and more organisations but the number of active people remained the same. This was confirmed by Petrov(as). Talking to people who organised different organisations or who planned to organise them, it appeared that the majority were conceived and founded in one's kitchen.[109] The issue of more formal characteristics such as statute, programme, committee, which would allow the organisation to function, were not seen as necessary.[110] That could be another reason why they so quickly appeared and then disappeared.

The Russians differed when it came to judging the 'many organisations' as a good or bad sign. Arefjeva argued that: 'There are a lot of Russian organisations because Russians are fed up with collectivity.'[111] In her opinion, Russians wanted to form organisations based on their needs. 'Lithuanian Russians' usually argued that it was positive to have a lot of organisations because 'everybody can find something for themselves'. 'People should be able to express themselves.' 'Russians of Lithuania', on the other hand, thought that it had a negative effect on the development of Russian culture in Lithuania. They pointed out that having a lot of organisations would not have been bad if they had concentrated on Russian problems and issues, and on the setting of a Russian agenda. Piotr Frolov argued that it was not a good idea to have a lot of different Russian organisations. He saw them as a part of the *divide et impera* policy, arguing that the government was encouraging a lot of different Russian organisations on purpose because it was then easier to rule over them.[112] He also pointed out that because the money was divided among the different Russian groups nobody received enough to finance their policies.

There were two Russian organisations mentioned by nearly all the people I interviewed, irrespective of what national group they belonged to; the Russian Cultural Centre and *Edinstvo*. They deserve special attention because they played an important role in mobilising the Russian population directly or indirectly for or against the cause of Lithuanian independence. The Russian Cultural Centre insisted that national difference did not prevent them from integrating into Lithuanian society. As one of its members pointed out: 'As long as Lithuania is a democratic state we shall be its citizens.' *Edinstvo* gave its support to the Soviet Union, arguing that only the Union could guarantee the equal treatment of all nationalities.

The Russian Cultural Centre

The Russian Cultural Centre was founded on 31 October 1988. As Russians would tell me later (in 1992 and 1993): 'All of us were members of the Russian Cultural Centre.' However, the Centre lost some of its supporters, especially when some leading members decided to openly support Lithuanian independence.

The Centre stated that it was not a political organisation.[113] 'We had to point out clearly that we are not a political organisation, that we are not an alternative movement in relation to Lithuanian awakening. We never wanted and still do not want to be a political organisation.'[114] The Centre declared that it was a Russian cultural organisation, whose aim was to cherish Russian culture in Lithuania. They argued that Russian culture 'has always existed in Lithuania in a symbiosis with other cultures'.[115] They were unhappy because 'new organisations' did not realise that and very often saw the Centre without a 'Lithuanian connection'. Their second aim was to introduce Russians to Lithuanian culture.

Members of the Russian Cultural Centre were unhappy with the way the Lithuanian independent state dealt with national minorities. They argued that there was no motivation to support the development of Russian culture (or the culture of other minorities) in Lithuania. They were especially unhappy with the rise to power of the LDDP because they claimed it was still loyal to its Marxist roots and talked about national minorities without doing anything for them. They compared it with the Soviet period which they insisted supported Soviet culture, never Russian, and they mentioned that the communist regime did much more for the Lithuanian and Polish cultures.[116]

Members of the Russian Cultural Centre were also unhappy with other Russian organisations who worked separately and often argued with each other. In their opinion there were a lot of arguments between different organisations which 'behaved like poorly brought up children'.[117] They rightly argued that more co-operation was needed.[118] However, they attributed this situation to the Soviet era when everything was provided by the state and very little initiative came from the grass-roots. They were quite pessimistic, first, in light of the Russian intelligentsia leaving the country[119] and, second, because national minorities as well as Lithuanians were suffering from the poor economic situation in Lithuania. As a result of the poor economic situation the minorities were oriented towards developing survival strategies and did not get engaged in minorities' organisations. The members felt that they were destined 'to exist in silence', without the possibility of their voice being heard.

Russian actors on the political stage – Edinstvo

A few Russians were critical of the Russian Cultural Centre from the day it was founded. They did not see it as an organisation which would protect their interests. They were especially worried about the stance taken by the Centre in the debate about the introduction of Lithuanian as the official language of the country. This discussion was an immediate reason to found *Edinstvo*. The organisation's declaration claimed 'that at present the country does not have sufficient experience in resolving the inter-ethnic problems which have accumulated'.[120] Therefore, they declared themselves in support of 'the interests and political rights of all citizens regardless of their nationality and religious faith'.[121]

Edinstvo, founded on 4 November 1988, adopted a programme which stressed their support for the communist ideology and the Soviet Union.[122] Like Interfront organisations in the other two Baltic states, *Edinstvo* represented 'Soviet rather than Russian sentiment'.[123] According to Petrov(as), '*Edinstvo* was an organisation which protected *nomenclature* and party principles.'[124] In his prison diary Valerii Ivanov called *Edinstvo* and the Communist Party *'ideinie satrudniki'* (people who share the same ideas).[125] The majority of people who founded and supported *Edinstvo* in Lithuania were Russian politicians, especially at the local level,[126] army personnel,[127] retired army officers,[128] managers and workers in the big factories, especially in military factories built in the 1960s.[129] It was revealed in the course of my interviews that Poles, Jews and Lithuanians were also members of this movement.[130] (The official name of the movement was *Venibe-Edinstvo-Ednosc* which means unity in Lithuanian, Russian and Polish.)

However, for people like Ivanov (the leader of *Edinstvo*), their nationality was an insignificant factor. Mikhael Bombin, the former Russian-Jewish dissident from Latvia, argues 'that you could not call the majority of post-war immigrants "Russians" since they had no religion and only economic and material aims'.[131] Tat'iana Pogozhilskaia stated that 'Ivanov did not feel Russian.'[132]

By the end of 1989, the majority of Russians felt alienated, isolated and frightened.[133] As was pointed out in Chapter 3, this was a period in which nationalist demands took over 'abstract democratic ideas'.[134] Vitalii Asovskii pointed out that 'Russians began to lose their sense of belonging to Lithuanian society and therefore it was easier to identify with *Edinstvo*.'[135] 'Lithuanian Russians' were ready to understand Lithuanians and wait in silence. They either quietly left *Sajudis* or adopted a silent role.[136] The other two groups of Russians did not feel that the Russian Cultural Centre was protecting them. The majority of 'Russians of Lithuania' saw *Edinstvo* as 'the only organisation which was protecting us'.

The beginning of 1989 brought with it a new word with a clear political message on the stage of Lithuanian history. Landsbergis, in a speech in Kaunas on 15 February 1989, started to talk openly about independence rather than sovereignty.[137] Reference to independence made the majority of Russians feel uncomfortable. But this was only the beginning. What was to emerge very soon was differentiation along ethnic lines, among *us* and *them*, good and bad, Lithuanians and Russians.[138] *Sajudis* lost its romantic aura for quite a few Russians as well as Lithuanians, and the rest of the Russians were, in their own words, in a 'state of shock'.

During the constituent congress of *Edinstvo*, held on 13–14 May 1989, a split appeared among the members of *Edinstvo*. According to the letter signed by the 25 (then former) members, it was claimed that a 'group of extremists from the movement's Vilnius city council, led by Ivanov, staged a well-rehearsed performance with dramatic appeals to delegates' feelings. …whipping up hysteria and playing a dangerous political game with unpredictable consequences.'[139]

According to my interviews, the atmosphere around the congress made quite a few 'Russians of Lithuania' reconsider the perception of *Edinstvo* as 'the only organisation protecting Russians'.[140] It is interesting to point out that what made them feel uncomfortable was a feeling that '*Edinstvo* was turning into the same type of organisation as *Sajudis*, a nationalistic one, declaring the living together of all nations but, at the same time, presenting Russians as victims and depicting Lithuanians as oppressors.' The language was the same but the roles had changed. Again the bottom line was *us* and *them*. Furthermore, some of the 'Russians of Lithuania' were wary of a possible connection between *Edinstvo* and the Communist Party (loyal to Moscow). For them there was no rationale in saving the Soviet Union especially in the light of the January events, and particularly after the putsch in August 1991.[141]

Do the Russians need a political party?

The third issue is the question of why Russians did not form a political party. I was usually given three answers. Most 'Russians of Lithuania' argued that they did not want a political party because it would be identified as pro-communist or pro-Russian, especially in the light of *Edinstvo*.[142]

A minority of the 'Russians of Lithuania' argued that for the last 50 years they 'were building socialism and making *Homo Sovieticus*' and did not think of themselves as Russians. Therefore, they argued that it was important for the Russians to have their own party and MPs. Among them were people who also thought that the political party should be based on the three largest Russian organisations in Lithuania, the Russian Cultural Centre (*Ruskii Kulturnii Centr*), the Russian Society (*Ruskoe Obshchestvo*) and the Russian Community (*Ruskaia Obshchina*). Frolov, the co-president of the last organisation, argued that it was very important for Russians to organise themselves along political lines. 'This is a very important time for Russians because it is difficult to take the role of a national minority. We have to make a basis for the future life of Russians and we also have to start from scratch. If we fail today there will be no Russian life here in five to ten years.'[143] However, he was not able to suggest why and how to organise a political party. The above quoted explanation could easily apply to a cultural organisation. Furthermore, I should add that I never encountered anybody from the other two organisations who mentioned the need to form a political party.

'Lithuanian Russians', on the other hand, argued that there was no reason to form a political party, primarily because Russians differed among themselves. They did not share Frolov's opinion that Russians should unite to survive because they lived in difficult times. 'We need more people to take care of our culture, especially among those who work in the governmental bodies. They can be either Russians or Lithuanians.'[144] They wanted representatives but at the same time they would argue that this was not a good enough reason to form a political party.[145] Their reasoning came from the understanding that Russians primarily faced a psychological challenge; they had to learn to be a national minority, to integrate into a new state and civil society and answer for themselves the question of what kind of Russians they were. Therefore, forming a political party would only slow down the process of integration and divide national communities, instead of making people realise that they should see themselves as citizens of Lithuania with Russian origins.

Could the Russians be a national minority?

Finally, the issue of being a national minority needs to be addressed.[146] I would not agree with Kasatkina's argument that at this early stage of national (re)awakening Russians were not at all a national minority but a 'subethnos' because they were not 'ready to take responsibility for the cultural and political life of their own community'.[147] From my own experience (as argued above), there was a constantly increasing sense of responsibility among Russians for their own cultural, political and religious life. The majority of them were confused about being a national minority. (The exception were 'Lithuanian Russians' who accepted they were a national minority and did not question their status as a minority at all.) How could a member of the Russian nation (the largest nation in the former Soviet Union) be a minority?

Two issues were important here. What it meant to be, first, Russian and, second, a Russian minority. The publicly dominant Lithuanian attitude towards Russians as well as differences within the Russian community also 'pushed' Russians to question the nature of their national identity.[148] This was a very difficult question for many of them to answer, as they often came from mixed marriages, were born in different places and had often moved frequently. It was difficult for the majority of Russians to face the consequences of the Soviet nationality policies on their own identity. This first step of facing 'who I am' was still on the agenda when I was in Lithuania. The second step would be to develop an awareness that s/he is a Russian in Lithuania and to try to learn about both Russian and Lithuanian history and culture. These issues were also connected with the issue of seeing themselves as members of a national minority.

As Frolov argued, it was difficult for Russians to accept the role of a national minority. Ironically, Russia's stance of not helping its fellow-nationals actually helped especially 'Russians of Lithuania'. 'New Russia' could not be their *otechestvo* (fatherland) because it did not address them at all as already pointed out. Furthermore, the new Russian state supported Lithuanian independence and, at the beginning, openly argued that it could not and should not take care of Russians who were Lithuanian citizens.[149] They saw Russia as their ethnic land, where their roots were, where their language came from as well as their culture.[150] Russia was on the other side of the border, and that could not be changed easily. All these issues, together with a slow awareness of the political history of the region, taught them to recognise that they were a national minority. Some 'Russians of Lithuania' stated that they were ready to live in Lithuania as a minority but claimed that Lithuanians were not ready to treat them equally. They also stated that they felt that the barriers were increasing and that they lived next to the Lithuanians or 'Lithuanian Russians' but did not mix socially with them. They shared the same geographical space but lived in a separate social space. Their worlds were moving apart. The rest of the 'Russians of Lithuania' in 1992 and 1993 were still not able to see themselves as a minority. They saw themselves as a part of the nation celebrated by the Soviet Union, a nation which brought victory to Eastern Europe in the Second World War. They believed that equality should entail a lack of distinction between majorities and minorities.[151]

'Soviet Russians' were not able to accept the role of a national minority primarily because they thought that they had outlived ethnic divisions. They saw national issues as being in opposition to internationalism in the same way that they saw capitalism as being opposed to communism and separatism to unity. Nationalism was dangerous because it was fighting communism and demanding the formation of a nation-state. Therefore it belonged to 'the dustbin of history', which would give them a clear political role in fighting 'bourgeois nationalism' in Lithuania.

Migration

As argued above, integration and collective mobilisation took place in Lithuania in relation to defining the role of Russians and their identity in the new state. The next response was migration. Migration was seen as 'a result of developing democracy',[152] as well as a result of political pressure.[153] Arvydas Juozaitis argued that the *Sajudis* 'turned towards a mystical nationalist spirit as well as violence and the use of physical power'.[154] As was pointed out in Chapter 3, during the Soviet period Lithuanians tried to prevent a large number of Russians and the Russian-speaking population from entering their republic.[155]

In the period of national reawakening and, later, independence Russians started to leave the country.[156] One has to point out that the emigration figures are higher than immigration ones for all national minorities except for Poles.[157] Russians mostly left for Russia, Belarus and Ukraine (in that order).[158] This does not mean that Russians were not leaving for other places but those numbers were very small and they were declining.[159]

If the negotiations with the USSR had been continually delayed all the time,[160] those with Russia ran comparatively smoothly[161] and within a year the Treaty on Friendly Relations and Good-Neighbourly Cooperation Between the Republic of Lithuania and the Russian Federation was signed by (the then) President of Russia Eltsin.[162] Lithuanian independence was acknowledged by Russia in the first article. In the fourth article, the right to apply for Lithuanian citizenship was extended until 29 July 1991 (the deadline was no longer 3 November 1989).[163] In the fifth article of the Treaty, the rights of ethnic, religious and language minorities in both countries to enjoy their culture, practise their religion and use their native language was acknowledged. In the sixth article, it was agreed that the immigration policies should be discussed in separate agreements linked with employment, resettlement and voluntary migration.

When it comes to resettlement and migration an important issue concerns the question of who were the people who were leaving the country. According to my interviews, the officers of the Soviet Army and their families had already left the country. I could not find any statistics on the Soviet Troops in Lithuania stating how many of them left in different years but we have to bear in mind that they were not welcome to stay in the country and also could not officially apply for Lithuanian citizenship.[164] 'I do not know the numbers when it comes to the officers of the Soviet Army, how many were here, how many left.'[165]

Vladimir Jarmolenka argued that data could be obtained neither from the Russian Embassy in Vilnius nor from Moscow.[166] According to my investigations, the other group of Russians who left the country were blue-collar workers working in the large Soviet enterprises that were closed down.[167] Vladimiras Gruzalis argued that out of 16 162 Russians who left Lithuania in 1992, 9927 were from Vilnius, Visaginas and Mazeikiai, where there were large Soviet enterprises.[168]

Audra Sipaviciene argued that there was a problem of a brain-drain because of the difficult economic situation and this especially took the form of migration to the West. Iasinskaia's opinion also supports this interpretation but highlighted that the migration of the skilled population occurred towards the East as well. She argued that not only blue-collar Russians but 'a lot of intellectuals already have left or are ready to leave Lithuania'.[169] She concluded, 'we are losing the best people'.[170]

The rise of a nationalistic attitude towards national minorities at the end of 1989 had a major impact on migration.[171] According to a survey done in 1991 by the Lithuanian State Centre on Ethnic Affairs, roughly 10 per cent of Russians wanted to leave the country.[172] A sociological survey carried out in 1991 showed that 57 per cent of Russians who decided to leave stated national enmity as a main reason.[173] Interpreting the results of another survey undertaken by the Sociological Centre at the House of National Minorities formed by the Lithuanian government in 1991, sociologist Eduardas Sviklas pointed out that Russians were not willing to give an explanation for leaving the country. In this survey 74.6 per cent of respondents did not answer the question. He argued that the nationalistic attitude of the Lithuanian government discouraged Russians from openly stating their opinion.[174]

From 1992 onwards, fewer Russians left.[175] Those who did leave gave repatriation and family reunion as a reason, leading Sipaviciene to conclude that 'all the talk about it [national tension] is more political game than reality'.[176] In her research conducted in 1992 among Russians in Visaginas who intended to leave for Russia, Kasatkina found that they had decided to leave because they could not find a job or argued that they had private reasons for leaving in relation to the education and future of their children.[177]

In a poll carried out in 1992 among Russians in Lithuania, one-fifth wanted to leave for Russia because of a lack of guarantees and freedoms, problems with occupational and professional education and personal family situations.[178] In particular, some of the 'Russians of Lithuania' were still pointing out in 1992 that national tension existed in Lithuania and they wanted to leave for Russia.[179] Their main problem was housing. Because of the increase in property prices in Russia, they would no longer be able to afford to buy apartments with the money they would have received from selling their apartments in Lithuania.[180] Some of them argued that Lithuania should compensate them, especially in light of the fact that 'the results of their work if they leave were going to be enjoyed by Lithuanians'. They also argued that if Russia was interested in helping people to move back to their homeland, then they should help them to find a way out.[181] Russian representatives in Lithuania argued that national tension existed but they also encouraged Russians to stay because 'it will take some time, not too long, for the situation to improve'. They added that moving to Russia 'should not be an emotional decision but one carefully thought through'. From this discussion it was obvious that Russia did not want more people to move back and tried to encourage them to stay in Lithuania. Nevertheless, in 1993 Gruzas reported that more than 2000 Lithuanian citizens had decided to give up their citizenship and 900 were still waiting to hear from the Lithuanian authorities. However, he was not able to say how many of them were Russians.[182] According to material collected by Gruzalis, at the end of 1992 there were no longer 9.4 per cent of Russians in Lithuania as in 1989 but 8.8 per cent.[183]

However, according to all the above quoted research, the majority of Russians pointed out that it would be difficult to leave the country. The main reason for this was that their families were in Lithuania as well as in Russia. In the course of my interviews, it was pointed out by those who were prepared to leave that although the economic situation in Russia was difficult, they would always be able to get support from their families, in the form of housing and food.

When I asked Russians what would have been their reason if they had decided to leave the country it was always connected with job prospects and education for their children.[184] Unfortunately, I did not meet that many Russians who had left Lithuania but those whom I did meet (when they came back to visit their friends who stayed in Lithuania) told me that they left because they could not find a job in Lithuania. They also pointed out that they had family outside Lithuania. They argued that their nationality made them the first to be made redundant and the last to be employed.[185] These answers clearly pointed out that there was more than one reason for migration; ethnicity played an important role as well as the political and economic situation in Lithuania and Russia.[186] Those who had family in other republics of the Soviet Union joined them. The others, especially married people with children, decided to stay. They judged that they did not have a future in Russia because of its difficult economic situation. On the other hand, at least one spouse had a job in Lithuania and they often had an apartment, however small it was. Furthermore, they pointed out that with the development of Russian business in Lithuania they had a chance to get a job because Russian bosses would prefer to employ 'their own fellow-nationals'.[187]

According to statistical data available from the Employment Office, unemployment among Russians and Lithuanians was not significantly different. This was confirmed by Povilas-Vytautas Ziukas, vice-minister at the Ministry of Social Security who argued that 'unemployment was stabilising and more and more working places have been opened. Although the job centres do not register nationality the research done by the Institute of Employment points out that there is less than 20 per cent of unemployment among national minorities and there is no discrimination towards national minorities.'[188] This figure of 20 per cent was a surprise because official unemployment was not that high (4.4 per cent in 1993).[189] However, research done by the Institute of Social Policy at the Ministry of Social Security points out that 'non-Lithuanians spend longer looking for a job'. Gruzevskis added that 'It is a shame we did not ask why. Is it because they do not have professional education or language skills? Certainly non-Lithuanians are more active in looking for a job.'[190]

According to material I collected in Lithuania and my interviews, it is difficult to generalise about why people decided to migrate. The rise of nationalism played an important role but this was not the only reason. As potential migrants pointed out, they no longer felt comfortable in a country that was only exhibiting its own national heritage while they also had economic problems. They decided to leave Lithuania because they hoped that Russia, or any other country, would provide better political and economic surroundings for their needs. But they were not always accepted openly by those countries.

Conclusion

In 1993, the majority of Russians in Lithuania were still trying to answer the question of who they were, where they belonged and how they could improve their position. Russian national identity was weakly developed in the Soviet Union due to its understanding in terms of 'coming together' and 'merging'. National identity among 'Lithuanian Russians' was formed in relationship with Lithuania and ethnic Russia. 'Russians of Lithuania' were forced into facing who they were and forming their own identity. 'Soviet Russians' continued to claim that national identity was outlived. This group of Russians were the most vocal and ready to fight for the 'brotherhood and unity' of the Soviet people.

This question of identity was combined with issues which they considered important in improving their position in Lithuania. This process also had implications for the Lithuanian majority because these communities had to learn to co-exist. Only 'Lithuanian Russians' found their place in the new Lithuania and felt integrated. They did not judge Lithuanian legislation as discriminatory although they agreed that nationalism at the level of everyday life still existed. Being a citizen of Lithuania and being able to cherish their culture were seen as an appropriate base to continue their life in Lithuania. 'Russians of Lithuania' were still engaged in a process of finding their place in a country which, despite its inclusive citizenship, did not welcome them. They started to feel more comfortable when they realised (especially after 1989 and 1990) that quite a few Lithuanians also did not feel comfortable with the rise of Lithuanian nationalism. From 1991 onwards, it was clear to them that they had witnessed the end of the Soviet Union and that it was up to them to build their life in Lithuania. Nonetheless, they continued to feel uneasy about being a national minority. The majority of 'Soviet Russians' left and there was a possibility that some of those who stayed reconsidered their position towards independent Lithuania, especially in the light of the putsch in 1991 which confirmed the end of the Soviet Union and the communist system. The policy of 'near abroad', introduced in 1993, argued that 'a special role in the post-Soviet space belonged to Russia'.[191] However, it did not address Lithuania on the same scale as the other former Soviet Union states, which had much larger Russian communities.[192]

At the same time, some Lithuanians began to stop distinguishing between *us* and *them* and between *our* Russians and *other* Russians. The rise of a nationalistic attitude in *Sajudis* made them withdraw from the movement and either join some other political parties or stay in the public arena without being affiliated to any political party, or withdrawing from public life altogether. I think it was all the above mentioned issues that enabled Eduardas Vilkas to conclude, 'We shall never have problems with Russians but Poles are different. The reason is history.'[193]

7
Polish Demands

Introduction

In this chapter the struggle of the Poles in defining their place in Lithuania will be analysed and different Polish identities will be introduced. These identities had been based on their understanding of what type of rights were necessary to preserve their national identity. In comparison with the Russians and Jews, all Poles in Lithuania believed in some form of autonomy, but varied according to whether they saw this in terms of territorial, political or cultural autonomy. However, all Poles felt that it was important to be able to have access to education in their own language, and therefore all of them agreed that there was a need for cultural autonomy in terms of a collective right. Language was seen as an important marker of national identity, especially given that some Lithuanians argued that Poles, particularly those in the rural South-East of Lithuania, were of Lithuanian origin. Furthermore, the tension surrounding this issue, together with 50 years of Soviet rule, resulted in a movement for territorial autonomy for the Vilnius (Wilno in Polish) and Salcininkai (Soleczniki) regions as well as the formation of a political party, the Union of Poles (*Zwiazeko Polakow na Litwie*). The collapse of the Soviet Union enabled Lithuania to take a much firmer stance and abolish the councils ruling in these two regions. It also influenced demands put forward by the Union of Poles which concentrated on cultural autonomy, although some of its members raised the issue of political autonomy as well.

The Polish minority is nearly as large as the Russian one, but there is a big difference between the two. The Poles live in the South-East part of Lithuania, in the Vilnius and Salcininkai regions (see Map 7.1). The majority of them are rural inhabitants.[1] Their educational level is the

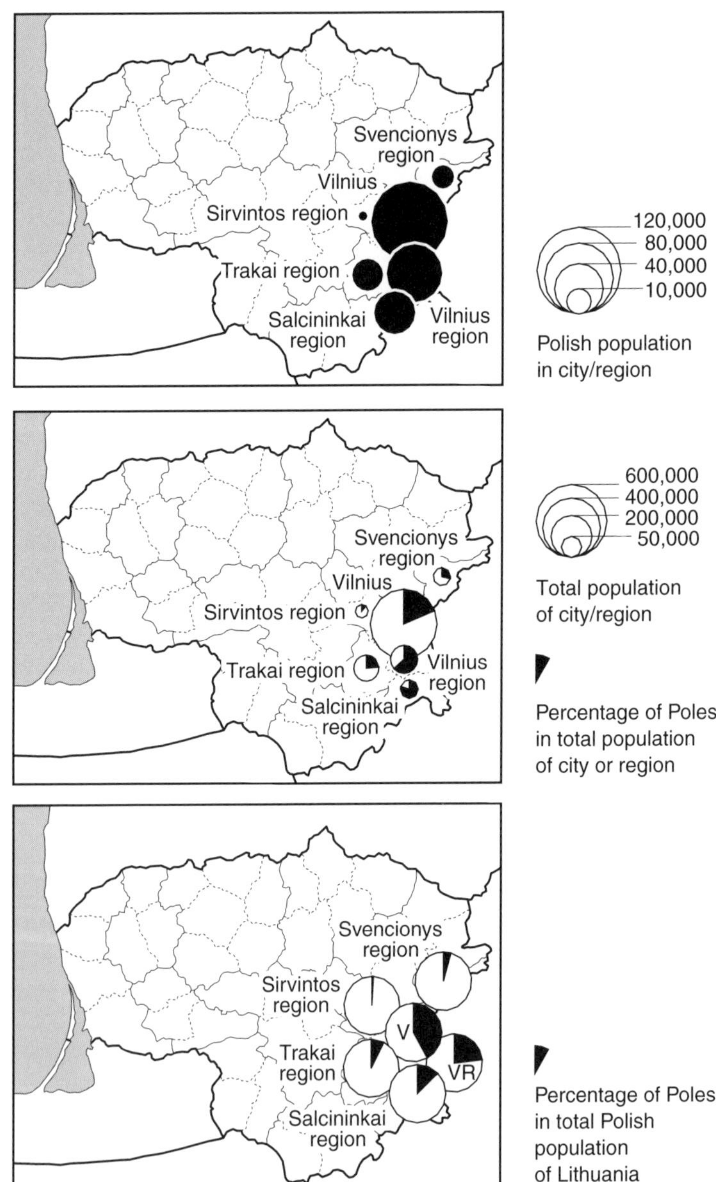

Map 7.1   Poles in Lithuania, 1989

lowest in Lithuania.[2] They are mostly part of a native population who have lived in these regions for centuries.[3] Between the two World Wars these regions were part of Poland. Following the First World War, the Poles emigrated to these regions and were rewarded with land. This fact is central to the problems connected with land reform. After the Second World War, the Polish intelligentsia left Lithuania for either Poland or, most commonly, the United States. The Polish population still suffers from not having an intelligentsia that could have played a central role in the development of national awareness.

How much do the Poles differ among themselves?

Introduction: the importance of the urban–rural divide and the language *po prostemu*

Before discussing types of identity among the Poles in Lithuania we have to refer to two issues which are closely related to identity, the urban–rural divide and the language *po prostemu*.

In Lithuania there is an urban–rural divide between Poles. My research revealed that this was acknowledged by both groups.[4] The rural Poles, known as *tutejszy*, felt that the urban Poles did not understand them because, whereas the identity of urban Poles had never been questioned, the rural Poles, on the other hand, had to face Lithuanians who questioned their ethnic origins.[5] There were claims in contemporary Lithuania that Poles, especially rural Poles, were in fact Polonised Lithuanians.[6] Eugenija Krukauskiene argued that sociological research carried out before independence in the South-East showed that passport identity and personal choice of identity had differed. She remembered a case, characteristic more for Poles than other groups, in which 'One individual said that he was a Pole. In his passport it was written Belorussian. His homeland was the Soviet Union and his mother tongue was Russian.'[7] In her research carried out in the South-East of Lithuania in 1989, she also suggested that there were 'Many more Poles according to their passports than their feelings'.[8] Lithuanian researchers also stressed that 'Only a minority among the Poles has Polish roots and most of these are people who live in the cities.'[9]

The rural Poles argued that they were conscious of their Polish identity and wanted to maintain this identity. The urban Poles and Poles from Poland made them feel uncomfortable because they had a condescending attitude to *tutejszy* and argued that they did not speak 'proper Polish'. Some of them argued that they were aware of this factor but they remained proud because they continued to speak their own language through centuries and they believed in the authenticity of their Polish identity in Lithuania.

Second, the language which rural Poles speak in the South-East is called *po prostemu* in Polish, *paprastoji* in Lithuanian and *po prostu* in Russian.[10] The Lithuanian and Polish perspectives on the language varied and were tinged with political connotations.

Before the Second World War, a Polish demographer Halina Turska carried out research on the language in the South-East of Lithuania.[11] Both Polish and Lithuanian communities in Lithuania made use of her research but in ways which emphasised different aspects. She argued that as a result of 'forced Russification' a lot of Lithuanians adopted 'their neighbours' Belorussian because it helped them in communication with the Russian bureaucracy and Polish neighbours'.[12] However, she added that in the larger part of the Vilnius region there was no Belorussian influence on the Polish language.[13] According to research that she conducted in 1933, rural Poles of the Vilnius region spoke either Polish alone or both Polish and *po prostemu* which she identified as the 'people's dialect' of the literary Belorussian, Lithuanian and Polish languages and which she sometimes refers to as Belorussian.[14] She clearly stated that the Polish language spoken in the villages of Lithuania has had elements of Belorussian in its phonetic, morphology and syntax: 'The Polish language adopted a whole range of foreign elements, primarily Belorussian.'[15] She argued that there were wide variations in the Polish spoken in the villages of this region. It tended to have much more Lithuanian and Belorussian influence than the Polish spoken in the cities or in the western or northern areas (around Kaunas and Zarasai).

The official Lithuanian position is that *paprastoji* is made up of the Belorussian language with the addition of many Russian and Polish words.[16] Research carried out in Poland on Polish minorities in Lithuania and Belorussia in the 1980s showed that 'Independently of the level of their knowledge of Polish, Poles speak a Belorussian dialect known as "*mowa prosta*"'.[17]

However, the Poles, especially from the Union of Poles, see *po prostemu* as a Polish dialect.[18] This statement is important because language was seen as a significant ethnic marker among the Polish community. Those Poles who were members of the Union pointed out that this dialect was spoken in Polish villages among *tutejszy*. The Polish minority in Lithuania claimed that they had been living in this region for centuries, and therefore they could not accept the suggestion that a process of Polonisation had taken place.

However, the rural–urban distinction and the language issue by no means encompass all the complexities of identity formation among the Poles in Lithuania. In order to understand such complexities, the same type of typology as in Chapter 6 will be employed.

'Lithuanian Poles'

'Lithuanian Poles', like the 'Lithuanian Russians' and 'Lithuanian Jews', supported the Lithuanian struggle for independence but, in comparison with the Russians, they were not ready to accept Lithuanian nationalistic behaviour. They emphasised that the Poles had also been suppressed during the Soviet era and thus believed that Lithuania should not make the same mistake as the Soviets in seeing them as 'enemies'.

'Lithuanian Poles' acknowledged that their self-understanding was shaped by their life in Lithuania. Their identity was influenced by being exposed to a mixture of different cultures, especially in Vilnius where these Poles lived. They cherished their Polish identity in 'conversation' with Lithuanians, Russians and Jews. They were therefore more receptive to their background in a socially mixed environment where these cultures were influencing each other. 'Lithuanian Poles' were brought up with these cultures and they realised and valued the influence that this had on their Polishness.

'Lithuanian Poles' argued that there was a need for education in Polish. They saw a need for cultural autonomy understood in terms of a collective right not like 'Lithuanian Russians' as individual rights. This was particularly connected with the Soviet era. They stressed that education in Polish during the Soviet era was poor and Soviet injustices had to be corrected with a guarantee that Polish culture would not be neglected. 'Lithuanian Poles' argued that Poles needed to acknowledge the fact that in some of their schools the curriculum was taught in Russian with their consent; 'Soviets did not always use force.'[19] Therefore, it was not enough for an individual to have a right to be educated in his/her language, rather the state had to introduce 'polyethnic rights' as collective rights which would give allowances to the Polish community in the form of, for example, keeping schools open even if there was an insufficient number of Polish-speaking pupils. Furthermore, 'Lithuanian Poles' addressed the issue of learning Lithuanian. They revealed that they had felt uncomfortable among Lithuanians until they had mastered their language. They saw the learning of the language as a gesture of good will which the Poles needed to show towards Lithuania. From a pragmatic point of view, it would make their situation easier because the Lithuanians would no longer see them as enemies. Furthermore, knowledge of the language would help the Poles to learn to get to know Lithuanian culture and respect the country.

After the Second World War and the exodus of the Poles, the Polish cultural institutions withered away and only societies promoting folklore remained open. There was, therefore, a belief in the need to revive the Polish intelligentsia because the Polish nation lacked those individuals who would have played a leading role in making and preserving national culture. The main concern of 'Lithuanian Poles' was higher education. Therefore, in 1991, they supported the foundation of the Polish University, which was still not officially recognised by the Lithuanian government in 1993.[20] According to Medard(as) Cobot(as) the University was seen as a political issue (a University of the Republic of Poland on the Lithuanian territory) and entailed the Poles being seen as enemies of Lithuania.[21] It should be noted, however, that it was not possible to study the Polish language and literature at the University of Vilnius.[22]

'Lithuanian Poles' acknowledged that, according to the letter of the law, they had been granted basic rights. However, Czeslaw Okinczyc pointed out that problems had already begun to develop in the Parliament because it 'did not devote enough time to deal with the interests of the Poles. Furthermore, the constant contact and dialogue with the Polish organisations (which had hardly existed) as well as with voters is of major importance.'[23] This group of Poles argued that the Polish community needed to encourage the Parliament to be constantly aware of Polish issues. They believed that joining the Union of Poles was not the only answer to solving the problems of the Polish community. 'Lithuanian Poles' acknowledged that Poles shared certain problems but also pointed out that the Poles differed very much among themselves. They emphasised that the most important division was that between urban and rural inhabitants.

'Lithuanian Poles' were ready to acknowledge that they themselves, not only Lithuanians, had a tendency to behave nationalistically. They also admitted to sometimes harbouring patronising attitudes towards Lithuanians which would be manifested in their belief that they belonged to a more developed cultural tradition. They also had a patronising attitude to their fellow-nationals which was particularly evident when they compared their Polish to that spoken by the rural population. However, according to my interviews, the Poles from Poland also addressed the language of 'Lithuanian Poles' as being poor in comparison with 'Warsaw Polish'.

'Lithuanian Poles' lived in Vilnius and mostly belonged to a very small group of Polish intelligentsia which did not leave Lithuania after the Second World War. In the period 1945–7, 180 000 Poles left Lithuania out of which 108 000 were Poles from Vilnius, leaving less than 20 000 Poles in Vilnius.[24]

'Poles of Lithuania'

'Poles of Lithuania' belonged to both urban and rural communities. Those who lived in urban areas were often the first generation of people who had left their rural communities and had gained an education. They were more politically active and joined the Union of Poles (analysed below). Rural Poles who belonged to this group were particularly worried about the status of the Lithuanian language as the only official language in the South-East of Lithuania. They also pointed out that the Poles should 'rule'[25] over the region in which they comprised a majority of the population.

Both rural and urban 'Poles of Lithuania' shared a common demand for cultural and political autonomy. They differed, however, when it came to how they perceived their cultural background. 'Poles of Lithuania' were aware of the hostile attitude of *Sajudis* who addressed the entire Polish community as 'Red Poles'.[26] Artur Plokszto argued that 'repression against Poles' had an established tradition both in Moscow and Lithuania. Moscow wanted Polish people to lose touch with their own culture and become Soviet people. Lithuania wanted to undermine Polish influence and culture, especially in Vilnius.[27] This deterred them from placing any obstacles in front of the exodus of the Polish population to Poland. They were particularly glad to see the departure of the Polish intelligentsia.[28]

'Poles of Lithuania' believed that 'once again' their community was neglected and discriminated against. For that reason they were oriented primarily towards their own community's needs and priorities. Therefore, they demanded cultural and political autonomy, understood as collective rights. In contrast to the 'Lithuanian Poles', they argued that to be able to preserve Polish identity cultural autonomy was not enough. Poles should be able to have political authority over the South-East because that was the only way to diminish the influence of the Lithuanian state and culture which had in the last 50 years been so influential in this area together with that of Soviet culture. Like 'Lithuanian Poles', this group was worried about the educational level of their community at the time and they were concerned about the various suggestions that the Poles were actually Lithuanians. They argued that the underfunding of their schools continued in the period of independent Lithuania. 'A letter from an ethnic Pole from Lithuania to *Gazeta Wyborcza* (25 September 1989) claimed that predominantly Polish regions receive 50 percent less funding from the Vilnius government than the Lithuanian ones.'[29]

Furthermore, the 'Poles of Lithuania' argued for 'special representation rights'. They argued that electoral boundaries should be defined along ethnic lines and also that ethnic parties should not have to pass the threshold to enter the Parliament. That would guarantee them a majority in the regional government. They made it clear in 1992 that they did not consider territorial autonomy a viable option. They argued that 'special representation rights' were needed because the Lithuanian state promoted its own culture and did not support minority cultures. 'Poles of Lithuania' feared that underinvestment in their culture, together with lack of assistance from Poland, might easily lead to the gradual disappearance of Poles in this region. Therefore, they argued that it was important to establish a Polish party. Only a Polish party would be able to address Polish demands and would allow them to have a significant effect on the Lithuanian Parliament.

While the 'Poles of Lithuania' saw themselves primarily as Poles whose fatherland had been taken away from them, they had nonetheless come to accept Lithuania as their new homeland. They had been living in Lithuania since the beginning of the Second World War, but largely as a result of a power game which enabled the 'fourth partition' of Poland. 'Poles of Lithuania' accepted and acknowledged that they lived in Lithuania, 'my second fatherland' as they called it, but still nostalgically thought about the past, especially the inter-war period, which they saw and interpreted as a period when their culture was particularly flourishing.[30]

In comparison with the 'Lithuanian Poles', urban members of this group saw themselves as being primarily influenced by Polish culture. 'Poland is the cultural centre for us.'[31] They were proud of their cultural heritage and proud to be Polish. They continually pointed out that 'all civilisation came to Lithuania through or from Poland'. Between the two World Wars they lived in a region where there were hardly any Lithuanians and where Polish culture had a much larger influence 'than the Jewish culture'. As already pointed out, rural members of this group put more emphasis on their local culture. Ryszard Maciejkaniec, a member of the Polish Union and MP, summarised these differences saying, 'Poland is Poland and the Vilnius region is the Vilnius region. We are Poles but a little different.'[32]

'Soviet Poles'

During my period of investigation, I did not come across any 'Soviet Poles'. Whereas the 'Soviet Russians' left written evidence, such as Ivanov's Prison Diary, the only evidence left about (though not by) the 'Soviet Poles' is in connection with the territorial autonomy of the Vilnius and Salcininkai regions. 'Soviet Poles' belonged to a group of Poles that had undergone the processes of Russification and Sovietisation.[33] They mostly went to Russian schools (though it should be noted that not all of the Poles who were educated in Russian were 'Soviet Poles'). However, this group mostly consisted of the Polish rural population whose educational level was rather poor. Anatol Lieven attended the founding congress of the new Autonomous Province in May 1991 and was struck by the 'limited education and horizons of the delegates, predominately village officials and collective farm managers'.[34] 'Soviet Poles' believed in communist ideology which kept alive the atrocities that Lithuanians had committed against the Jews as well as the Poles in the South-East. Communist propaganda constantly reminded them of the massacres committed by 'police battalions' in the Second World War.[35]

According to my interviews, 'Soviet Poles' consisted of 'conservative Poles' who favoured the Soviet Union and the communist regime. However, the members of the Union of Poles also saw them as a group concerned with the rights of the Poles in Lithuania. These members argued that the demand of 'Soviet Poles' for autonomy was fuelled by Lithuanian nationalistic behaviour, in other words, that they did not have the choice. 'Soviet Poles' were worried about the rights of the Polish minority but their attitude towards the Lithuanian authorities was not one that favoured the opening up of dialogue. The Lithuanian authorities were not ready to discuss the Polish minority issues without reference to the Vilnius question and without demanding from the Poles (both in Poland and Lithuania) that they should condemn Zeligowski and Pilsudski. The Lithuanian national reawakening made 'Soviet Poles' concerned that their ideology and power might be diminished.

In summary, while there is evidence to suggest that differences between groups of Poles in Lithuania existed, they had certain features in common. In comparison with the Russians, the Poles felt strongly that their rights had been curbed. They saw themselves as an indigenous population who had the same rights as Lithuanians. The Poles did not want to be seen as a people with a localised rather than a national identity. This was especially the case during the Lithuanian reawakening period. They remembered (through individual or collective memory) the Second World War and the Lithuanian take-over of this region as well as the exodus of the Polish population. They argued that their local identity did not conflict with their identity at the national level.[36] The Poles did not want to be addressed as 'Red Poles' or to be told that they were Lithuanians. They were alarmed when they came to register for Lithuanian citizenship and were told their names would not only be written in Lithuanian but also Lithuanised.[37] I would argue that the sentiments surrounding this issue were to provide the initial stimulus for Poles to organise their own political party, or to join the communist leadership in the Vilnius and Salcininkai regions. Before addressing these two issues we shall summarise their concerns in relation to citizenship rights which were highlighted by all the Poles whom I interviewed.

Polish perception of their citizenship rights

Discussion with the members of the Polish community,[38] regardless of their political affiliation, brought out five issues. Four will be discussed in this section. The fifth one, concerning the importance of Vilnius to Poles, will be discussed later in this chapter.

1. Land reform had been discussed regularly by the Polish population and according to Maciejkianiec, Chairperson of the Polish Faction in the 1990–2 Lithuanian Parliament, was 'the main reason' why Poles felt that they suffered from discrimination.[39] It is one of the most substantial problems which Lithuanian governments have faced since independence. The major problem was in the South-East of Lithuania. This region was a part of Poland between the two World Wars. As pointed out in Chapter 2, Poles were encouraged to immigrate to this region. The land reform in Lithuania was based on two principles.[40] The main principle argued that the land should be returned to its pre-socialist owners. The second one, which was complementary, argued that collective farms should be privatised. Poles who moved there between the two World Wars were treated as 'occupiers' and because of that they were not able to claim the land back. Although this suggestion was dismissed, many Poles were still unable to claim their land back in 1993 for two reasons. First, they could not get hold of the land ownership documents which could be either in Poland or in Belarus. The LDDP, therefore, decided that 'all different types of documents, with the holder's name on it, issued between 1920–1939 are valid'.[41] The *Sajudis* government argued that the documents concerning land ownership should have

been issued in 1940, the year after Lithuania regained the Vilnius region.[42] The second reason was that the Parliament was still discussing land reform. Erevistas Raisuotis argued, 'Between the two World Wars quite a lot of people came here and we cannot acknowledge their right to the land.'[43] This position 'hurts only Poles because there were no Lithuanians in this region between the two World Wars'.[44] The Poles saw an ethnic dimension in it and the LDDP government, aware of this complaint continually emphasised the fact that land was limited. They argued that they inherited all these problems from the *Sajudis* government which rushed into land reform without thinking it through.[45] Raisuotis stated, 'The present government was aware of all the problems and, therefore, decided to introduce a project for each single village. This means that the reform will be sorted out by 1998.'

Another problem concerned the land around big cities, especially Vilnius. The city authorities claimed to need it for development. According to the Union of Poles, MPs, members of the Army and the judiciary had started to build their homes on some of this land. The local community was very upset because they felt cheated. As an example, Plokszto described an incident in the village of Gudeliai where the Army came and started shooting at the villagers who complained because they had heard that some houses were to be built in their village. After this event, which the Army described as 'manoeuvres', the 'people from the city' started to build houses because they had been issued permits during the *Sajudis* government.[46]

2. Higher education was the main topic of Polish educational discussion. The problem was approached from two angles: higher education in Polish at the University of Vilnius, and the functioning of the Polish University. While legislation allowed education to be undertaken in the native language, many Poles gained higher education, especially since independence, in Lithuanian.[47] Polish primary and secondary schools were seen as being of poor quality and for the Poles a possible explanation could be related to, in the words of Apolonia Skakowska, 'The policy of the *Sajudis* government to put into these regions only half the money which it puts in other regions'.[48] Poles argued that it was very difficult, after finishing secondary school, to enrol at the University of Vilnius for three reasons; the bad reputation of Polish schools, poor knowledge of Lithuanian and, finally, their nationality, which, they said, did not help them to win a place to study in Lithuania. Skakowska argued that in 1992/3 there were 200 Poles studying in Poland because they could not find a place in Lithuania.[49]

She claimed that usually the Poles who left for Poland did not come back. In the same academic year, 100 Poles studied at the University of Vilnius.[50]

Because of the above mentioned concerns the Polish University was founded and it started to unofficially enrol students from 1991, although in 1993 they had not yet received a permit for which they had applied in 1989.[51] The representative of the LDDP government, after nearly eight months in power, declared, 'I do not know why the University is still not registered, maybe because the registration is connected with obtaining premises.'[52] Zbigniew Siemenowicz argued that the best example of the Lithuanian authorities' opinion of the University was its refusal to allow an American Pole to buy a building and donate it to the University. Cobot(as) compared this University with a Polish University that had been founded after the Second World War in Chicago, and which had been closed down after seven years because the Poles realised the need to pursue their education in English.[53]

3. According to the Union of Poles, the Polish population in Vilnius should have at least three buildings returned to them, the Theatre building, the Building of the Friends of Science, and the Scout building. Their argument was that since so many buildings in the Old city were built with Polish money, they should at least have the three most important buildings returned to them.[54] They suggested that the government was 'afraid to return some buildings as they would then be obliged to return the rest'.[55] The Union of Poles claimed that they did not want more buildings back because they were unable to finance their maintenance or use them in any way. All three buildings, especially the second one, the Building of the Friends of Science, had an important role in the history of the Polish community in Vilnius. 'The Building of the Friends of Science was built in 1913 with Polish money. This foundation had the role of promoting national awareness and education among the Poles. It contained several libraries which are now scattered around Vilnius.'[56] The importance of this building shows the vital role of memory in shaping national identity. This is a crucial element in bringing back their perceived golden age. The other vital element is the Polish University. The Lithuanian government claimed that this building would be returned. However, 'At the moment in this building there are paintings which were moved here from the Cathedral. We are building a gallery near the Piatnickaja Church and as soon as it is finished we shall return the building to the Poles. I have seen all

the documents.'[57] Vladimiras Gruzalis also pointed out, 'There are documents which show that Poles and Belorussians gave the money towards this building.' This statement has to be seen in the light of the argument which states that 'Vilnius is a melting pot and very often it was a non-Lithuanian capital at different points in history.'[58] The Poles realised that the Scout building would not be returned because it had been given to the American Embassy. According to Gruzalis, the Theatre building still housed the Russian theatre and was also claimed by the Lithuanian Youth Theatre. Plokszto argued that he was 'personally sceptical about the Polish theatre. For our community it is enough to have two–three performances per month. People do not have money to go to the theatre.' Skakowska pointed out that, according to the Foundation Charter of the Polish theatre, 'Only Polish can be spoken in that building.'[59] She added that there was no chance of retrieving this building back. 'Eight times the government told us "no" because they argued that the building belongs to the Lithuanian Youth Theatre. Their administration is already there.' In relation to the building issue, they made a first draft of a business scheme which included ideas concerning how Polish culture could be financed through business grants and rent. 'We would like to offer to Polish companies premises for their offices in Lithuania. We would like to encourage the opening of a Polish restaurant.'[60] The scheme was not as developed as the Russian one, but it was moving in the same direction.

4. Poles disapproved of using only Lithuanian names for their towns, villages, regions, etc. in the South-East of Lithuania. 'Arunas Eigirdas removed the Polish names of streets and towns.'[61] Poles argued that they would like to be able to officially use Polish names for these places in addition to the Lithuanian ones. Therefore, they were pleased with the decision of the LDDP government to begin implementing the Law on National Minorities which included, as analysed in Chapter 4, the Polish way of spelling their surnames in Lithuanian passports (their first names were spelled in the Polish way).[62] The Poles wanted to be able to spell their surnames in the Polish way. Mindaugas Stakvilevicius argued, 'Polish names in passports are spelled in the Lithuanian way because of the computing facilities.'[63] These two issues can be seen as minor, but they are important to the Poles as they are connected with their identity both at the group and individual level.

Some 'Poles of Lithuania' talked about economic autonomy, i.e. the need to have Polish factories and businesses, without giving details about how this could be done. However, all of them indicated that they were against territorial autonomy.[64] They indicated that, in relation to the above analysed issues as well as the issues of the Vilnius question analysed below they needed, in Kymlicka's terms, 'polyethnic' and 'special representation rights'. They needed these rights as a group, not only as individuals. They were afraid that the bias towards the Lithuanian language and culture would undermine political and economic support for their language and culture. As a result, they would be disadvantaged and would opt to assimilate into the dominant culture. According to the Lithuanian laws, they were granted 'polyethnic' rights as individuals. However, the laws did not always work in practice. For example the 'Poles of Lithuania' argued that, while they had a right to be educated in Polish, the state was not ready to invest in Polish schools.[65] As a result, the level of education continued to be low and some Poles chose to send their children to Lithuanian schools. However, the last statement contradicts the data which point out that both the number of Poles attending full time general education and the number of schools were growing.[66] With regard to 'special representation rights', according to the 1992 Electoral Law, the national minority parties did not need to satisfy the threshold of 4 per cent.[67] Furthermore, the Poles fought against the proposed changes of electoral boundaries for two reasons; first, they wanted their opinion to be at least heard if not 'amplified' and second, they did not want to belong to the city of Vilnius. Because the city was growing so fast, they would each be able to claim only 0.2 hectares of their land back.[68] Their argument for these two types of rights followed the argument put forward by Iris Young and Will Kymlicka.[69] The Poles argued that the state supported the majority culture. They believed that cultures should be treated equally and fairly. If their language and culture were not protected they would not be able to exercise their rights as individuals. They felt vulnerable, first, because their language and culture were not adequately acknowledged and sometimes threatened, such as in the case where they were described as 'Polonised Lithuanians'. Second, they did not have their own intelligentsia and did not see how, under contemporary circumstances, it could be formed. They saw the intelligentsia as a vital element in continuing their life in Lithuania.

The Union of Poles

The Union of Poles was founded on 5 May 1988. Plokszto, Leader of the Union of Poles in 1992, argued that the Poles founded their own political party because they had lived in the South-East of Lithuania since the fourteenth century and thus desired 'to rule over the region in which they lived'. In accordance with their party programme they were in support of a democratic state and the equal rights of all people. They believed in the principle that Lithuania as a democratic state should preserve its multicultural character. They suggested that administrative and linguistic borders should coincide and that minority languages should be used both in the governmental offices and in formal communication. Minorities should be able to obtain education at all levels in their native languages. In the language of collective rights, as discussed in Chapter 1, they asked for 'polyethnic rights' and 'special representation rights'. They also argued that Lithuanian should be taught in all the minority schools but at a higher standard than was currently the case. They also demanded the registration of the Polish University, the right to spell their names in Polish, to have at least one TV channel broadcasting in Polish and more financial support for the media and literature in minority languages.[70] The aim of the Union was the national rebirth of the Poles of Lithuania, promotion of Polish education at all levels and contribution to the public, economic and cultural development of the Vilnius region as an integral part of Lithuania.[71] The Union warned that there was a danger of Lithuania forgetting about its minorities as a result of the small size of the minority population.

An important question at this point was why the Poles needed to have political control over the Vilnius and Salcininkai regions. They argued that 'this region is a mixture, it is neither Lithuania nor Poland'.[72] However, they reasoned that the majority of the population who lived in these regions were Poles and therefore 'they should rule over Vilnius and Salcininkai regions'.[73] Furthermore, they did not see Lithuania as a democratic state but as a state with a government that was turning more and more nationalistic. They did not trust *Sajudis* which they saw as an organisation that was curbing their rights.[74] They also felt that the Lithuanian government saw them as a threat to Lithuanian independence especially because of the demand for Polish autonomy which will be analysed later in this chapter.

In the course of my interviews, it became clear that the Union of Poles was viewed by a minority of Lithuanians as a 'nationalistic party' whose aim was to 'rule' over the South-East instead of entering into a democratic dialogue. However, a considerable number of Lithuanians pointed out that the Union had been changing its political attitude towards Lithuania, taking on a more conciliatory attitude. Arunas

Eigirdas argued that the Union was collaborating with those who demanded territorial autonomy and who wanted to secede from Lithuania. He pointed out that in December 1991 the Union of Poles demanded restoration of political and economic rights and also supported the introduction of new territorial-administrative units which would enable Poles to secure their political autonomy[75] (as will be discussed later in this chapter). Just ten days before the deadline to register for the October 1992 elections the Prosecutor-General's Office demanded that the registration of the Union of Poles should be annulled because of what was seen as a hidden agenda to weaken the integrity of the Republic of Lithuania through the creation of a Polish territorial entity. However, the Ministry of Justice concluded that there was no evidence of the Union's unconstitutional activities[76] and added that there were only a few individuals within the Union who violated Lithuanian legislation. According to the documents which I collected, primarily from the General Prosecutor's Office and the State Security Department, there were individuals within the Polish community who, as members of the Lithuanian Communist Party loyal to the CPSU, acted against the Lithuanian Constitution because they were in support of the Soviet Union's territorial integrity and its communist system. But it was not clear from these documents that they were also members of the Union of Poles.[77] The members of the Union argued that they had not changed their opinion but had been constantly arguing that there was a problem with the rights of the Polish minority. They also stated that they had urged the Poles to take part in the Lithuanian referendum on independence in February 1991 and support Lithuanian independence.

The Union of Poles saw itself as the main representative of the Polish minority. According to the membership figures, the Union had only 10000 members in 1992, comprising 2.7 per cent of Poles.[78] (This percentage coincides with the percentage of votes which the Union received in the October 1992 elections.) Those Poles who supported the Union believed that it was the only party which gave priority to national minorities and their various problems. Its membership mostly lived in urban areas and consisted mainly of 'Poles of Lithuania'. 'Lithuanian Poles' argued that Poles differed politically and should, therefore, address Polish issues through different political parties. According to my interviews, the Union of Poles was not seen as a party which represented the Polish minority in Lithuania. This was also supported by the election results in 1990 and 1992. In the first elections the Union of Poles won three seats and in 1992 four seats respectively.[79]

Polish passivity

The majority of the Polish community was politically passive. In the 1992 elections a 'little over 40 per cent of Poles bothered to vote at all'.[80] What is even more interesting is that the turn-out for the elections for the local councils in the Vilnius and Salcininkai regions was so low that 'Several elections have been invalidated'.[81] The elections took place on 22 November 1992. Romualdas Ozolas, as Chairperson of the Parliamentary Committee on Regional Issues, held a press conference on 4 December 1992 and declared that in Salcininkai region only 14 out of 29 electoral districts had a turn-out of more than 50 per cent of voters. In the Vilnius region only 3 out of 47 electoral districts had more than a 50 per cent turn-out.[82]

Polish passivity has to be seen primarily in terms of their lack of involvement in politics. Politics was seen as a sphere which was outside both the reach and influence of 'ordinary people'. First, this was revealed by the widespread sentiment of 'What difference does it make if I vote?'[83] It is also important to remember that rural Poles in the course of this century have experienced eight different types of ruler. Second, I noticed that quite a few rural Poles were scarcely aware of political events, including, for example, the 1992 general and local elections. Even if it was acknowledged that rural Poles did not follow the Lithuanian mass media, we have to bear in mind that the Union of Poles was especially active in the South-East. One example are leaflets printed in Polish and Russian (on the same page) asking the people to vote for a Union candidate. 'Take power in your own hands. Finish the governor's rule, plundering the land and brutal colonisation in the Vilnius region. The future of the Vilnius region depends on your vote.'[84] However, even the Union was not ready to address Polish passivity. 'We are not interested in all that. What matters is that we won.'[85] This suggested that the development of political awareness was not a concern. People were, once again, treated as voting machines.

Furthermore, I would argue that another possible explanation for passivity is related to the Soviet years which did not encourage interest in politics except at a formal level, literally in the form of casting a vote. The substance of politics was excluded from discussion and debate. An additional reason for the passivity was that the low level of education in general did not encourage the Polish population to develop an interest in, and involvement with, the political sphere.

It is important to stress that the majority of Poles were also culturally passive. The poor educational level of the Poles did not allow them to organise themselves. Therefore, all the Poles whom I interviewed argued that education in Polish was of vital importance. Polish schools stayed open after the Second World War only in the Vilnius region but this was seen by the Poles as 'a miracle'. For Lithuanians this was seen as a totalitarian way to prevent the development of Lithuanian culture and they argued that it was a policy that overlooked the fact that some of these Poles were actually Lithuanians who were Polonised.[86] According to Skakowska, those Polish schools that remained open were underfunded during the Soviet period and both the Russian and Lithuanian schools were favoured.[87] Furthermore, mixed schools were introduced in which the Poles were always deprived of education in Polish.[88] Poles chose Russian, rather than Lithuanian, schools because they assumed that the knowledge of Russian would help their children to become more socially mobile. This decision was helped by the fact that etymologically Polish is closer to Russian than to Lithuanian. As a result, in 1989 9.2 per cent of Poles considered Russian their mother tongue (57.9 per cent of them spoke Russian).[89] Cobot(as) pointed out that the Poles were especially keen to use Russian in the public sphere. Krukauskiene argued that in the Salcininkai region in 1989 'The data ... show that 81 per cent of inhabitants write their applications to their management in Russian (7.4 percent in Polish, 6.3 percent in Lithuanian). ... The point is that only 44 percent of the respondents studied in Polish schools, the others who thought of themselves as Poles, studied in Russian schools.'[90]

The exception to this cultural passivity were the 'Poles of Lithuania' who argued that they needed more support from the state. They wanted, as analysed above, at least a few buildings to be returned to the Polish community to allow them to organise their activities and raise money via different business schemes. Furthermore, they asked for more TV and radio programmes in Polish.[91]

The small number of Poles who did organise clubs were mainly involved in promoting issues related to Polish folklore.[92] On the other hand, a small group of urban Poles argued that the Poles should show more initiative. 'Lithuanian Poles' declared that 'ordinary people' spoke *po prostemu* and watched only Polish or Russian television. They wanted rural Poles to realise that it was important to learn Lithuanian and to become integrated into Lithuanian society, as argued on the pages of *Znad Wilii*, a weekly newspaper started by Okinczyc in 1989.[93] From 1 July 1992 the radio station under the same name started broadcasting in Polish, Lithuanian and Russian.[94] There was another independent newspaper published by the Union of Poles, *Nasza Gazeta* and a journal *Magazyn Wilenski*. In 1992–3 there were another four newspapers published in Polish which were subsidised by the Lithuanian state.[95]

'Here everything is about history': the Vilnius question[96]

The Vilnius question has been of major importance for Poles and Lithuanians in Lithuania, Poles in Poland and for both states. It is a question of how history is viewed and interpreted. Lithuanians saw Vilnius as its capital and the Eastern Provinces as a part of Lithuania. The Poles pointed out that between the two World Wars Vilnius was a Polish city which had, since the fourteenth century, been under Polish influence. In contrast, Lithuanians argued that although the Poles had influence they never succeeded in Polonising the majority of the population. One has to recognise, of course, that in the last 100 years Vilnius was first a city with a Jewish majority, then a Polish majority, while in the last 50 years Vilnius has primarily been a city with a Lithuanian majority.[97] The Polish (and Jewish) influence should not be overlooked but the Lithuanian influence should also be acknowledged.[98]

Here it is important to point out the role of memory in national reawakening, or as Antonia Byatt put it, 'the importance of memory in the constitution of life'.[99] National identity is based on memory.[100] Nations always hope to recreate their distinctive culture and to regenerate their distinctive community through the lines of descent. They often share a belief that their nation is superior to other nations. This belief is common not only among the so-called 'chosen people' but also among small nations who would like to draw strict lines between *us* and *them* (the *them* being both other nations who share the same territory as well as neighbours). When it comes to small nations, the whole nation is mobilised, rather than just the elite, because it is often believed that preserving national identity is a question of life and death for the nation. There is a sense among these nations that they are endangered by larger nations. Therefore, very often the territory is invested with a sacred significance that has to be preserved for generations to come. Distinctive events, celebrated in the history of the nation, and distinctive people, born on that territory, make that territory a 'promised land'.[101]

Memories such as these were sacred to Lithuanian nationalists. Those who were members of *Vilnija*, a political organisation which was openly against Lithuanian national minorities, went a step further and identified Lithuania and its land with Lithuanians only and argued that Poles should be re-Lithuanised. *Vilnija* was never supported by *Sajudis* but '*Sajudis* was not always openly against it.'[102] Following *Vilnija*'s line of argument, the Poles were called *tuteisai* (in Lithuanian), understood as uneducated people who were therefore unable to trace their Lithuanian roots.

As previously pointed out, the Poles were alarmed with these statements. 'Soviet Poles' established territorial autonomy, as it is going to be analysed in the following part of this chapter. 'Poles of Lithuania' differed among themselves. While rural Poles supported territorial autonomy, urban Poles acknowledged that the Vilnius and Salcininkai regions were a part of Lithuania in which the Poles were the dominant ethnic group and that they should therefore have political control over these regions.[103] Some of them also pointed out that the Vilnius and Salcininkai regions were a part of Lithuania because of the 'fourth partition' of Poland. 'Lithuanian Poles' argued that the regions belonged to Lithuania, whatever its past political allegiance. However, they also stated that there was a large Polish minority in these regions and Lithuania should cater for the specific needs of the Polish population.

As Tomas Venclova argued, the main problem with Lithuanian political life was its orientation towards the past.[104] Eigirdas argued that Lithuania and Poland had to enter into a dialogue over their past so as to be able to put it aside.[105] And that obsession with the past clearly showed in Lithuania's attitude towards Poland. It can be argued that Lithuanian politicians were so preoccupied with the past that they tended to overlook the Lithuanian present or future.

If we follow the negotiations, which began in December 1989 and culminated in the signing of the Treaty on Friendly Relations and Good-Neighbourly Cooperation Between the Republic of Lithuania and the Republic of Poland in April 1994, we can see that two issues were responsible for postponing its signing; the treatment of the Polish minority in Lithuania and the Vilnius question. The Polish side expressed its concern with the treatment of the Polish minority, seeking to point out that the situation could be solved by applying or improving the Lithuanian legislation. The Lithuanian response was always the same; this is an internal issue and Poland should not interfere in the internal affairs of an independent state. However, the Polish government claimed that it did not want to interfere in the affairs of the ethnic Poles because they saw this group as being manipulated by Moscow and they did not want to be involved in policies that were formulated in Moscow.[106] Nevertheless they believed, according to a leaked *aide-memoire* of the Polish Foreign Ministry (November 1990),[107] that if the Poles had been given 'polyethnic rights' they would never have asked for territorial autonomy. Certain sectors of the Polish *Sejm*, such as the Christian National Union and Stanislaw Tyminski's Party X, demanded territorial autonomy for the Poles in Lithuania but they were always overruled by others who claimed that it was an internal Lithuanian issue.[108]

Despite arguing that history should be left aside, the Lithuanian side stressed that it was imperative for Poland to condemn 'General Zeligowski's aggressive act of 1920'. This situation did not change substantially when the Lithuanian Democratic Labour Party came to power in November 1992, partly because of its own national agenda and partly because of pressure from the opposition, which drew attention to the LDDP's communist past, forcing it to take a firm stand toward Poland.

From the very beginning of the Treaty negotiations, Poland was asked to acknowledge Lithuania's post-Second World War boundaries, declare that it did not have any revanchist claims and denounce its political as well as cultural imperialism.[109] During the Treaty negotiations, Poland acknowledged Lithuania in its post-Second World War borders but did not want to discuss in any further detail the events of the past, especially the events of inter-war period.[110] The official line of different Polish governments was that the discussions about history had to be left to historians.[111] Until 26 April 1994, when the Treaty on Friendly Relations and Good-Neighbourly Cooperation Between the Republic of Lithuania and the Republic of Poland was signed,[112] the Vilnius question was the main source of dispute. In the final analysis, it was of vital importance of Lithuania 'To mention the annexation of Vilnius either in the main agreement or when Poland disagreed, the Lithuanian side suggested to move history to a separate declaration that would be signed simultaneously ... '.[113] The issue was settled as 'Inviolability of borders, ... (and) territorial integrity'.[114]

During these negotiations Poland attempted to demonstrate its support for the Lithuanian independent state by offering hospitality to the Lithuanian government in exile during the January events in 1991 and the Moscow coup in August 1991. Furthermore, it chose not to support the Poles who proclaimed territorial autonomy within Lithuania.

Territorial autonomy

In Lithuania the Polish question was always of greater importance than the Russian one. Eduardas Vilkas argued in 1992 that the Polish question was going to stay the most important issue for many years to come.[115] The main reason was not only the Vilnius question but also the demand for and establishment of an autonomous region. The Poles, especially those from the South-East, were perceived by the Lithuanian authorities as a group which could endanger Lithuanian independence. The Poles saw the language laws[116] as concessions to Lithuanians which, at the same time, took their rights away.[117] They argued that the language laws did not 'provide legal guarantees for the development of other languages, including Polish and Russian'.[118]

This lack of language provision fuelled the demand for territorial autonomy.[119] Already from the middle of 1989, there was a desire among the 'Soviet Poles' for territorial autonomy which they established in September 1989 and further confirmed after Lithuanian independence in May 1990. It was revealed in the course of my interviews that most of the leaders of the Vilnius and Salcininkai regions were in support of the Soviet Union but this did not apply to all the Poles in these regions.[120] Furthermore, the Soviet Union supported these two regions in their demands for autonomy. Finally, the Soviet Army still remained on Lithuanian territory and Lithuanians were worried that the Army could become involved.[121]

I shall argue that the demand for and establishment of an autonomous region should not only be seen in terms of the desire of all Poles to stay within the Soviet Union, but also as the result of fears among the Polish population that rights were under threat. Fears developed because the Poles did not know the legislation (the majority did not speak the Lithuanian language). They were also manipulated by the leadership in the regions. *Sajudis* who had the majority in the Lithuanian government did not try to win over the Poles. The majority of Poles were worried about their rights and were not in support of communism. Those in support of autonomy led the movement because of fears of losing power as well as because they disagreed with the Lithuanian legislation on minorities.

Using the documents which I collected in Lithuania, I shall analyse the issue of Polish autonomy because it was seen as important not only in 1989 and 1990 but also, as pointed out in Vilkas' quote, it has continued to be a very important issue ever since. The demand for territorial autonomy has been a perennial and contentious issue between the Poles and Lithuanian authorities.

Some villages in the Vilnius and Salcininkai regions proclaimed the formation of national-territorial units in June 1989 and put forward 'The demand to form an autonomous oblast for Poles'.[122] This step was criticised by the Parliament which issued a statement (23 June 1989) pointing out that 'The Poles' cultural autonomy is a reality today',[123] and asked Poles to take part in the making of the Draft Law on National Minorities. The Lithuanian political elite saw the Polish demands simply in terms of 'being manipulated' by the communists loyal to Moscow.[124] They did not want to consider the possibility that territorial autonomy was a response to the fact that the existing legislation did not cater sufficiently for the rights of national minorities. As some members of the Lithuanian authorities themselves admitted, some of their first legislation was a result of 'hasty decisions', a phrase which was used in the context of the Decree on Language.[125]

As a result of a lack of communication between the Lithuanian government and the leaders of the Regional Council as well as of the loyalty which some leaders had for the Soviet Union, the Salcininkai Polish Autonomous Region was formed on 6 September 1989. According to its declaration the main concern was the use of minority languages. It was also argued that political rights of national minorities were violated. The declaration had only five articles, of which the first one acknowledged Lithuanian, Polish and Russian as official languages. Ten days later the Vilnius Regional Council declared autonomy within the Soviet Socialist Republic of Lithuania.[126]

On 21 September 1989, the Parliament passed a resolution annulling the decisions of the two regional councils because they 'contradict Lithuania's Constitution'.[127] However, another resolution was passed at the same session of the Parliament and a Nationalities Committee was set up. As Virgilijus Cepaitis commented at the time, the Lithuanian Parliament 'realised that the nationality question should have its legal framework'.[128] This statement did not prevent Antanas Kulakauskas arguing that *Sajudis* had only 'very general policies on national minorities and nothing in detail'.[129] My interviews with Ozolas and Eugenij(us) Petrov(as) revealed that the Parliament was primarily afraid of the possibility of a 'new Nagorn-Karabagh'.[130]

The formation of an independent Communist Party and the declaration of Lithuanian independence[131] resulted in the decision of the Salcininkai Regional Council to proclaim the Lithuanian Soviet Socialist Republic's Polish National Territory's Region of Salcininkai (on 15 May 1990). They decided to stay within Lithuania but did not accept 'the anti-constitutional acts of Lithuania's present Parliament'.[132] On 24 May the Vilnius Region's Council followed in Salcininkai's steps. (That very day Lithuania suspended its declaration on independence.) In Lithuania this was the period of the Soviet blockade which did not apply to the

Vilnius and Salcininkai regions. Furthermore, the people from these regions were drafted into the Soviet Army.[133]

During the months devoted to the negotiations with the Soviet Union, the Lithuanian authorities stayed firm in their belief that the Poles were used 'in the interest of Moscow' and Landsbergis commented that 'The talks may be delayed by the intentions of a certain part of the population in South-East Lithuania to proclaim the area a Polish autonomy within the Soviet Union. ... He hoped the population there will not get lured by the promises of Moscow emissaries, who are soon expected to come to South-East Lithuania.'[134] This type of comment was due to the increasing influence of the right-wing within *Sajudis*, which was hardly ready to compromise (as is discussed in Chapter 3).

However, responding to the influence of the members of government who were more prepared to negotiate with the Poles, the government used a mixed approach which consisted of both conciliatory measures and a firm stand. On 25 September 1990 the Law on Political Parties was adopted, which stated that the parties of other states could not operate on Lithuanian territory. As a consequence, the Lithuanian Communist Party, loyal to Moscow, was outlawed. This decision triggered the creation of the Polish National Territory on 6 October 1990.[135] It meant that the leadership of the Territory was considering secession. It was revealed in the course of my interviews that the leadership was seen as pro-Soviet, although there were claims that certain members of the leadership were in favour of joining Poland. Ozolas stressed four reasons in his report that fuelled the establishment of the Polish National Territory: 'The problem of the use of the Lithuanian state language, of the Polish language, and of the languages of the other national minorities in Eastern Lithuania, the problems of education and higher education, culture, and economy'.[136] He acknowledged the right of minorities to use their native language but did not provide further details. Ozolas also proposed preparing and submitting to the government a series of urgent measures. First, the government was obliged to draw up a long-term higher educational programme for national minorities before 1 May 1991. Second, the government was obliged to draw up a new administrative-territorial division of the Republic before 31 May 1991.[137]

After promising a 'series of urgent measures', the Parliament passed a Law on Direct Administration in Territorial Units on 27 December 1990. This law was opposed in the Parliament by all the members of the Polish Faction and the Regional Council which continued to ignore the letter of the law.[138]

The language issue, the way the Lithuanian government dealt with the two regions and the land reform are crucial in trying to understand the support among the leaders of the Salcininkai and Vilnius Regional Councils for the August coup in 1991.[139] It is important to stress that the leaders also differed among themselves. According to my interviews, they were not a homogenous body, as was often assumed.[140] The leaders differed when it came to the issues of Lithuanian independence which some of them supported. All of them agreed that their rights, understood as minority rights, were violated, as previously pointed out. Even if they had some doubts about Soviet ideology the official Lithuanian behaviour did not help in winning their trust and support.[141] A considerable number of Poles, Lithuanians and Russians argued that there was support for the putsch in 'Lithuanian councils but they were not abolished'. The members of the Polish Faction agreed that the leaders of the regional councils supported the putsch but they also pointed out that the day before the decision to dissolve the regional councils, the Salcininkai Regional Council decided that their leaders should be dismissed because of their support for the putsch. Nevertheless, the whole council was blamed and dissolved.[142] Arvydas Juozaitis argued that this decision 'destroyed the trust that the Poles had for the Lithuanian authorities'.[143] Furthermore, the Poles complained that they were again being treated as a homogeneous group. 'The views of this group of communists cannot be made synonymous with the position of the whole Polish community.'[144]

The Polish faction within the Parliament continued to press for local elections in the Vilnius and Salcininkai regions to take place by March or April 1992 because direct rule was imposed for only six months. I would argue that they hoped that the informal assurance given to the Polish Foreign Minister, Krzystof Skubiszewski, would support their proposal. However, the Parliament stood firm by the proposal made by its own Commission in December 1991 and postponed elections for 'several months'.[145] Petrov(as)[146] argued, in March 1992, that there were two reasons why the elections should be postponed for another six months, explaining that according to the law direct rule could be 'extended under extraordinary conditions'.[147] First, the former deputies of the dissolved regional councils were still active in the *apylinke* councils (the smallest administrative units in Lithuania which were never dissolved). These were (ironically) the councils which, according to the Lithuanian officials, carried out 'quietly and successfully' privatisation of land. Second, there were certain forces within the Union of Poles, former Communist Party (loyal to Moscow) activists, which were still advocating anti-Lithuanian policies. Petrov(as) also added that criminal proceedings against the councils' deputies and other officials who acted against the Republic of Lithuania were a precondition for the election and they had not started at that point in time. Furthermore, the Law on De-Sovietisation had not been adopted.[148] As far as the last two points are concerned, it was hardly the fault of the Poles that the criminal proceedings had not started and that the Law had not been adopted. With regard to the issue of dissolved councils, the political involvement in the territorial autonomy of the former deputies meant that the Polish community in the South-East was not able to elect its political leaders.

On 23 July 1992 the Lithuanian Parliament finally voted to hold the elections in the two regions on 22 November 1992. As already pointed out, the turn-out was low so the elections had to be repeated and in February 1993 the two Regional Councils were formed and started functioning.[149]

In summary, Gorbachev openly argued that Lithuania could declare independence but the Klaipeda and Vilnius regions would have to remain part of the Soviet Union.[150] Therefore, Polish autonomy, being supported by the Soviet Union, was a threat to Lithuanian independence. However, the Lithuanian authorities, being under the influence of the right-wing of *Sajudis*, did not try to win over the Polish community. They adopted a firmer approach and refused to address Polish demands and criticised them for being a 'tool' in Moscow's hands. Some leaders of the two Councils were in support of the Soviet Union but the rest of the Polish population in that region wanted to have a right to 'rule' in these two regions because they made up the majority of the population there. They argued that they were discriminated against and wanted more understanding and support from the Lithuanian government.

Conclusion

In the period immediately after independence, the articulation of 'one-dimensional' thinking was dominant; whoever did not agree with *us* was against *our* sovereignty and independence. Verbally fighting for democracy, Lithuania reproduced a type of thinking they had been used to. Once again we had to face the one and only truth which, needless to say, is fundamentally anti-democratic. Personally, I was reassured by the willingness of the people to struggle against these sentiments. I did not always feel that there was a guaranteed space to express different opinions. Even if this space existed according to the letter of the law, people did not trust such a freedom because it had never been a part of their experience. Different opinions were, according to their experience, usually condemned and that type of reality did not cease to exist. While the form stayed the same the content changed. *We* and *they* were understood in different terms and that understanding had an emotional charge as well. Therefore, first, it was difficult to acknowledge and to come to terms with the disappointment with the way one's *own* state is run, especially if one was supporting a struggle for independence. Second, it was even more difficult to bear a stigma that one is against one's own state. That is the reason why different opinions could not be heard, although they existed. I would argue that support for my thesis may be seen in all the various opinion polls which never predicted the landslide victory of the Lithuanian Democratic Labour Party.[151] As in Soviet times, the citizens of Lithuania kept their thoughts to themselves but they were able in 1992 to act according to these thoughts. And they silently acted accordingly. The citizens of Lithuania proved to be more democratic than Landsbergis who announced that they were not ready for democracy. Despite their lack of familiarity with a democratic culture, they used democratic tools to express their opinion.

When it comes to the democratic tools, some Poles had previously not been able to use them. Only after the elections were announced, the Lithuanian Parliament finally voted, on 23 July 1992, to hold elections in the Vilnius and Salcininkai regions. Although this decision, in my opinion, was part of a pre-election campaign it came too late to win the trust of the Polish people. As I already pointed out, they hoped that the LDDP would enable them to exercise their rights as well as improve the Lithuanian legislation. However, the Party did not fulfil their expectations.

Politically active Poles argued that the Polish question still existed in Lithuania and that different governments were not ready to address this issue. The 'Lithuanian Poles' saw this question in terms of obligations which should be undertaken by both Lithuanians and Poles. The 'Poles of Lithuania' saw the existence of this question as a result of the Lithuanian state not fulfilling its role in protecting the Polish minority. The 'Soviet Poles' argued that it could be solved only if the communist ideology was prevalent.

This chapter has sought to emphasise the importance of taking account of the different perspectives of the community, rather than just the most vocal lobby which was expressed in the form of the Polish demand for autonomy. This demand has to be seen as a belief in communist ideology and a wish to stay in power as well as the inability of the *Sajudis* government to consider the minority issues. The national minorities had to struggle for these issues to be acknowledged and considered. However, the push towards prolonging a Soviet society was understood as a Polish demand, the demand of all the Poles. And here the vicious circle started, in which there was a dualistic opposition of *us* against *them*. The Poles and the Lithuanians who were primarily ready to turn towards their own communities and criticise these communities were ignored. And that brings us back to the point already argued that a space in which different opinions could be expressed was not encouraged, despite all the claims that civil society had been developing. Difference within one's *own* community and even less differences among *their* community, especially during the 'difficult times', were neither acknowledged nor welcomed.

8
Jewish Answers

Introduction

A problem arises when a common territory is a sacred locality for different nations. Vilnius has a very special meaning not only for Lithuanians and Poles but also for Jews. The Jews referred to the city as a Lithuanian Jerusalem because of its importance as a Jewish cultural centre since the time of their arrival during the reign of King Gediminas. In the independence period, *Sajudis* sought not only to continue the reaffirmation of Lithuanian culture and history but also, by insisting on their own interpretation of culture and history, to draw ethnic boundaries which did not appreciate the co-existence of different cultures on the same territory. From this perspective, the territory belongs either to *us* or *them* and it cannot be shared. The politisation of history which took place during the period of national awakening meant that the memory of Vilna (Jewish name for Vilnius), and for that matter also Wilno, was swept aside and the memory of Vilnius was to predominate.

As pointed out in Chapter 2, the Jews were the largest ethnic minority in the pre-Second World War independent Lithuania. Over 90 per cent of Lithuanian Jews were killed during the Second World War.[1] In the 1970s, Jews from Lithuania and other parts of the Soviet Union were allowed to leave the country and emigration started again in the period of *perestroika* and independence. This raises the question; why isn't independent Lithuania a contemporary home to Jews? The answer is primarily related to two issues which are interconnected – the Holocaust and anti-Semitism. Anti-Semitism is often seen as a major reason for the Holocaust. The Holocaust and anti-Semitism were the most important issues for the Jews who stayed in Lithuania. The memory of the Holocaust and the reality of anti-Semitism influenced Jewish lives, especially because there was a feeling among the Jews that the Lithuanian government was not ready to take responsibility for the Holocaust. Therefore, nearly all the Jews I interviewed argued that there was no future for Jews in Lithuania. They predicted that Jews would continue to leave the country. However, those who decided to stay tried to cherish the Jewish culture while recognising that it was not possible to revive the 'glorious past' of previous centuries.

At present the Jewish community is one of the smallest national minorities in Lithuania. However, they are by far the most educated.[2] They are mostly an urban population concentrated in three cities: Vilnius, Kaunas and Klaipeda.[3] They are the oldest population and a group with a much higher death than birth rate.[4] Until the Second World War, they were the largest minority. As a result of the Holocaust 'Jews of Lithuania' argued that the Jewish question did not exist in Lithuania, and that a population of 5000 Jews made them insignificant.[5]

In this chapter I shall highlight the importance of memory and the interpretation of history in forming Jewish identity as well as in defining their relations with the state of Lithuania and its people. This chapter will start with an analysis of the contemporary Jewish community which can be broadly divided into two main groups with regard to how they approached the task of constituting Jewish identity in Lithuania and how they dealt with the memory of the Holocaust. Memory is vital in a decision to take an active part in Lithuanian politics and society. The Jews did not think that they could influence the politics of (citizenship) rights because they were such a small community that their opinion did not need to be taken into account. They saw the issue of how to approach the Holocaust as the precondition for becoming involved in Lithuanian politics. It will be seen that the Holocaust provided a vital element in the formation of Jewish identity in Lithuania and shaped the relationship between Jews and the Lithuanian majority. Furthermore, this chapter will continue with an analysis of how these very emotive episodes in the past have been approached by the *Sajudis* and LDDP governments. In the final section we shall deal with Jewish emigration which was seen as one of the possible and the most common answers to the historic memory of the Holocaust.

Different Jews and the Holocaust

Despite being a small community, the Jews were a heterogeneous body.[6] Like the Russians and Poles, their identities were shifting in nature. The

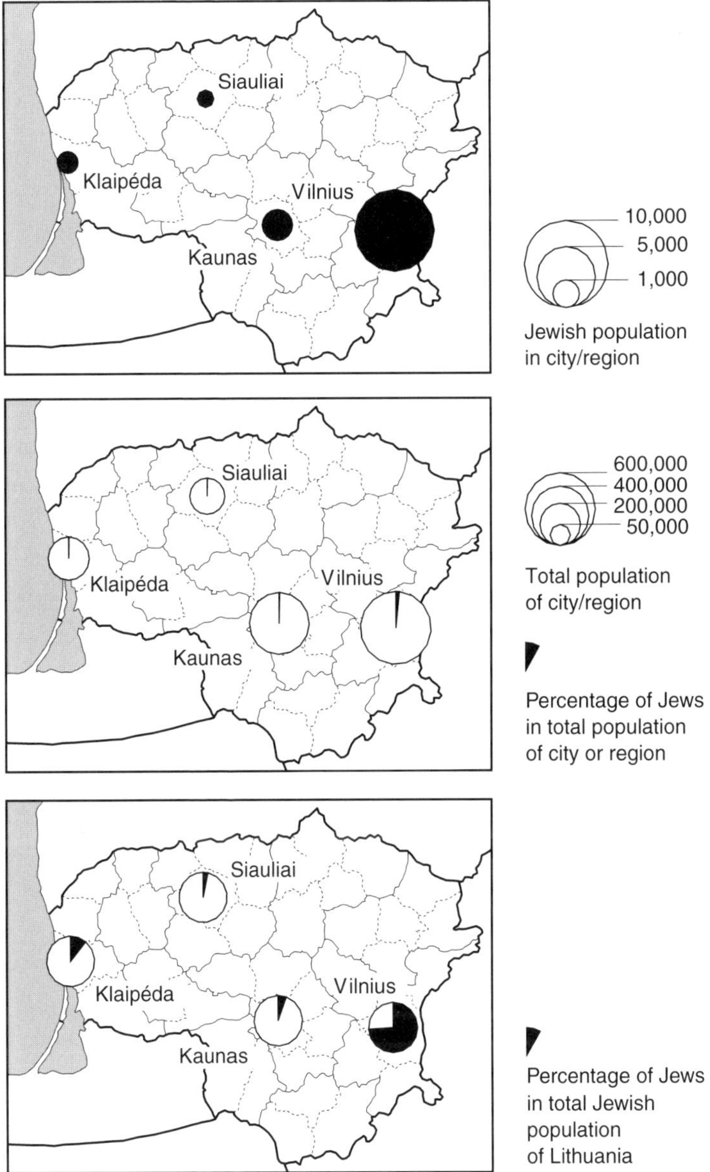

Map 8.1   Jews in Lithuania, 1989

legacy of the Holocaust together with the political and cultural situation in independent Lithuania are important in my typology of the Jews. The Jews did not discuss economic problems on the same scale as Russians but these problems certainly played an important role in the decision to leave Lithuania. In comparison with many Russians and Poles, the Jews whom I interviewed were in support of Lithuanian independence and were familiar with Lithuanian culture. Although more than half of them considered Russian their mother tongue, they were also fluent in Lithuanian.[7] Jews differed in their opinion of the degree to which Lithuania was truly a democratic society. They were sceptical about the willingness of the government to accept minority cultures and their histories and were critical of the government's attitude to the Holocaust.

The Holocaust in contemporary Lithuania – Jewish perspectives

While the Holocaust was universally condemned by the Jews, they approached it in different ways. Grigorii Kanovich, President of the Lithuanian Jewish Community, argued that the Holocaust meant there was no future for Jews in Lithuania. 'Of course, we cannot state with certainty that we know where (i.e. which countries) it will be calm and good for us, but we can boldly state, without falling into the sin of exaggeration, that we know where it was and still is bad for us. For this knowledge we have occasionally paid with our lives.'[8] He argued that it had been difficult for Jews to continue living in Lithuania with the memory of the Holocaust. In Lithuania they were surrounded by so many memories of Jewish life and culture but all these features belonged to a past which could not be reborn. In Lithuania, therefore, there was no Jewish question because there were hardly any Jews left and those who wanted to live within their own community did not have the opportunity to do so. As he pointed out, the rate of mortality exceeded that of births and 'soon there will be no more than 800 Jews in Lithuania'.[9] Kanovich felt this was yet another place which Jews had to leave if they wanted to preserve their identity. 'Here it is a desert for the Jews and our cultural centres and schools are oases which only underline the existence of the desert.'[10] He pointed out that there were still elements of anti-Semitism in everyday life.[11]

On the other hand, Misha Jakobas, President of the Jewish Community of Vilnius, argued that the Jews were capable of, and had an obligation to, find the strength to revive the Jewish community that had existed before the Second World War.[12] In the view of Jakobas, the Holocaust was one of the most tragic events in Jewish history but Jews should struggle on, as they always had done in the past. In his opinion the Holocaust could not be simply explained in terms of 'they killed us only because we were Jews'. He did not believe that 'working for NKVD/KGB' was an explanation because it was known that 'Lithuanians also worked for these bodies and that not only Lithuanians were sent to Siberia by the Soviet regime but also Jews'. He argued that the Holocaust was also a very important issue for Lithuanians which they had still not come to terms with. He hoped that a Lithuanian democratic future would change Lithuanian attitudes towards the Jews and enable all its citizens to feel and be treated equally. He pointed out that in the immediate future some Jews would leave Lithuania and there would be a maximum of 2000 Jews left in Lithuania but he thought that they would leave for economic rather than political reasons.

Finally, Sergei Rapoport, a sociologist, argued that there was a mythology built around the Holocaust which constructed the Jews as both a suffering and chosen people. 'Very often the martyrdom of the Jewish population is looked at through the prism of the other ideology – "chosen people". "We have suffered because we are very special…Jews are chosen to be victims and to be punished."'[13] He pointed out that this mythology of Jewish martyrdom very often produced anti-Semitism, and he further argued that the Jews were not always prepared to come to terms with this.[14]

This thesis relates to two other issues which I believe to be very important. First, it is not only the case that Jews themselves pointed out that they were a chosen people but it is also important to bear in mind that they were seen by other ethnic communities as essentially different. 'Because of his early, medieval association with the idea of exclusion, the Jew remains forever in the mind of the West the most readily available and imaginative target for exclusion, the most essential outsider of society.'[15] On the level of everyday life they are approached through ethnic stereotypes which describe them as being rich, community oriented, helping exclusively their own fellow-nationals, being influential, etc. It was frequently remarked upon by Lithuanians that Jews received a considerable amount of support from the Jewish community abroad.

Second, Jews are not the only people who see themselves as chosen and they are not the only group who suffered genocide. Therefore, Rapoport's thesis, seen in this context, is interesting because it addresses the issue of the relation between a minority and the state and the question of whether it is possible to be involved in a society in which genocide was committed. I would argue that his analysis raises the issue of what should be done to allow for a Jewish life in Lithuania.[16]

Different Jews

These different understandings of the Holocaust played an important role in the definition of Jewish identity in Lithuania. The issue of identity was related to the major concern of Jews which was to find their place in a newly independent country that was on the road to democracy. According to my interviews with the Jews, I could not identify anyone that, following the typology of the previous chapter, may be termed 'Soviet Jew'. I was told that 'the Jews also joined *Edinstvo*' but nobody was able to provide me with information to allow me to trace these people, as was the case with the 'Soviet Poles'. Furthermore, I could not find any written evidence about or by 'Soviet Jews'.

'Lithuanian Jews'

The term 'Lithuanian Jews' will be employed to describe those Jews who became involved in the independence movement and then continued this involvement after the establishment of independence. According to my interviews, only a small minority of the Jews in Lithuania had been actively involved in the national reawakening. While they all said that they valued the existence of Israel, they saw Lithuania as their country, their motherland. They emphasised that Jewish life and the Jewish community would never exist on the same scale as before the Holocaust and they argued that one should cherish what was left.

The 'Lithuanian Jews' were critical of the Soviet period. They saw the Soviet Union as a state which had curtailed their rights. They had suffered during Soviet times because their religion, culture and language were suppressed. Lithuania was the only part of the Soviet Union in which the number of Jews in the central political and party bodies reflected the number of Jews in the wider population of the republic.[17]

The 'Lithuanian Jews' argued that there was a future for the Jews within the boundaries of independent Lithuania. They were satisfied with the letter of the law although they pointed out that they would have liked the Lithuanian state and people to take more account of what had been done to the Jews during the Second World War. However, they would always acknowledge that there had been Lithuanians who had helped the Jews during the war. They pointed out that those Lithuanians or their offspring had been, or should have been, commended. While this group saw their future in Lithuania the Holocaust was an important issue for both the Jews and the Lithuanians.

The 'Lithuanian Jews' concentrated their efforts on education in Yiddish and Hebrew, often from a very early age. In 1992 there was a kindergarten and a primary school in Yiddish. The director of the school argued that it was impossible to enrol all the children who applied for the school because of its limited capacity. Furthermore, there was not a sufficient supply of teachers who could teach in Yiddish and Hebrew. Finally, there was a demand from the older generation to introduce classes both in Yiddish and Hebrew and these were well attended. This situation reflected exactly what Kanovich argued, namely that his mother tongue was taken away from him.

The other issue which was raised by a small minority within the same group was religious freedom. There was a small group of Jews around the Orthodox synagogue who put a lot of effort into reviving the Jewish religion and they were satisfied that there was a guaranteed space for religious practice and tolerance in independent Lithuania.[18] It is interesting to point out that the younger generation around the Orthodox synagogue was not brought up according to Orthodox Judaism. They argued that they had chosen Orthodoxy because it seemed to be the most appropriate way to lead a Jewish life. They had only ever experienced the Orthodox synagogue, and had never encountered the liberal or reformist alternatives. I was told that the rabbi, who came from London, introduced the teaching of the Orthodox synagogue as well as enabling and encouraging studies of Tora and Talmud, which attracted quite a few people both to the synagogue as well as to religious workshops and lectures.

Like the 'Lithuanian Russians' and 'Lithuanian Poles', the 'Lithuanian Jews' saw their future in Lithuania because they felt that an independent Lithuania enabled them to develop and cherish their own identity. They stressed the fact that their Jewishness was shaped by their existence in the independent Lithuania. Members of this group had been politically active and influential. Some of them argued that they were used by the Lithuanian political elite, on the one hand, to show the West that they were not anti-Semitic and that the new state was a true multi-ethnic society and, on the other hand, because of their foreign contacts.[19] The Jewish community saw the 'Lithuanian Jews' as their main spokespersons.

'Jews of Lithuania'

Among the 'Jews of Lithuania' two groups could be distinguished; while both groups shared a process of defining their own identity, they differed in their readiness to organise along ethnic lines. Some of them decided to think through their identity on their own or within a close and closed circle of friends and family. Some others thought that they should organise cultural and religious organisations and within their community define identity and restart developing Jewish culture and heritage. The other important feature of 'Jews of Lithuania' was an ambivalent set of attitudes in which they were, on the one hand, keen to leave the country (mainly for Israel) while, on the other hand, they were also prepared to continue living in Lithuania.

The 'Jews of Lithuania' shared with their fellow-nationals an interest and a concern for education in Yiddish and Hebrew. This was seen as a part of their heritage that had been taken away from them. Some of them also saw this revival of Yiddish and Hebrew as a means of assimilating into the new Israeli society.

This group saw Jewish social and cultural life in Lithuania as coming to an end; the close of yet another Jewish chapter. The Jewish community was getting smaller and smaller and soon it would be impossible to continue to live as a Jew in Lithuania. Their analysis was very much influenced by the Holocaust. They saw it as a turning point in the life of the Jewish community in Lithuania. The Soviet era continued this trend by destroying Jewish culture.[20] The Jews stayed in the Soviet Union because they were compelled to do so. This was testified by the fact that when emigration laws were relaxed they applied for visas in vast numbers and left the country (as analysed later in this chapter). Emigration on the same scale continued after *perestroika*. In the opinion of 'Jews of Lithuania', this process would continue to the point where there would be hardly any Jews left in Lithuania. Once again it can be seen that the Holocaust was an important issue in approaching and understanding the life of the Jewish community. 'Jews of Lithuania' believed that if the Jews wanted to continue their life as Jews they should leave Lithuania. It was felt that even independent Lithuania was not able to come to terms with its past. And even if it did make an attempt to negotiate with past events, it would be unable to ensure the continuity of the Jewish culture. The 'Jews of Lithuania' wanted an official apology, such as that which Jews had received from Germany.

Not all the 'Jews of Lithuania' considered leaving Lithuania. Even if they agreed that there was no future for Jewish culture in this country, many Jews pointed out that they were too old to leave, bearing in mind that Jews were the oldest population in Lithuania. These older members of the 'Jews of Lithuania' would stay in Lithuania and, being in the latter stages of their lives, they saw the possibility of looking for their Jewish identity freely which meant that they could 'revive' the

Jewish organisations, community and culture and explore their identity. The 'Jews of Lithuania' agreed with the 'Lithuanian Jews' that the letter of the law made them equal citizens. Furthermore, they pointed out that they were able to claim back some of their property. 'Jews of Lithuania' acknowledged that this claim should only be partial because the community was so small that it would not be able to maintain and look after all the formerly Jewish property. They felt more 'at home' in the independent Lithuania than in the Soviet Union. However, they still felt that there were some elements of anti-Semitism in Lithuania; it was not on a large scale 'but it still exists'. While they were grateful to Lithuania for its religious freedom, they lived in the shadow of the Holocaust which primarily shaped their search for identity.

What was specific about the Jews in Lithuania was their assimilation into the Russian and Lithuanian nations. These were the people who came mostly from mixed marriages.[21] Some of them did not feel that their Jewish origins defined them at all while the others kept an interest in Jewish issues. Unfortunately, I did not meet enough of this group of people to be able to analyse them in more detail. Therefore, I am not sure that Jonathan Weber's argument that the concept of assimilation has different and complex meanings for the Jews is right. Assimilation includes openness of the host culture to accept Jews. From the Jewish point of view:

> Reworking of the traditional Jewish culture from the inside implies a simultaneity of contradictory goals: retaining group identity while also finding ways of allowing it to disappear. The culture of assimilated Jews is thus very complicated and is full of new inconsistencies, based on the selective rearrangement of traditional forms of behaviour.[22]

Jewish life in Lithuania is defined by history. Every Jew that I interviewed referred in some way to the Holocaust. As analysed above, the Jews differed in their approach to the Holocaust, and the question of how to live with it, but they agreed that it was an important marker for their community. They also insisted that it was an important event in Lithuanian society.

The Holocaust in contemporary Lithuania –
a formula of symmetry

Some 'Jews of Lithuania' argued that if it was indeed the case that 'some Jews were poisoned by communism' it was also the case that 'some

Lithuanians were poisoned by anti-Semitism'. They pointed out that they felt more comfortable among Germans who were ready to simply say, 'I am sorry for what my nation did to yours.'[23] They wanted to hear the same sentence from Lithuanians. What they heard was a 'formula of symmetry' which equated Jewish and Lithuanian sufferings during and after the Second World War.[24] In this conception the Jews were partly held responsible for the deportation of the Lithuanians to the Soviet Union. They were presented as members of the Communist Party and of NKVD/KGB. A member of LAF, describing the events which took place on 25 June 1941[25] in the Lietukis garage, which was on Vytautas Prospect (the same Vytautas who granted the charter to the Jews) argued:

> According to my information, the majority of those killed were investigators of the security organs and heads of the 'special departments' of enterprises and institutions; they were killed as officials rather than as representatives of a certain nationality. It turned out that the majority of the victims were Jews.[26]

This logic of symmetry is exemplified by Liudas Truska who, while admitting that there was no ground for holding Jews responsible for the independence lost in 1941, immediately pointed out that Lithuanians also could not be blamed for killing Jews. 'Just as there is no basis to claim that the Jews are subverts of Lithuanian independence, and for identifying them with Communists and members of the KGB, there is also no basis to the claim that the Lithuanians are "Jew-killers".'[27] He argued that only 3000 Lithuanians could be found guilty of killing Jews, but then qualified this by saying that there was an equal number of Lithuanians who saved Jews. Even when Lithuanians admitted that some of their nation killed Jews they labelled them as 'criminals', 'hooligans' and talked about occasional incidents and 'clashes' with Jews.[28]

Lithuanians preferred to talk about the people who saved the Jews and argued that the majority of Lithuanians helped the Jews.[29] It seemed that the Lithuanian state was employing an argument developed by some members of the Lithuanian émigré community, which pointed out that before the war the Lithuanians and Jews had lived in peace and that the Jews had also been granted national autonomy. From this viewpoint, it was stressed that Lithuanians had also suffered under Nazi occupation, that local Jews were annihilated by the Germans and that only a small minority of Lithuanians took part in killing Jews.[30]

The last three points are either directly or indirectly stated in the Declaration on the Genocide.[31]

At the same time, the Lithuanian government wanted to point out that it continued to be sensitive towards the local Jews whose predecessors were killed in Lithuania. 'The Lithuanian Republic, since its independence, has been seeking to remedy the grievances committed towards the Jewish community.'[32] The Jews were quite sceptical about this statement, including even the Lithuanian Jews who supported the *Sajudis* from 1988. Irene Veisaite, a supporter of *Sajudis*, remembers its First Congress:

> They were going on and on about Lithuanian victims and sufferings, and I suddenly thought, what the hell am I doing here? My mother was a victim, my whole family, my three-year-old cousin, and they have no place here, not even a mention. But then, I thought, it is the first time that Lithuanians can talk about their sufferings, about the truth. We must understand their happiness and share it…but to this day (11 May 1992), there have been only a very few statements from the intelligentsia, and a few official gestures concerning the Lithuanian role in the Holocaust.[33]

They did not feel that enough space was given to national minorities and they felt marginalised once again, especially when the independence of Lithuania started to turn into independence for Lithuanians.

Furthermore, the Jews were unhappy when the Lithuanian government proclaimed the 23 September 'Genocide Day of the Jews'. It is interesting to point out that not a single Jew mentioned it to me in their interviews. My impression was that they saw it as a token gesture. This is confirmed by Anatol Lieven.[34] It appeared as something that was conceded in order to mollify criticism. Therefore, is this a beginning of 'an uncontroversial route to reconciliation' as Lieven argues?[35]

After proclaiming 23 September the Genocide Day, the Lithuanian Parliament introduced on 7 November 1990 a Resolution on Putting in Order the Graves and Cemeteries of the Victims of Genocide of the Jewish People and the Marking of the Heritage. This Resolution was not implemented in all districts and towns[36] and therefore on 2 August 1991 a new Resolution was introduced. It is interesting to point out that the Parliament ordered that 'all graves and cemeteries of the victims of genocide of the Jewish people must be put in order not later than 23 September of the current year – the day of genocide of the Jewish people', and when it comes to the old Jewish cemeteries they 'must be put in order by the autumn of the current year, and in separate cases, taking into account the scope of work – not later than 1 October 1992'. One could argue that the Lithuanian authorities were keen to show that they were taking the Jewish issue seriously and with all due respect. 'During 1991 in 30 towns and districts 130 cemeteries and 102 graves had been put in order. On 20 June 1991 a monument was unveiled in memory of the Jews who were killed during the war.'[37]

On 23 September 1992 the Lithuanian authorities organised a ceremony in the Lithuanian Parliament and Landsbergis presented medals to Lithuanians, or their families, who had helped to save Jews. When I asked about Russians and Poles who had helped the Jews, nobody was able to give me an answer. On 23 September 1993 a monument on the site of the Vilnius Ghetto was unveiled with an inscription in Yiddish and Lithuanian saying: 'In memory of the martyred and the fighters of the Vilnius Ghetto, 1941–1943'. Another memorial plaque was placed on a former Jewish cemetery, which had existed since 1487 and was destroyed by the Soviet regime in 1950.

However, the Lithuanian leadership did not change its attitude towards the Holocaust and the involvement of Lithuanians. They continued to emphasise their view that only a few people had committed crimes, while also reiterating that some Lithuanians were involved in helping the Jews.

Rehabilitation of Lithuanians who took part in the Holocaust

A contentious issue in relation to the Holocaust was connected with the rehabilitation of some Lithuanians who took part in the Holocaust.[38] The Jewish community wanted the Lithuanian government to apologise to the Jews for the Holocaust; as Willy Brandt and Lech Valensa had done.[39] They felt that the Declaration on Genocide was well written but they pointed out that Lithuanians were not ready to admit that the majority of Jews were killed by Lithuanians.[40] In the Declaration it was argued that the Supreme Council 'notes with sorrow, that among the executioners serving the occupants, there were Lithuanian citizens'.[41] Furthermore, it was not implemented in practice. As an example the Jews mentioned a case which happened in Autumn 1991 when 30 people who took part in the genocide were rehabilitated.[42] Some of these 30 people were still rehabilitated in 1993. Those Jews interviewed, especially 'Jews of Lithuania', argued that among high-powered people there was a small minority who were anti-Semitic and the best supporting argument was the rehabilitation of Lithuanians who killed Jews. The rehabilitation caused an outcry all over the world which brought the representative of the Wiesenthal Centre to Lithuania and provoked a protest from the Israeli government. The general public was informed about it through three articles published in *The New York Times* on 5, 8 and 10 September 1991.

Two demands were a common feature in this protest; the first raised the question of the identity of the 'participants in genocide' and the second consisted of a demand to publish the names of the people who were rehabilitated. The Lithuanian government responded by saying that it only rehabilitated the people against whom war crimes could not be proved. The Lithuanian Procuracy issued an official statement on 7 September 1991 stressing that all applications were considered carefully. It added that the Soviet judgements in many cases were unjust.[43] However, two days later a statement was issued by the Lithuanian Parliament which pointed out that

> Isolated cases may have occurred where law enforcement officials gave insufficient attention to the proposals of citizens willing to provide newly incriminating evidence; or questions relative to this issue received from abroad were not answered in due time. Mistakes may have been made because the office of the Procurator General of the Republic of Lithuania based its conclusions exclusively on material it had at its disposition – material provided by the USSR KGB – and irresponsibly relied upon it.[44]

The main problem with these two statements is that they contradict each other – if the Procuracy thought that according to the KGB files unjust decisions were made and, even more importantly, the documents themselves were questionable, why in that case did it rely upon them as argued in the statement?

As a result of the above mentioned protest, the *Sajudis* government proposed to form a joint Israeli–Lithuanian delegation which was going to deal with this issue. When the Labour government came into power they repeated the invitation and a pilot delegation arrived in Lithuania on 21 June 1993. According to Dov Levin, who was a member of the Israeli delegation, it was estimated that the number of people who were rehabilitated were more than 30 000. But it was not just the number of people who were rehabilitated that was important but also the question of how to identify a 'participant in genocide'. According to to the Lithuanian explanation, only the people who were actually involved in killing were treated as participants. The Labour government agreed that participants should be classified as all those who had participated in the persecution of the Jews because of their ethnic identity or religion. However, when the Israeli representatives arrived in Vilnius the Speaker of the Lithuanian Parliament, Ceslavas Jursenas, told them that 26 410 requests for rehabilitation were submitted while 655 were turned down and 24 132 were granted. And out of these, six were revoked and eight were to be reviewed.[45]

It should be pointed out that there was no legal remedy for unjustified rehabilitation in the Law on Rehabilitation and this was confirmed by the Prosecutor-General, Arturas Paulauskas. He added that a presidential decree was needed to overcome this problem. From the legal point of view, this is a completely impossible situation.[46]

President Brazauskas confirmed that there had been some cases of wrongful rehabilitation and agreed to review them 'as needed'.[47] The Lithuanian government also applied a formula of symmetry in these discussions by proposing a bilateral agreement between Israel and Lithuania on the extradition of war criminals.

However, the issue of memory and selective memory in particular has to be seen in the Soviet context. Three issues have to be pointed out in this regard. First, during the Second World War Stalin tried very hard to show the world, and particularly Lithuanians, that they were fighting against the Germans for Soviet Lithuania. Stalin made particular use of the Jews who fought in the Lithuanian Division for this purpose.[48] Second, the Soviet command tried to stress that the Germans committed all the atrocities against the Jews, not the Lithuanians.

Third, after the Second World War the new Soviet government brushed the issue of the Holocaust aside. The Jews who were killed in the Holocaust were presented as Soviet citizens. They were not mentioned on monuments such as Babi Yar or in the Great Soviet Encyclopaedia which gives information about every nationality which fought in the Second World War. It was only in 1988 that Jewish names were added to a memorial stone in Paneriai (a suburb of Vilnius) commemorating the death of more than 100 000 Soviet citizens.[49] The synagogues which were ruined were completely destroyed and the monuments with Jewish names removed in accordance with the aim of the official policy which subscribed to the full assimilation of Jews.[50] As Nora Levin argued the 'black years' started after the Second World War, despite an effort to form the Birobidzhan Autonomous Province and despite the reawakening of Jewish life there. Anti-Semitism was a part of Soviet political life.[51] Everything Jewish was seen in terms of the past, as a part of history of which no one could be proud because it was labelled as 'bourgeois nationalism'. Mikhail Suslov simply summarised this attitude: 'We have no intention of reviving the dead culture.'[52] Brushing aside the memory of the Holocaust also meant forgetting about the Lithuanian and other people who saved Jews. Maybe that is a reason why there were only a few names which were usually repeated.[53]

Jewish emigration

The Holocaust played a significant role in the decision of Jews to leave Lithuania. The majority of them felt that they could not integrate into a society which was responsible for the annihilation of over 90 per cent of its Jews. Furthermore, they reckoned that they were too small a group for their opinions to be considered. When Jews were allowed to leave they went mainly to Israel or America.[54]

Throughout the whole of the post-Second World War period, there was a process of Jews leaving Lithuania. The Jews felt discriminated against in the Soviet Union. As in other parts of the Soviet Union, the Lithuanian Jews argued that they were not able to enter higher education because of the quota system and emphasised that they had difficulty finding employment.

According to research done among Lithuanian and Latvian Jews who emigrated to Israel,[55] Jews felt rejected by both the Balts and Russians. They argued that the Balts perceived them as surrogate Russians (which was worse than being seen as proper Russians) because they were attached to Russian culture and language.[56] They argued that the Russians were keen to take advantage of them, deflecting national tension away from themselves. They left not only because they were dissatisfied with the Soviet policies towards Jews, but also because of economic factors, though this was not always acknowledged.[57] Furthermore, another two issues should be addressed. First, that Jews had a place to migrate to, in other words they were in a position to choose where to settle. Second, they were encouraged to leave not only by their Jewish friends but also by their non-Jewish friends.[58] It is interesting to quote both Lithuanian and Jewish opinion on this issue. 'In the depths of our souls we felt that they were not leaving us Lithuanians, but that a common woe had affected us.'[59] 'The day comes to say goodbye to our neighbours. It is not easy. We have many good friends among the teachers. At the same time I cannot forget the great evil that some Lithuanian people had done. They helped the Nazis to kill.'[60] Therefore, the best solution, in the eyes of both nations, was for the Jews to leave.[61]

In the decade after the relaxation of emigration laws (i.e. in the 1970s) nearly 10 000 Jews left Lithuania.[62] The majority of them left for Israel.[63] They joined nearly 60 000 Lithuanian Jews who had been living in Israel.[64] Lithuania was not only the republic of the Soviet Union with the highest relative number of Jews who emigrated (46.7 per cent) but it also had the highest relative number of *refuseniks*, 1.91 per cent.[65] *Perestroika* meant that Jews were allowed to apply for Israeli visas and consequently leave the country. The independence period again saw a large number of Jews leaving the country.[66] According to the Population Census in 1989 there were 12 392 Jews in Lithuania (0.3 per cent of the total population).[67] In 1993 all the Jews I interviewed agreed that there were no more than 5000 Jews in Lithuania.[68] These Jews argued that the decision to leave Lithuania was no longer political, as was the case during the Soviet period. Jakobas argued that economically 'There is no light at the end of the tunnel' and therefore the Jews decided to leave. Furthermore, they were left to live with a Holocaust memory which encouraged them to leave Lithuania. This memory was interpreted by Kanovich as a guideline 'to live in a place where one's own nationality lives'. Finally, as in the other parts of the Soviet Union, Jews felt that anti-Semitism was still alive in Lithuania. For instance, Simon Alperovich argued, that 'Anti-Semitism is a part of everyday life'. Arvydas Juozaitis argued that it existed but 'the Jews make too much out of it'.[69]

Conclusion

We are still left with the question of how much this analysis can help us in understanding why 'The war was a catastrophe for the Jews, but was a far worse catastrophe for the Lithuanians'.[70] First, it has already been pointed out that these two communities lived separately between the two World Wars. Social, religious and cultural differences kept them apart and although they shared the same territory this common territory had a different meaning, understanding and past for these communities. Social interaction was therefore negligible. It was only in independent Lithuania (between the two World Wars) that the Jews started to learn the Lithuanian language and their culture. They were already familiar with Russian, Polish or German languages and cultures and they showed respect towards them, which cannot be said on the same scale for Lithuanian culture which was seen as a culture based on folk roots.[71] For Lithuanians the Jews were alien, foreign. Their language, alphabet, culture and religion were different, not known to

Lithuanians at all. Second, the rise of anti-Semitism in the rest of Europe also affected Lithuania. Did the seed fall on fertile ground because there were grievances against the Jews who were perceived as economically more successful than the Lithuanians in their own country? It was pointed out that Jewish economic influence declined in the mid-1920s, which might lead us to conclude that the rise of anti-Semitism was happening at the same time as the decline of Jewish economic power. Is it possible that the characteristic of being seen as a power-losing and wealth-losing people made them a target? Social discrimination against the Jews developed when Lithuanians and Jews began to compete for the same jobs. Furthermore, Lithuania as a nation-state between the two World Wars saw the Jews as an influential group and sought to underline this by offering them national autonomy. This coincided with the Jewish interest in self-preservation, in cherishing their own culture and slowly learning about Lithuania. One can argue that, although in the past these two communities lived separate lives quite peacefully, at this moment in history the fact of being unfamiliar with each other possibly allowed for prejudices to be developed and accepted. As Plato pointed out, persuasion comes from opinions which are changeable and last as long as the argument takes place, not from truth. Therefore, the Jews could be labelled 'red' and 'guilty' for Lithuania's loss of independence. As Hannah Arendt argues, 'political anti-Semitism developed because the Jews were a separate body, while social discrimination arose because of the growing equality of Jews with all other groups'.[72]

Has the above analysis helped to understand why so many Jews were killed? I myself doubt it and feel that all these rational answers help to form a mosaic of understanding but that mosaic is far from finished, with elements still missing. Why, with a few exceptions, are Lithuanians unable to confront what happened during the war? I would argue that their confrontation would help us to understand much more about the tragic events for both Lithuanians and Jews. In the period of national reawakening and the process of celebrating one's own past it is difficult to confront events which might cast a different light on one's own nation. Antanas Terliackas argues that the Lithuanians should learn 'to appreciate the scale of tragedy and the degree of guilt of the generation of 1940s. Then, after getting rid of preconceptions, to better understand Jewish people, its culture and tradition. Only thus can we arrive at coexistence, mutual understanding, and co-operation.'[73]

As has been pointed out, the LDDP government was slowly moving towards discussing the issue of Lithuanian responsibility towards the

Holocaust. According to my interviews in 1992 and 1993, Gediminas Kirkilas was not the only Lithuanian politician who openly admitted, 'We Lithuanians committed crimes.' There were only a few Lithuanians who were prepared to express such a sentence. However, the LDDP government pointed out that it was important to acknowledge the long history of Jews in Lithuania, as well as the need to undertake more research on this issue. As a result, on 22 March 1993 a Centre for Judaic Studies was opened at the University of Vilnius. Gestures like this one did not prevent the majority of Jews I interviewed from arguing that there was no future for Jews in Lithuania.[74] If the Population Census of 1989 is compared with the estimate of population in 1992, it can be seen that, in three years, more than half of the Jewish population left Lithuania.

The majority of Jews supported *Sajudis* in its struggle for independence but did not want to get directly involved in the Lithuanian national movement. They wanted the Lithuanian state to deal with the issue of the Holocaust but they desired more than just token gestures.

They founded different Jewish organisations or were active in the newspaper *Jerusalem of Lithuania*. In October 1989 the first issue of the Jewish newspaper *Jerusalem of Lithuania* was published. This newspaper should be seen as a part of the national reawakening in Lithuania which was giving support to all forces who supported the Lithuanian struggle for independence. Therefore, it is not a surprise that it was supported by *Sajudis*. The newspaper was concerned with Jewish national self-identification and reports about different events in Lithuania and abroad. However, a very important issue was the relation between the Lithuanian majority and the Jewish minority. Therefore, it had to deal with the issue of the Holocaust and was ready to hear the Lithuanian side and give a forum to different opinions among the Jewish community, which was not always accepted, especially by the Jews who left Lithuania.[75] It also strongly attacked anti-Semitism in contemporary Lithuania.

So did every single Jew in Lithuania. Alperovich referred to numerous examples of continuous anti-Semitism, mentioning the newspapers *Terminus* and *Pozicija*, as well as citing an article called 'Jews and the KGB' that was published in *Lietuvos Aidas* by a former member of the Parliament (Varanauskas). He also referred to a statement by an officer of the Lithuanian Army (Svarinskas) who argued that the Jews deserved what they had experienced.[76] He was unhappy that the Lithuanians were not ready to address their own anti-Semitism.[77] Being a lawyer himself, he pointed out that the main issue in Lithuania was not the law but anti-Semitism in everyday life which allowed the law to be implemented in the 'wrong way'. As an example he pointed out that 'The Declaration on the Genocide is all right from the legal point of view. However, the way it is carried out is wrong. The judicial decisions are now carried out by administrators who rehabilitated the Lithuanian soldiers who committed crimes against the Jews.'

What is interesting is that the Jews did not discuss Lithuanian legislation concerning citizenship issues in relation to their community. In the course of my interviews, they expressed a general satisfaction with the legislation.[78]

Most of the Jews I interviewed agreed that the Jewish community was only going to get smaller and that it would be difficult to continue Jewish life in Lithuania. Some of them were ready to leave but some of them decided to stay and try to continue Jewish life. People who decided to stay there tried to define their Jewish identity and how it related to Lithuania. The majority of them were still in the process of raising questions about their own people, its history and its languages (Hebrew and Yiddish). A small number of them found an answer in the Orthodox synagogue. Some others said, 'It does not mean a lot to me to be a Jew in Lithuania.'[79] What all of them had in common was a belief that the only way for Lithuania to come to terms with its past and to learn to live with its minorities was to build a democratic society which would be able to accept Lithuanian minorities together with their cultures and histories.

9
Postscript

Concluding remarks on events until 1993

Although the language of *Sajudis* emphasised the rule of law, democracy and the role of citizens, its rhetoric in the late 1980s became increasingly nationalistic, as red, green and yellow (the colours of the Lithuanian national flag) became more conspicuous. In the words of Landsbergis,

> We adopted an attitude to foster exactly civil consciousness and thereby to create opportunities for everybody to self-determine, to feel, to become and to be the citizen of Lithuania. ... We... are still looking for civil society, that is, a society of human beings who consider the Fatherland as a real and valuable entity. One may recite a certain maxim, the locution of ancient Romans: for the true citizen, to die for the Fatherland is a sweet death.[1]

It is a paradox that the rise of civil society allowed nationalism to develop into a fully fledged movement and that nationalism acted as an 'enemy' of civil society and impeded its growth. In comparison with the Soviet era, a space officially existed but it was permanently invaded by the national agenda.

> We are now going through an awakening period of the nation which is based on a peasant culture. It is very difficult to reach the same level of national identity as in Europe and we should not try to take a short-cut. Here there is no modern education system. The most important problem is that there is not a sufficient thinking through of different issues, and it is very important to develop this,

if we would like to reach a European level. People have to be aware of two things, to understand the nature of an individual and to understand that society is based upon a social contract, a contract between individuals.[2]

In this context, citizenship proved to be a dynamic principle or a 'history of struggle' for individual and collective rights to be acknowledged and exercised. Citizenship entails a membership in a community and, as such, depends on the way the rights are defined in the letter of the law. Legislation is of vital importance because it sets criteria for membership. In Lithuania, these criteria allowed for citizenship based on an inclusive principle. However, legislation, though a necessary prerequisite, was not alone sufficient for citizens to be able to exercise their rights. In Lithuania, there was an increasing tension between citizenship and nationalism. The national minorities argued that this tension did not allow them to exercise their rights and become active citizens in Lithuanian society. Furthermore, this tension forced them to become less active in the Lithuanian national movement. Their responses were either to leave the movement altogether, to withdraw from the public sphere, or to become engaged along ethnic lines, culturally and politically.

The national minorities felt that the question of how to define a (true) Lithuanian also had relevance to themselves. They had to find an answer to the question of who was a (real) Russian, Pole or Jew. This issue was also important in relation to their duty towards the 'Fatherland', to use the phrase of Landsbergis in the above quote. Although the majority of members of the national minorities felt that Lithuania was their homeland, they wanted Lithuania to be a multicultural society. The obsession of the Lithuanian national movement with Lithuanian history did not embrace the minorities' histories on the territory of Lithuania. They were seen as endangering the existence of the Lithuanian state, and this was particularly true of Polish culture. The Lithuanian national movement felt uncomfortable with what they saw as the dominance of Polish culture, the association of Russians with rulers and especially Soviet might, and finally the perceived insulation of the Jewish community. Minorities' histories in this land, throughout centuries, were different. Therefore, there were different responses, demands and answers raised by the national minorities. An irony is that this perception of Polish culture, Soviet might and Jewish closeness were all linked to the past. There were hardly any Jews left in Lithuania. The Poles stressed the view that Polish culture had been destroyed in Soviet Lithuania. The Soviet might threatened independent Lithuania up to 1991. However, despite the past nature of these features, the Lithuanian national movement did not try to gain the support of its minorities. On the contrary, its rhetoric became increasingly nationalistic. However, this rhetoric made the differences within the Lithuanian community more visible. Even more importantly, some of them expressed opposition against the nationalistic rhetoric and this was, needless to say, welcomed by minorities.

A small number of the national minority population felt that during the Soviet era their national identity was neglected because it was under the pressure of Sovietisation. The Lithuanian national movement forcefully introduced the rest of this population to the nationality question, which insisted on preserving differences among national groups. Therefore, all of them had to face the question of who they were. This question was a painful issue for the majority of the national minority population especially because it was raised against a background which concentrated on celebrating the Lithuanian nation. The celebration of a collective ideal was a familiar process to these people but this time it was not the working class but the nation which was elevated on a pedestal. Minorities were not included in this celebration. Furthermore, Russians were addressed as 'occupiers', Poles were called 'Red Poles' and Jews were reminded of their support for communist ideology. Ethnic differences were not appreciated. The majority of national minorities were taken aback and confused. They did not know how to approach the question of who they were. Most of the members of the minority groups withdrew from public life and were passive. Passivity must be seen in relation to the Soviet era as well as the result of the rise of Lithuanian nationalism. In both cases, passivity was imposed on the minorities because they were marginalised by the majority. Those who got involved, organised themselves into different types of organisations. Their choice of organisation was determined by their relation towards independent Lithuania and how they envisaged their cultural and economic future in this country.

The 1992 election result should not only be seen as an LDDP victory but also as a judgement on the *Sajudis* reign. Both Lithuanians and national minorities hoped that the LDDP would tone down the nationalistic rhetoric. The Poles acknowledged that the LDDP had made positive first steps in implementing legislation concerning minority rights, especially the use of minority languages in public offices. The majority of Russians I interviewed were disappointed because in their opinion LDDP did not have a policy on national minorities. All of them admitted that there was less pressure on the minorities after the 1992 elections but at the same time there was still no dialogue. The Jews were satisfied with the willingness of the LDDP government to address the issue of the Holocaust. However, the only forum in which minority issues were raised was in the government.[3] Otherwise there was 'silence'. The national minorities were not prepared to collaborate against this silence. They argued that their circumstances differed and that there was a need to raise awareness about specific issues among their respective communities.

In assessing the years from 1988 to 1993, one can see that this was a turbulent time for national minorities in Lithuania. As my research pointed out, although the Lithuanian legislation complied with international regulations, national minorities still had grievances which prevented them from becoming active citizens. There was less and less respect for diversity and there was a tendency towards homogeneity. While at the beginning of 1988 important steps towards the establishment of civil society had been taken, from late 1989 onwards nationalist rhetoric became more conspicuous and impeded such developments. People had been learning the language of civil society and had entered the space which was no longer covered by the 'big brother'. However, new cards were asked to be shown at the door; this time not of the Communist Party but the national ones. In August 1993 the Soviet Army left Lithuania. 'Lithuania will be finally independent', I heard from quite a few of my interviewees.

1993 to the present

What has changed since 1993 for the national minorities? According to the present Lithuanian government the Russian population 'have psychological problems concerning their identity... even though their ethnic rights specifically and their human rights in general are fully protected by the law'.[4] As far as the Poles were concerned, they were seen as a group which was privileged during the Soviet period. The Lithuanian authorities argued that despite having schools in Polish and other cultural institutions 'Russification of the Poles was obvious'.[5] Jews were seen as a privileged minority in the first Lithuanian Republic and they were annihilated by the Nazis and discriminated against during the Soviet period.[6] The government pointed out that Lithuania had been committed to its minorities since independence. Its policy document is a typical example of what has been already pointed out, that there has not been a dialogue between national minorities and Lithuanian authorities.

The demographic picture of Lithuania is slowly changing. Russians started to leave in the period of national awakening and their emigration reached a peak in 1992. As a result, it is estimated that the number of Russians today is just above 300 000 which means that more than 10 per cent left the country or around 40 000 people.[7] Jews also left Lithuania and their number today is a half of what it used to be in 1989.[8] The number of Poles who stayed in Lithuania did not change.[9]

A major concern of the national minorities is how to be integrated into Lithuanian society. When I met Halina Kobeckaite in 1992, she told me that there was a large number of Russian cultural and religious organisations, especially in comparison with the Polish and Jewish equivalent.[10] In 1998 there were more than 50 Russian and Polish cultural and religious organisations and nearly 30 Jewish ones.[11] There was a tendency, especially among Russians, to try to unite these different organisations but these attempts usually failed.[12] There were also quite a few attempts to form a Russian political party, such as that of Piotr Frolov in 1993.[13] On 28 October 1995 the first Russian political party was founded, the Union of Russians in Lithuania. Its first chairperson was Sergei Dmitriev. The aim of the party was 'the promotion of the interests, language, cultural and educational rights of Lithuania's 310 000 Russians'.[14] This party took part in the 1996 elections but it did not cross the threshold of 5 per cent so it does not have any representatives in the present Lithuanian Parliament (*Seimas*). The party did not have much support among the Russian community. Some Russian organisations gave their support to the Polish Electoral Action[15] which was formed in the autumn of 1994 when the Election Law changed, allowing only political parties to take part in elections.[16] The party was especially concerned with the language rights of Lithuanian national minorities. This has to be viewed in the perspective of discussions about a new language law. It was proposed that Lithuanian should be the only language in the country. At the beginning of 1995, the period given to national minorities to learn Lithuanian expired. During a heated discussion in the *Seimas*, the Polish Faction argued for amendments which would allow for minority languages to be used in areas where they made up the majority. This group also argued that Poles should be allowed to spell their names and names of the places in which they live in the Polish way. However, a new Language Law was adopted on 31 January 1995. Ceslavas Jursenas, LDDP MP and speaker in *Seimas*, argued 'The forcible assimilation is undemocratic and has no future...The only thing I always stress: If you live in Lithuania, learn Lithuanian.'[17]

The number of Russian and Polish pupils who are taught Lithuanian in their schools has been growing since 1989. 'About 13 percent of ethnic Russian children attended schools with Lithuanian language instruction in 1989. There were 31 percent of such children in 1993, according to a survey conducted by the Lithuanian Institute of Sociology and Philosophy. Experts say such figures will be much higher in 1998.'[18] However, the major problem was the quality of teaching of Lithuanian. This was an important reason behind only a small number of Russian children leaving Russian schools for Lithuanian ones.[19] The Lithuanian authorities argued that there had been a positive response from the Poles in the South-East after they had introduced longer hours of teaching Lithuanian, started to teach Lithuanian in the first class and improved the quality of teaching.[20]

Since 18 May 1998, the Polish University has been registered by the Department of Law of the city of Vilnius as an independent body, under the name of *Universitatis studiorum Polona Vilnensis*. It is still unable to issue diplomas so students often go to Poland to complete their studies. Since 1991, the number of students has dropped and in 1998 there were 39 students studying law and 15 students doing an MA degree in primary school teaching.[21]

Although the number of national minorities who learn Lithuanian has been growing, there is still a demand, especially in the South-East, that minority languages should be treated equally with Lithuanian. This was the reason why the Vilnius region decided on 7 January 1998 that Lithuanian and other minority languages were the official languages of this area. Arunas Eigirdas repeated that this region was again 'a card in the hand of a foreign country (Russia)' and he added that the Polish Electoral Action had been involved in this decision. He claimed that once again the rationale for the existence of a Polish party was stirring a conflict with the Lithuanian government.[22] The chairperson of the Polish Electoral Party, Jan Senkewicz, stated that he was 'ready for discussion about territorial autonomy of the Vilnius region'.[23] His statement was criticised by the members of the Polish ethnic community who argued that the idea of autonomy was discredited because it was promoted by the people who were against Lithuanian independence. Whereas in 1989 the whole of the Polish community was engaged in discussing the Language Law, in 1998 only politicians were engaged in the debate.[24]

Another issue which is connected with the Vilnius province (under which are the Vilnius and Salcininkai regions) is related to land reform and the expansion of the city of Vilnius. Edvardas Makelis, the

Agriculture Minister, argued in November 1998 that 'wrapping up this programme may take another four years'.[25] The Poles are against the expansion of Vilnius. They argued that only 10 per cent of land restitution cases had been settled in the Vilnius region in comparison with 50 per cent in the rest of the country.[26] They wanted the Lithuanian government, first, to address the land restitution cases before they made decisions on city expansion. At the end of 1998 only 60 per cent of land restitution cases had been resolved in Lithuania.[27]

In the post-1993 period, relations between Jews and Lithuanians continued to be defined by the issue of the Holocaust. In 1995 the Prime Minister, Adolfas Slezevicius (whose parents were honoured for rescuing two Jewish families during the war), argued that there were 'hundreds' of Lithuanians who collaborated with the Germans in the murder of the Jews. When Brazauskas visited Israel in March 1995 he repeated the same sentence. As was previously pointed out it would be more accurate to talk about thousands. Nevertheless, both of them were attacked in the Lithuanian press for 'bowing down to Jewish pressures'.[28] Emanuelis Zingeris argued in 1995 that 'the difficulty is that the Lithuanian government is clearly far ahead of popular opinion, which is not even ready for a calm discussion of the problem'.[29]

In 1995 the LDDP government decided to form a commission which would co-ordinate events to mark the 200th anniversary of the death of Gaon Elijah, an internationally known Jewish scholar from Vilnius.[30] 1997 was a year of remembering the Jewish heritage in Lithuania. There were a series of conferences organised as well as cultural events throughout the year. In the same year a commission was formed to clarify current and historical problems between Jews and Lithuanians.[31] The Holocaust still remains the central issue because the present government, as quoted above, declared that the Nazis should be held responsible. The Lithuanian Jewish Community, while arguing that the Holocaust and anti-Semitism were still important issues, declared nonetheless that the community had to carry on and concentrate on issues such as 'preserving national identity, cultural and educational issues, restitution problems, help for socially needy people and problems of students and youth'.[32] In February 1998, the Centre for Tolerant National Identity and Mutual Understanding Between Lithuanians and Jews was formed. Markas Zingeris, its representative and a writer, argued that it was important to 'encourage positive rather than negative examples of Jewish–Lithuanian relations'.[33] All these events and commissions are important in building bridges between these two communities, possibly even more so than the well publicised case of Aleksandras Lileikas who has been on trial because of his 'responsibility for genocide of Lithuanian's residents'.

Many of the issues raised by the national minorities continued to exist after 1993. However, they were no longer seen as conflicts but as matters which could be settled. Of course, some conflicts have occurred, especially between the Poles and the two Lithuanian governments (1992–6 and one elected in 1996). However, they have not captured the attention of the minority communities and Lithuanians on the same scale as they did in the late 1980s and early 1990s. I would argue that this is primarily related to the mellowing of nationalistic rhetoric. An important achievement of the LDDP government was the policy of avoiding conflicts as far as possible. As a result, the Russians have been increasingly integrating into Lithuanian society. The Jews still raise the issue of the Holocaust but are ready to take a more active part in Lithuanian society. The Poles continue to argue that their grievances concerning land reform and the expansion of Vilnius have not been dealt with. However, they agree that the LDDP government made attempts to improve education in Polish. The period 1993 onwards has been a period in which both the Lithuanian authorities and minority populations have been learning the language of democracy, which has entailed coming to terms with differences and the question of how to live with them.

Appendixes

Demographic data

Table A1.1a   Population of Lithuania (in %)

Nationality	1857	1897	1923
Lithuanians	75.6	61.6	69.2*
Russians	1.4	4.8	2.5
Poles	5.6	9.7	15.3
Jews	10.7	13.1	8.3
Belorussians	0.3	4.7	0.4
Ukrainians	0.1	0.1	0.0
Germans	5.1	4.4	3.4
Others	1.2	1.6	0.9

Source: Lietuvos respublikos gyventoju demografine statistika (tautiniu aspektu), p.6.
*These data include the data for Klaipeda region from 1925, and Vilnius region from 1931.

Table A1.1b   Population of Lithuania (excluding Memel) according to Race (1923 census)

	Lithuan.	Jews	Russian	German	Poles	Letts (Latvia)	Others
Number	1 701 863	153 743	54 881	29 231	65 599	14 883	8771
Per cent	83.88	7.56	2.70	1.44	3.23	0.73	0.44

Source: The Baltic States, p.30.

Table A1.1c Population of Lithuania according to Nationality after the Second World War

Population	1959	1970	1979	1989
Total	2 711 400	3 128 200	3 391 500	3 674 800
%	100	100	100	100
Lithuanians	2 130 800	2 506 700	2 712 200	2 924 300
%	79.3	80.1	80.0	79.6
Russians	231 000	268 000	303 500	344 500
%	8.5	8.6	8.9	9.4
Poles	230 100	240 200	247 000	258 000
%	8.5	7.7	7.3	7.0
Jews	24 700	23 600	14 700	12 400
%	0.9	0.8	0.4	0.3
Belorussians	30 300	45 400	57 600	63 200
%	1.1	1.5	1.7	1.7
Ukrainians	17 700	25 100	32 000	44 800
%	0.7	0.8	1.0	1.2
Others	26 800	19 200	24 500	27 600
%	1.0	0.5	0.7	0.8

Source: *Lietuvos respublikos pagrindiniu tautybiu gyventojai*, p.1.

Table A1.1d Estimated Population in Lithuania by Nationality

Population	1995	1996
Total	3 717 700	3 711 900
%	100	100
Lithuanians	3 022 400	3 023 000
%	81.3	81.4
Russians	310 900	307 500
%	8.4	8.3
Poles	259 200	257 900
%	7.0	7.0
Jews	5 900	5 600
%	–	–
Belorussians	55 900	55 200
%	1.5	1.5
Ukrainians	37 700	37 300
%	1.0	1.0
Others	25 700	25 400
%	0.7	0.7

Source: *Lietuvos statistikos metrastis, 1996*, pp.33–4.

Table A1.2a   Russians according to Place of Birth in 1989

	Lithuania	*Russia*	*Ukraine*	*Belorussia*	*Other*
Number	171 025	129 465	10 251	10 710	23 004
%	49.7	37.6	3	3.1	6.7

Source: *Lietuvos respublikos gyventoju demografine statistika (tautiniu aspektu)*, pp.58–9.

Table A1.2b Poles and Jews who were Born Outside Lithuania and were Residents of Lithuania in 1989

	Poles	*Jews*
Number	32 300	5 400
%	12.8	43.7

Source: National Minorities in Lithuania, 1992, p.11.

Table A1.3a   Immigration to the Baltics from the Other Soviet Republics, 1946–89

	Estonia *1946–89*	*Latvia* *1947–88*	*Lithuania* *1951–89*
Total number of immigrants	1 158 600	1 517 800	1 093 500
Net immigration	365 900	445 200	311 000
Average immigration per annum	8 300	10 600	8 000

Source: Ole Norgaard *et al.* (1996), p.170.

Table A1.3b Migration to/from Russia, 1959–90 and 1959–96

Migrants	*to Russia*	*from Russia*
1959–90	266 139	394 162
1959–96	309 161	408 457

Source: Given to me by Virgilia Eidukiene, Head of Statistics Section, Lithuanian Department of Statistics, 1 December 1997.

Table A1.3c Migration by Nationality from 1987 to 1995 with the Republics of the (Former) Soviet Union

Nationality	In-migration		Out-migration	
	number	*%*	*number*	*%*
Total				
1987	22 464	100	14 534	100
1988	21 899		14 855	
1989	16 755		15 439	
1990	13 197		19 827	
1991	10 709		18 085	
1992	6 206		27 324	
1993	2 682		15 076	
1994	1 557		3 418	
1995	1 870		2 916	
Lithuanians				
1987	4 082	18.2	3250	22.4
1988	3 956	18.1	2749	18.5
1989	3 767	22.5	1831	11.9
1990	3 299	25.0	1586	8.0
1991	2 894	27.0	1454	8.0
1992	2 109	34.0	1379	5.1
1993	1 055	39.3	521	3.5
1994	479	30.8	162	4.7
1995	456	24.4	145	5.0
Russians				
1987	9 841	43.8	6 697	46.1
1988	9 856	45.0	7 194	48.4
1989	7 370	44.0	8070	52.3
1990	5 675	43.0	11 896	60.0
1991	4 659	43.5	10 163	56.2
1992	2 490	40.1	16 162	59.2
1993	979	36.5	9 309	61.7
1994	581	37.3	2 094	61.3
1995	821	43.9	1 864	63.9
Poles				
1987	1 444	6.4	756	5.2
1988	1 393	6.3	749	5.1
1989	1 051	6.3	701	4.5
1990	1 055	8.0	793	4.0
1991	532	5.0	917	5.1
1992	343	5.5	1 062	3.9
1993	177	6.6	429	2.8
1994	97	6.2	128	3.7
1995	87	4.7	91	3.1

Table A1.3c   (continued)

Nationality	In-migration		Out-migration	
	number	%	number	%
Jews				
1987	153	0.7	76	0.5
1988	152	0.7	63	0.4
1989	111	0.7	49	0.3
1990	132	1.0	198	1.0
1991	98	0.9	76	0.4
1992	28	0.4	68	0.2
1993	15	0.6	27	0.2
1994	11	0.7	19	0.6
1995	12	0.6	6	0.2
Ukrainians				
1987	2 612	11.6	1 531	10.5
1988	2 427	11.1	1 684	11.3
1989	1 865	11.1	2 073	13.4
1990	1 848	14.0	2 576	13.0
1991	1 061	9.9	2 197	12.1
1992	478	7.7	3 809	13.9
1993	140	5.2	2 381	15.8
1994	101	6.5	364	10.7
1995	127	6.8	280	9.6
Belorussians				
1987	2 810	12.5	1 289	8.9
1988	2 379	10.9	1 382	9.3
1989	1 398	8.3	1 631	10.6
1990	1 056	8.0	1 784	9.0
1991	721	6.7	2 254	12.5
1992	419	6.8	3 495	12.8
1993	152	5.7	1 652	11.0
1994	124	8.0	346	10.1
1995	150	8.0	224	7.7
Other				
1990	132	1	994	5
1991	744	7	1 024	5.7
1992	339	5.5	1 349	4.9
1993	164	6.1	757	5.0
1994	164	10.5	305	8.9
1995	217	11.6	306	10.5

Sources: Lietuvos respublikos gyventoju demografine statistika (tautiniu aspektu), p.54. (The data for other nationalities was not given for the period 1978–89). *Statisticheskii ezhegodnik Litvi, 1990*, pp.18–19; *Statisticheskii ezhegodnik Litvi, 1991*, p.17; *Statisticheskii ezhegodnik Litvi, 1992*, pp.28–9; *Lietuvos statistikos metrastis, 1993*, p.41; *Lietuvos statistikos metrastis 1994–1995*, p.53; *Lietuvos statistikos metrastis, 1996*, p.48.

Table A1.3d   Migration by Nationality to Other Countries except the Soviet Union from 1987 to 1989

Migration/ Nationality	In-migration		Out-migration		Net migration
	number	*%*	*number*	*%*	
Total					
1987	1 367	100	1 337	100	30
1988	1 361		1 259		102
1989	2 156		2 198		−42
Lithuanians					
1987	108	8.1	236	17.6	−128
1988	96	7.0	188	14.9	− 92
1989	104	4.8	381	17.3	−277
Russians					
1987	775	58.0	528	39.5	247
1988	671	49.3	447	35.5	224
1989	891	41.3	479	21.8	412
Poles					
1987	92	6.7	92	6.9	0
1988	102	7.5	43	3.4	59
1989	618	28.7	142	6.5	476
Jews					
1987	9	0.7	123	9.3	−114
1988	1	0.1	267	21.2	−266
1989	2	0.1	756	34.4	−754
Ukrainians					
1987	156	11.6	152	11.4	4
1988	224	16.5	107	8.5	117
1989	260	12.1	168	7.6	92
Belorussians					
1987	97	7.2	95	7.1	2
1988	68	5.0	79	6.3	−11
1989	69	3.2	84	3.8	−15

Source: *Lietuvos respublikos gyventoju demografine statistika (tautiniu aspektu)*, p.55.

Table A1.3e　Emigration to CIS and Other Countries

	1991	*1992*	*1993*	*1994*	*1995*
Total	20 703	28 855	15 990	4 246	3 773
CIS – total	17 401	26 948	14 866	3 356	2 856
Russia	9 746	15 726	10 558	2 452	2 248
Belarussia	4 072	6 230	2 439	548	362
Ukraine	2 754	4 248	1 623	265	188
OC – total	3 302	1 907	1 124	890	917
USA	362	428	234	199	182
Canada	30	54	27	22	31
Israel	1 142	451	368	281	337
Poland	725	181	50	75	38
Germany	253	307	191	180	250
Estonia	70	49	34	6	8
Latvia	614	327	176	56	52

Source: Lietuvos statistikos metrastis, 1996, pp.46–7. The data for 1989 and 1990 do not exist.

Table A1.4　Ethnic Minorities according to their Native Language (in %)

Nationality	*Year*	*Native l.*	*Lithuanian*	*Russian*	*Other*
Russians	1970	97.8	2.0		0.2
	1989	95.6	4.1		0.3
Poles	1970	92.4	3.1	3.8	0.7
	1989	85.0	5.0	9.2	0.8
Jews	1970	61.9	2.8	35.0	0.3
	1989	35.7	6.7	56.8	0.8

Source: National Minorities in Lithuania, 1992, p.17. Lietuvos respublikos gyventoju demografine statistika (tautiniu aspektu), p.60.

Table A1.5a   Russians in Lithuania in 1989

City/Region	Total population of city/region	Number of Russians in total population of city/region	Number of Lithuanians in total population of city/region	% of Russians in total population of city/region	% of Russians in city/region in total population of Russians
Vilnius	576747	116618	291527	20.2	33.9
Klaipeda	202929	57204	127757	28.2	16.6
Kaunas	418087	34823	367941	8.3	10.1
Siauliai	145629	15343	123840	10.5	4.5
Ignalina R.	59757	23559	23408	39.4	6.8
Trakai R.	81232	9651	46801	11.9	2.8
Svencionys R.	38004	6152	18001	16.2	1.8
Zarasai R.	25970	5544	17963	21.3	1.6

Source: *Lietuvos respublikos pagrindiniu tautybiu gyventojai*, p.5 and pp.29–38. The last column is calculated by author and the total is 81.1%.

Table A1.5b   Poles in Lithuania in 1989

City/Region	Total population of city/region	Poles in total population of city/region	Lithuanians in total population of city/region	% of Poles in total population of city/region	% of Poles of city/region in total population of Poles
Vilnius	576 747	108 239	291 527	18.8	41.9
Salcininkai R.	41 347	32 891	3 871	79.6	12.7
Sirvintos R.	21 713	2 408	18 563	11.1	0.9
Svencionys R.	38 004	10 934	18 001	28.8	4.2
Trakai R.	82 321	19 365	46 801	23.8	7.5
Vilnius R.	94 131	59 812	19 549	63.5	23.2

Source: *Lietuvos respublikos pagrindiniu tautybiu gyventojai*, p.5 and pp.29–37. The last column is calculated by author and the total is 90.4%.

Table A1.5c　Jews in Lithuania in 1989

City	Total population of cities	Jews in total population of city	Lithuanians in total population of city	% of Jews in total population of city	% of Jews in cities in total population of Jews
Vilnius	576 747	9 109	291 527	1.6	74
Kaunas	418 087	1 359	367 941	0.3	11
Kleipeda	202 929	681	127 757	0.3	5.5
Siauliai	145 629	420	123 840	0.3	3.4

Source: Lietuvos respublikos pagrindiniu tautybiu gyventojai, p.5 and pp.29–30. The last column is calculated by author and the total is 93.9%.

Table A1.6　Population by Nationality Living in Urban and Rural Areas in 1989

Nationality	Urban	Rural
Total	2 486 832	1 187 970
%	67.67	32.33
Lithuanians	1 899 162	1 025 089
%	64.95	35.05
Russians	309 116	35 339
%	89.74	10.26
Poles	148 945	109 049
%	57.73	42.27
Jews	12 210	104
%	99.15	0.85
Others	117 399	18 389
%	86.35	13.65

Source: National Minorities in Lithuania. Vilnius, 1992, p.13.

Table A1.7　Population by Nationality in Relation to the Categories of Employment in 1979 and 1989 (in %)

Nationality	Workers	Office employees	Collective farmers	Others
Lithuanians	55.2	21.9	22.8	0.1
	54.3	28.3	17.1	0.3
Russians	58.4	37.7	3.8	0.1
	55.6	41.0	2.9	0.5
Poles	71.6	12.0	16.2	0.2
	69.4	17.7	12.2	0.7

Source: Lietuvos respublikos gyventoju demografine statistika (tautiniu aspektu), p.43. The data for the Jews were not available.

Table A1.8a Population by Nationality Employed in Material Production and Non-material Production in 1979 and 1989 (in %)

Nationality	Material	Non-material
Total		
1979	77.8	22.1
1989	74.8	24.7
Lithuanians		
1979	78.4	21.4
1989	74.8	24.7
Russians		
1979	72.0	27.8
1989	71.6	27.8
Poles		
1979	82.9	17.0
1989	80.1	19.4

Source: Lietuvos respublikos gyventoju demografine statistika (tautiniu aspektu), p.46. The data for the Jews were not available.

Table A1.8b Population by Nationality Employed in Material Production in 1979 and 1989 (in %)

Nationality	Industry	Agriculture	Transport	Communi-cations	Building	Trade and public catering	Other branches of material productions
Total							
1979	28.9	23.7	5.4	1.3	10.8	6.6	1.8
1989	29.5	17.7	5.9	1.2	10.6	7.1	2.8
Lithuan.							
1979	26.8	26.1	4.5	1.2	11.1	6.7	2.0
1989	28.0	20.2	4.9	1.2	10.6	7.2	2.7
Russians							
1979	38.8	5.7	8.7	1.5	9.7	6.1	1.5
1989	36.4	4.9	9.8	1.4	10.3	6.0	2.8
Poles							
1979	31.3	24.5	7.5	1.5	8.5	7.2	2.4
1989	33.0	16.5	8.5	1.4	9.7	8.3	2.7

Source: Lietuvos respublikos gyventoju demografine statistika (tautiniu aspektu), pp.47–8. The data for the Jews were not available.

Table A1.8c   Population by Nationality Employed in Non-material Production in 1979 and 1989 (in %)

Nationality	Housing, public utilities and services	Health care and social welfare	Education	Culture and arts	Science and related services	Banking and state insurance	Admini-stration	Social organisations
Total								
1979	2.9	4.5	6.4	1.2	2.1	0.5	4.1	0.4
1989	3.3	5.5	8.1	1.5	1.8	0.5	3.6	0.4
Lithuan.								
1979	3.0	4.7	6.8	1.3	1.9	0.5	2.8	0.4
1989	3.4	5.9	8.6	1.6	1.7	0.6	2.5	0.4
Russian								
1979	2.6	3.4	5.3	0.9	3.5	0.5	11.1	0.5
1989	2.9	4.1	6.9	1.1	2.5	0.4	9.4	0.5
Poles								
1979	3.0	3.4	4.6	0.7	1.8	0.4	2.8	0.3
1989	3.4	3.9	5.6	1.0	1.7	0.4	3.0	0.4

Source: *Lietuvos respublikos gyventoju demografine statistika (tautiniu aspektu)*, pp.49–51. The data for the Jews were not available.

Table A1.9   Mother's Nationality of New-Born Children Whose Father Was Not of the Same Nationality as the Mother

Year/ Total	Lithuanian	Russian	Polish	Byeloruss	Ukrainian	Jewish	Other
1970 12.9%	34.2	27.3	21.2	10.5	3.3	0.8	2.2
1975 14.2%	35.3	27.6	21.4	8.7	4.4	0.6	1.4
1980 16.4%	6.9	51.1	45.9	69.5	75.6	32.3	57.8
1985 15.9%	6.8	46.8	46.2	67.5	71.5	29.1	72.6
1990 14.9%	6.1	54.5	45.1	71.2	75.9	39.5	72.4
1991 13.9%	5.8	55.2	45.1	72.6	78.2	64.1	74.6
1992 12.9%	5.5	56.3	42.6	79.3	80.3	45.7	64.1

Sources: *Statisticheskii ezhegodnik Litvi 1991*, p.12; *Statisticheskii ezhegodnik Litvi 1992*, pp.21–2.

Education

Table A2.1 Population by Nationality in Relation to Educational Level in 1970, 1979 and 1989 (calculations are made by taking 1000 people from each ethnic minority over the age of 10)

Nationality	HE	SSE	CE	ISE	PE
Lithuanians					
1970	46	55	66	189	384
1979	74	101	130	231	333
1989	109	176	220	172	249
Russians					
1970	74	95	161	248	266
1979	118	146	233	229	200
1989	172	211	267	152	156
Poles					
1970	15	23	59	196	412
1979	28	57	158	238	366
1989	50	137	277	175	264
Jews					
1970	236	93	213	77	211
1979	326	141	208	147	142
1989	385	179	195	110	114

HE – higher and incomplete higher education
SSE – special secondary education
CE – comprehensive education
ISE – incomplete secondary education
PE – primary education

Source: National Minorities in Lithuania, 1992, pp.23–4.

Table A2.2   Number and Percentage of Students According to the Language of Education

	Total	Lithuanian	Russian	Polish
1990/1				
No.	67 312	60 658	6 393	261
%	100	90.1	9.5	0.4
1991/2				
No.	59 571	54 857	4 473	210
%	100	92.1	7.5	0.4
1992/3				
No.	55 263	51 899	3 044	175
%	100	94	5.5	0.3
1993/4				
No.	48 389	45 815	2 119	169
%	100	94.7	4.4	0.3
1994/5				
No.	45 448	43 521	1 318	155
%	100	95.8	2.9	0.3

Sources: *Statisticheskyi Ezhegodnik Litvi, 1992*, p.144. *Lietuvos statitikos metrastis, 1994–1995*, p.411.
Higher education consists of three stages: Bachelor's degree, Master's degree and Doctor's degree.

Table A2.3   Number and Percentage of Students by Nationality

	Total	Lithuanians	Russians	Poles
1992/3				
No.	55 263	50 082	2 753	1 502
%	100	90.6	5	2.7
1993/4				
No.	48 099	44 228	2 111	1 130
%	100	92.3	4.1	2.3

Sources: *Statisticheskyi Ezhegodnik Litvi, 1992*, p.145. *Lietuvos statistikos metrastis, 1993*, pp.341–2.
See also: *National Minorities in Lithuania*, 1992, pp.22–4.

Table A2.4 Number of Pupils in Full-time General Education by Language of Education

	Total	Lithuanian	Russian	Polish
1989/90	501 700	398 400	50 800	4 100
1990/91	499 700	401 800	49 800	4 500
1991/92	499 700	401 800	49 800	4 500
1992/93	497 400	406 500	47 000	5 600
1993/94	496 660	422 429	58 802	15 313
1994/95	509 209	434 706	57 740	16 613
1995/96	520 704	447 281	55 373	17 898

Sources: *Lithuania's Statistics Yearbook, 1991*, p.117. *Statisticheskyi Ezhegodnik Litvi, 1992*, pp.125–6. *Lietuvos statistikos metrastis, 1996*, p.478.
Full-time general education consists of three stages: primary (classes 1–4), basic (classes 5–9) and secondary (classes 10–12).

Table A2.5 Number of Schools in Full-time General Education by Language of Education

	Total	Lithuanian	Russian	Polish
1989/90	2 040	1 801	85	44
1990/91	2 058	1 822	83	46
1991/92	2 058	1 822	83	46
1992/93	2 131	1 887	87	53

Sources: *Lithuania's Statistics Yearbook, 1991*, p.117.
Statisticheskyi Ezhegodnik Litvi, 1992, pp.125–6.
See also: *National Minorities in Lithuania, 1992*, pp.19–22.

Table A2.6 Number of Pre-School Institutions by Language of Instruction

	1992	1993	1994
Total Sch.	1048	809	747
Children	91 733	78 596	85 492
%	100%	100%	100%
Lithuanian Sch.	846	664	617
Children	76 455	68 741	76 509
%	83.4%	87.5%	89.5%
Russian Sch.	64	39	31
Children	12 917	8038	6954
%	14.1%	10.2%	8.1%
Polish Sch.	8	8	9
Children	2329	1817	2005
%	2.5%	2.3%	2.3%
Jewish Sch.	1	–	–
Children	32	–	–
%	0%	0%	0%

Source: *Lietuvos statistikos metrastis, 1994–5*, pp.412–13.
See also: *National Minorities in Lithuania*, 1992, p.18.

Mass media

Table A3.1   Number and Percentage of Newspapers, Magazines and Other Periodicals by Language of the Text

	1990		*1991*		*1992*		*1993*		*1994*		*1995*	
Total Newspap.	324	100%	381	100%	413	100%	393	100%	445	100%	477	100%
Lithuan.	273	84.3%	328	86.1%	353	85.5%	336	85.5%	384	86.3%	412	86.4%
Russian	40	12.3%	39	10.2%	43	10.4%	38	9.7%	38	8.5%	44	9.2%
Polish	8	2.5%	9	2.4%	8	1.9%	8	2.0%	11	2.5%	11	2.3%
Yiddish	1		1		1		1		1		1	
English	1	0.3%	2	0.5%	5	1.2%	6	1.5%	6	1.4%	6	1.2%
Total Magazines	159	100%	221	100%	237	100%	212	100%	269	100%	321	100%
Lithuan.	125	78.6%	195	88.2%	210	88.6%	192	90.1%	237	88.4%	277	86.3%
Russian	29	18.3%	18	8.1%	12	5.1%	6	2.8%	7	2.6%	11	3.4%
Polish	1	2.5%	3	1.4%	3	4.2%	2	4.7%	2	0.7%	1	0.3%
English	4	0.6%	4	1.8%	10	1.3%	10	1.0%	21	7.5%	30	9.3%

Source: *Lietuvos statistikos metrastis, 1996*, p.496.
See also: *National Minorities in Lithuania*, 1992, pp.24–6.

Table A3.2 State Radio and Television Programmes and Average Broadcasting Time (ABT) a Day (in Hours) by Language of Broadcasting

	1992	1993	1994	1995
Radio prog.	15 450	15 239	15 156	16 102
ABT	42.2 h.	41.8 h.	41.5 h.	46.6 h.
Lithuanian	14 017	13 596	13 755	14 699
	38.3 h.	37.2 h.	37.7 h.	40.3 h.
Russian	758	899	685	684
	2.1 h.	2.5 h.	1.9 h.	1.9 h.
Polish	183	169	176	179.5
	0.5 h.	0.5 h.	0.5 h.	0.5 h.
English	375	458	417	417
	1.0 h.	1.3 h.	1.1 h.	1.1 h.
Other	117	118	123	122.5
languages	0.3 h.	0.3 h.	0.3 h.	2.8 h.
Television prog.	4197	3903	3647	4299
ABT	11.5 h.	10.7 h.	10.0 h.	12.24 h.
Lithuanian	–	3476	3401	4088
		9.5 h.	9.3 h.	11.2 h.
Russian	–	105	79	87
		0.3 h.	0.2 h.	0.2 h.
Polish	–	86	27	26
		0.2 h.	0.1 h.	0.07 h.
Other	–	236	140	198
languages		0.7 h.	0.4 h.	0.77 h.

Sources: *Lietuvos statistikos metrastis, 1994–5*, p.432. *Lietuvos statistikos metrastis, 1996*, p.494.

In 1995 there were 21 municipal and 24 private radio and TV companies which were not included in the above table. 'In Hebrew 40 min. radio coverage and TV broadcast.' *National Minorities in Lithuania*. Vilnius: Department of Nationalities of the Government of the Republic of Lithuania, 1992, p.26.

Questionnaire

A

1. What are citizenship rights?
2. Are your rights respected?
3. If not, can you legally fight for your rights?
4. Is there any organisation to help you?
5. How would you describe the evolution of inter-ethnic relations in ithuania?
6. Is nationalism in Lithuania a result of inter-ethnic relations in the states of the former Soviet Union?
7. How to explain a different understanding of inter-ethnic relations and their goals?
8. What does it mean to be Russian or Polish or Jewish or Lithuanian?
9. What kind of argument would you put forward to explain a need for domination of one nation?
10. Does it matter what the nationality of your neighbours/workmates is?
11. What do you feel for Russia, Poland, Israel, Lithuania?
12. Which political organisation do you support or are you a member of?

B

1. Gender
2. Age
3. Citizenship
4. Nationality
5. Parents' nationality
6. Partner's nationality
7. Educational level
8. Mother tongue
9. Other languages
10. Place of birth
11. How long have you been living in Lithuania?
12. History of employment

Leaflet

(English translation. Original in Polish and Russian.)
Take power into your own hands. Finish the governor's rule, plundering the land and brutal colonisation in the Vilnius region. The future of the Vilnius region depends on your vote.

Notes

1 Conceptual and Methodological Issues Concerning Citizenship Rights of National Minorities

1. The Lithuanian national movement is analysed in Chapter 3.
2. L. Barrington (1995) 'The Domestic and International Consequences of Citizenship in the Soviet Successor States', *Europe–Asia Studies*, vol.47, no.5, pp.733–9. R. Brubaker (1992) 'Citizenship Struggles in the Soviet Successor States', *International Migration Review*, vol.26, no.2, pp.279–86. O. Norgaard *et al.* (1996) *The Baltic States After Independence.* Cheltenham: Edward Elgar, pp.183–8. G. Smith, A. Aasland and R. Mole (1996) 'Statehood, Ethnic Relations and Citizenship', in: G. Smith, ed. *The Baltic States: The National Self-Determination of Estonia, Latvia and Lithuania.* Basingstoke: Macmillan, pp.188–92. As is going to be analysed in the following chapters quite a few of my respondents also supported this thesis.
3. See: Appendix: Demographic Data: Tables A1.1a, A1.1b, A1.1c, A1.1d.
4. 'Children's years' means the formative years in the process of nation-building (in our case 1988–93).
5. As will be analysed in Chapter 4 Lithuania was the first republic of the Soviet Union to make the Lithuanian language the official state language, on 19 November 1988.
6. Local level is used in the sense of maintaining autonomy and space within which to pursue new initiatives. It means that one has to take into account both a geographic area and social relations which are constituted there. When it comes to ethnic community a certain place gets a subjective dimension – it gets a particular value.
7. S. Tarrow (1994) *Power in Movement: Social Movements, Collective Action and Politics.* Cambridge: Cambridge University Press, p.76.
8. In the words of Vaclav Havel the regime attempted to fill people's stomachs in order to empty their minds.
9. We are not primarily interested in legal and philosophical definitions of citizenship but in socio-political ones. Legal definitions consider what kind of rights and duties citizens have towards a nation-state and, also, rights and duties of a nation-state towards its citizens. Philosophical definitions, being of normative type, concentrate on the concept of a just state, its duties towards its citizens and the relationship between citizens. These two definitions relate their discussion to the nation-state, understood as a neutral and abstract concept. Socio-political definitions agree that citizenship cannot be understood outside the nation-state but argue, first, that a nation-state has its socio-historical context and, therefore, specific social, political and economic relations have to be taken into account. Second, a nation-state is only one level on which citizenship can be exercised. Other levels are local levels from regional government to more local governing bodies, local community, family etc. K. Faulks (1998) *Citizenship*

in Modern Britain. Edinburgh: Edinburgh University Press, pp.2–5. See also: B.S. Turner, ed. (1993) *Citizenship and Social Theory*. London: Sage.

10. I.M. Young (1990) *Justice and the Politics of Difference*. Princeton: Princeton University Press, pp.183–91.

11. Ibid., p.191. A. Phillips (1993) *Democracy and Difference*. Cambridge: Polity Press, p.95.

12. W. Kymlicka (1995) *Multicultural Citizenship*. Oxford: Clarendon Press, pp.26–33.

13. They did not use the term 'collective rights' because it reminded them of their Soviet past.

14. Tamara Resler argues that the emphasis on multiculturalism should be regarded as a guarantee of rights of national communities. T.J. Resler (1997) 'Dilemmas of Democratisation: Safeguarding Minorities in Russia, Ukraine and Lithuania', *Europe–Asia Studies*, vol.49, no.1, p.101.

15. M.A. Vachudova and T. Snyder (1997) 'Are Transitions Transitory? Two Types of Political Change in Eastern Europe Since 1989', *East European Politics and Society*, vol.11, no.1, pp.18–19.

16. Between 1991 and 1992 three documents were of major importance in institutionalising minority rights: the Document of the Copenhagen Meeting of the Conference on the Human Dimension, the Report of the July CSCE Meeting of Experts on National Minorities in Geneva, and the 1992 Helsinki Document 'The Challenges of Change'. See: K. Koch (1993) 'The International Community and Forms of Intervention in the Field of Minority Rights Protection', in: I.M. Cuthbertson and J. Leibowitz, eds., *Minorities: the New Europe's Old Issue*. Boulder, Col.: Westview Press for the Institute for EastWest Studies, pp.253–72.

17. Interview with E. Petrov(as), 25 June 1993. He was a Russian, a member of *Sajudis*.

18. In the first two elections in Lithuania, in 1990 and 1992, the threshold for the Union of Poles did not exist, for all other parties it was 4 per cent.

19. L. Guinier (1991) *The Triumph of Tokenism*, cited in: A. Phillips (1993), p.22, footnote 16.

20. Ch. Mouffe (1995) 'Pluralism and the Left Identity', in: M. Waltzer, ed., *Towards a Global Civil Society*. Oxford: Berghahn Books, p.297.

21. Ch. Mouffe (1992) 'Introduction', in: Ch. Mouffe, ed., *Dimensions of Radical Democracy: Pluralism, Citizenship, Community*. London: Verso, p.13.

22. D. Harvey (1993) 'Class Relations, Social Justice and the Politics of Difference', in: J. Squire, ed., *Principled Positions: Postmodernism and the Rediscovery of Value*. London: Lawrence and Wishart, pp.112–15.

23. A. Giddens (1994) *Beyond Left and Right: The Future of Radical Politics*. Cambridge: Polity Press, p.104.

24. J. Keane (1988) *Democracy and Civil Society*. London: Verso, p.x.

25. A. Melucci (1989) *Nomads of the Present*. London, Hutchinson Radious, p.172.

26. J.A. Hall (1995) 'In Search of Civil Society', in: J.A. Hall, ed., *Civil Society: Theory, History, Comparison*. Cambridge: Polity Press, p.16.

27. See also: R. Dahrendorf (1990) *Reflections on the Revolution in Europe*. London: Chatto and Windus, pp.95–7.

28. J. Luik (1991) 'Intellectuals and their Two Paths to Restoring Civil Society in Estonia', in: Z. Rau, ed., *The Emergence of Civil Society in Eastern Europe and*

the Soviet Union. Boulder, Col.: Westview Press, pp.77–93; M. Ryabchuk (1991) 'Civil Society and National Emancipation: The Ukrainian Case', in: Z. Rau, ed., pp.95–112.

29. E. Gellner (1994) *Conditions of Liberty: Civil Society and its Rivals*. Harmondsworth: Penguin.

30. J.I. Dawson (1996) *Eco-nationalism: Anti-nuclear Activism and National Identity in Russia, Lithuania and Ukraine*. London: Duke University Press, p.6.

31. Ibid., p.51. The *Zemyna* Club was founded in late 1987 and described itself as an 'independent environmental association'. *Zemyna* is the Goddess of the Earth in the Lithuanian pagan mythology. The chairperson of the *Zemyna* Club, Zigmas Vaisvila, became the Chairperson of the Ecological Committee of *Sajudis* in June 1988.

32. N. Lomaniene (1994) 'On Lithuanian Nationalism: the Movement and the Concept', in: N. Lomaniene and M.P. Saulauskas, eds., *Social Change*, vol.1. Vilnius: Independent Institute for Social Research, p.29.

33. Ch. Mouffe (1995), p.296.

34. J. Cohen (1995) 'Interpreting the Notion of Civil Society', in: M. Waltzer, ed., *Towards a Global Civil Society*. Oxford: Berghahn Books, p.36.

35. M. Hroch (1993) 'From the National Movement to the Fully-Formed Nation: the Nation-Building Process in Europe', *New Left Review*, no.198, p.12.

36. Quoted in: R. Szporluk (1989) 'Dilemmas of Russian Nationalism', *Problems of Communism*, vol.38, no.4, p.35.

37. M. Hroch (1993), p.12.

38. R.J. Dalton, M. Kuechler and W. Buerklin (1990) 'The Challenge of New Movements', in: R.J. Dalton and M. Kuechler, eds., *Challenging the Political Order*. Cambridge: Polity Press, pp.3–20.

39. R. Brubaker (1992) *Citizenship and Nationhood in France and Germany*. Cambridge, Mass.: Harvard University Press, p.xi.

40. V.S. Vardys and J.B. Sedaitis (1997) *Lithuania: the Rebel Nation*. Boulder, Col.: Westview Press, p.221.

41. M. Hroch (1993), p.17.

42. M. Hammersley and P. Atkinson (1996) *Ethnography: Principles in Practice*. London: Routledge, p.136.

43. I interviewed 87 people altogether, 30 Russians, 15 Poles, 10 Jews and 32 Lithuanians.

44. T. May (1997, second edition) *Social Research: Issues, Methods and Process*. Buckingham: Open University Press, p.87.

45. Ibid., pp.119–20.

46. He was a member of *Sajudis* (and since 1993 of *Tevynes Sajunga*, the Homeland Union). At the first Congress of *Sajudis* he was elected a member of the National Council being responsible, together with Virgilijus Cepaitis, Georgii Efremov and Bronius Kuzmiskas, for minority relations. He has also been active in defining Israeli–Lithuanian relations. However, I had a chance to talk to his secretary who provided me with a lot of information on Jews in Lithuania. In the 1990–2 Parliament there were 14 MPs who belonged to Lithuanian national minorities, 10 Poles, 3 Russians and 1 Jew. In the 1992–6 Parliament there were 10 MPs who belonged to Lithuanian national minorities, 6 Poles, 3 Russians and 1 Jew.

47. 'At the same time it should be noted that there are distinct advantages in combining participant observation with interviews; in particular, the data from each can be used to illuminate the other.' M. Hammersley and P. Atkinson (1996), p.131.
48. See: Appendix: Questionnaire.
49. T. May (1997), p.111 (emphases by the author).
50. M. Hammersley and P. Atkinson (1996), p.132 and p.156.
51. 'Where the aim is generalisation to some finite set of cases, rather than development and testing of the theory, it may be possible to assess the typicality of the case or cases studied by comparing their relevant characteristics with information about the target population, if this is available in official statistics or in other studies.' Ibid., p.44.

2 National Minorities Issues between the Two World Wars

1. All the other minorities in independent Lithuania together numbered as many as the Jews. See: Appendix: Demographic Data, Tables 1a and 1b and Figure 2.1.
2. It is important to make a distinction between national and nationalistic. I understand a starting point of 'national' to be respect towards one's own national culture. 'Nationalistic' primarily relates to the *other* who is described in negative terms.
3. A treaty is an agreement between the governments of two or more states. A declaration is a formal statement intended to create, preserve, assert or testify to a right. Therefore, the treaties could be concluded only with the already recognised states and Lithuania was not one of them in 1919 when it sought to be a member of the League of Nations. L. Rutherford and S. Bone, eds. (1993) *Osborn's Concise Law Dictionary*, eighth edition. London: Sweet and Maxwell.
4. Quoted in H. Arendt (1950, second, enlarged edition) *The Origins of Totalitarianism*. London: George Allen and Unwin Ltd, p.270.
5. C.A. Macartney (1934) *National States and National Minorities*. Oxford: Oxford University Press, pp.195–6.
6. Ibid., p.220.
7. P. de Azcarate (1945) *League of Nations and National Minorities: an Experiment*. Washington, DC: Carnegie Endowment for International Peace, p.14. He was a Director of the Minority Questions Section of the League of Nations.
8. Ibid., pp.21–7.
9. H. Arendt (1950), p.272.
10. P. de Azcarate (1945), pp.92–3.
11. The Peace Conference appointed the New State Committee to deal with minority (as well as economic) issues. The Committee demanded that the minority legislation should not be changed without the approval of the League. This demand was accepted.
12. 'Article 9. Poland will provide the public educational system in towns and districts in which a considerable proportion of Polish nationals of other than Polish speech are resident adequate facilities for ensuring that in the primary schools the instruction shall be given to the children of such Polish

nationals through the medium of their own language. This provision shall not prevent the Polish Government from making the teaching of the Polish language obligatory in the said schools.

'In towns and districts where there is a considerable proportion of Polish nationals belonging to racial, religious or linguistic minorities, these min-orities shall be assured an equitable share in the enjoyment and application of the sums which may be provided out of public funds under the State, municipal or other budget, for educational, religious and charitable purposes.

'The provisions of this Article shall apply to Polish citizens of German speech only in that part of Poland which was German territory on 1 August, 1914.' C.A. Macartney (1934), p.505.

13. 'Article 10. Educational Committees appointed locally by the Jewish committees of Poland will, subject to the general control of the State, provide for the distribution of the proportional share of public funds allocated to Jewish schools in accordance with Article 9, and for the organisation and management of these schools.

'The provisions of Article 9 concerning the use of languages in schools shall apply to these schools.

'Article 11. Jews shall not be compelled to perform any act which constitutes a violation of their Sabbath, nor shall they be placed under any disability by reason of their refusal to attend courts of law or to perform any legal business on their Sabbath. This provision, however, shall not exempt Jews from such obligations as shall be imposed upon all other Polish citizens for the necessary purposes of military service, national defence, or the preservation of public order.

'Poland declares her intention to refrain from ordering or permitting elections, whether general or local, to be held on a Saturday, nor will registration for elections or other purposes be compelled to be performed on a Saturday.' Ibid., pp.505–6.

14 Ibid., pp.234–5.

15. Ibid., p.238.

16. Interview with Ona Ruzelyte, 27 November 1992. She was a lawyer working at the Institute of Sociology, Philosophy and Law.

17. See: *League of Nations – Official Journal*, vol.2, no.8, October 1921, under: 'Dispute Between Lithuania and Poland', pp.869–80. 1. The Memorandum from the Polish Group of Deputies in the Diet of Western Lithuania to the League of Nations, Kowno, 19 June, 1921 'in defence of the human, civic and national rights of the Poles in this country. All efforts made with this object within the country itself have hitherto proved fruitless…' (p.873). 2. The Memorandum from the two Polish deputies in the Diet of Kowno to the League of Nations, Kowno, 7 July, 1921 'against being addressed as Polish-speaking Lithuanian nationals' (p.873). See also: vol.3, no.4, April 1922, under: 'Dispute between Lithuania and Poland', p.327: Two telegrams from the Polish minister for foreign affairs (23 and 25 February 1922) arguing that there are 117 Poles in custody for political offences in Kowno among whom more than 30 contracted typhus and six died.

18. C.A. Macartney (1934), p.259.

19. M. Narushevitch. Sixteenth Session of the Council, held at Geneva from Tuesday, 10 January, to Saturday, 14 January, 1922. Wednesday, 11 January,

1922 at 10.30 a.m.: Protection of Minorities in Estonia, Latvia and Lithuania. *League of Nations – Official Journal,* vol.3, no.2, February 1922, pp.89–90.
20. Ibid., p.491.
21. During the Peace Conference the Lithuanian leaders made the official declaration (5 August 1919) with regard to the rights of the Jewish minority which meant a Jewish dream coming true – national autonomy. For Jews it did not matter that it was only a 'proclamation of intent' and, therefore, was not legally binding. It seemed to them that the Lithuanian state had every intention of enforcing it. E. Mendelsohn (1983) *The Jews of East Central Europe: Between the World Wars.* Bloomington: Indiana University Press, p.220. The same type of declaration was given by Ernestas Galvanauskas, Prime Minister, and (once again) Augustinas Voldemaras, Foreign Minister, during the Conference on Jewish Autonomy in January 1920. S. Gringauz (1952) 'Jewish National Autonomy in Lithuania (1918–1925)', *Jewish Social Studies,* vol.14, no.3, p.234.
22. H. Arendt (1946) in her review of Oscar Janowsky's book on Nationalities and National Minorities argues: 'It should be remembered that the Jews played a very important, if not decisive, role in the drafting of the minorities treaties at the close of the First World War, when every care was taken to grant them protection and freedom of national development in several European states.' *Jewish Social Studies,* vol.8, no.2, p.205.
23. *League of Nations – Official Journal,* vol.3, no.2, February 1922, pp.89–90.
24. As quoted in E. Mendelsohn (1983), p.219.
25. A. Lieven (1994) *The Baltic Revolution: Estonia, Latvia, Lithuania and the Path to Independence.* New Haven: Yale University Press, pp.146–7; E. Mendelsohn (1983), pp.218–29.
26. N. Berdichievsky (1992) 'The Baltic Revival and Zionism', *Lituanus,* vol.38, no.1, p.75. See also: S. Gringauz (1952) 'Jewish National Autonomy in Lithuania (1918–1925)', *Jewish Social Studies,* vol.14, no.3, July 1952, p.230; A.E. Senn (1959) *The Emergence of Modern Lithuania.* New York: Columbia University Press, pp.10–11.
27. I. Cohen (5704-1943) *Jewish Community Series: Vilna.* Philadelphia: The Jewish Publication Society in America, p.385.
28. Ibid., pp.385–6.
29. In the middle of the sixteenth century it was reported that there were 72 religions and sects in Vilnius. This was a period when the first Jewish Council was founded in 1533 and when the first synagogue was opened in 1573. In the eighteenth century Vilnius was seen as a centre of the Orthodox rabbinical resistance to the messianic movement of Hassidim founded in Poland in the first part of the same century. The leading figure of the Orthodox resistance was Gaon (Genius), Rabbi Elijah ben Solomon Zalman. He is famous not only because of his disputes with the Hassidim movement and his preaching against it (he even declared it heretical), but also because of his study of the Talmud. Vilnius had dozens of prayer-rooms in which the Talmud was studied and which attracted Jews from different parts of Europe to study there. In one hundred years (from the end of the seventeenth century to the end of the eighteenth century) the Jewish population tripled; from 415 to 1300. This was a period when Vilnius was named the 'Lithuanian Jerusalem'.

30. Neither Poles, Russians nor Germans were granted their own ministry in the Lithuanian government of 1918. M.M. Laserson (1941) 'The Jewish Minorities in the Baltic Countries', *Jewish Social Studies*, vol.3, p.275.
31. On 18 September 1917 the Provincial Council (*Taryba*) was elected to serve as a provisional government. This decision was made under the auspices of the German government and the High Command as Lithuania was overrun by the German Army in 1915. Lithuania declared independence on 16 February 1918, and on 2 November 1918 the *Taryba* drew up a Provisional Constitution.
32. 'The *kehilla* was defined as a medieval public law body with the right to impose taxes and issue ordinances regarding religion, education, philanthropy, and the function of registering births, marriages and divorces.' S. Gringauz (1952), p.235. See also: M. Friedman (1976) 'The Kehillah in Lithuania 1919–1926: a Study Based on Panevezys and Ukmerge (Vilkomer)', *Soviet Jewish Affairs*, vol.6, no.2, p.83.
33. S. Gringauz (1952), p.234.
34. It met for the first time on 11 January 1920.
35. M. Friedman (1976), p.85.
36. Ibid., p.85; S. Gringauz (1952), p.236.
37. 'Annex 339, Protection of the Minorities in Lithuania. Eighteenth Session of the Council, 12 May 1922, at 11 a.m.', *League of Nations – Official Journal*, vol.3, no.6, June 1922, p.587.
38. They were Dr Samson (Shimshon) Rosenbaum, Vice-Minister for Foreign Affairs, Dr Nahman Rachmilevitch, Vice-Minister for Trade and Industry, Dr Jacob Wigotski (Yaakov Vygodski), Minister for Jewish Affairs, later replaced by Dr Max Soloveitchik (because Wigotski decided to stay in Vilnius).
39. A.P. Blaustein and G.H. Flanz, eds. (1992) *Constitutions of the Countries of the World: Lithuania* by G.H. Flanz. New York: Oceana Publications, Inc., Dobbs Ferry, p.37.
40. 'Article 7 The State language is the Lithuanian Language.
    It shall be determined by law in which districts and in which public offices other languages beside Lithuanian may be used.
    Article 18 Citizens shall be equal before the law.
    The rights of a citizen cannot be restricted on account of his religion, race or national origin.
    Article 27 Cognisant of the value of religion in the life of a person, the State recognises the existing churches in Lithuania and equivalent religious organisations.
    Other churches and equivalent religious organisations may be recognised by the State if their doctrines and rituals are not contrary to morals and public order.
    Article 28 The churches and equivalent religious organisations recognised by the State may freely teach their doctrines, perform their services, maintain houses of prayer, and operate religious schools for the preparation of their clergy.' Ibid., pp.58–63.
41. C.A. Macartney (1934), pp.406–10.
42. Ona Ruzelyte pointed out that one possible reason why the national autonomy 'never in total came through' are the Lithuanian authorities who from

the legal point of view tried to curb its importance. Interview with Ona Ruzelyte, 27 November 1992. See: J. Hiden and P. Salmon (1994) *The Baltic Nations and Europe: Estonia, Latvia and Lithuania in the Twentieth Century.* Harlow: Longman, p.47. Christian Democrats were a dominant party in the period between 1920 and 1926. They formed (together with the Farmers' Alliance and the Labour Federation) governments in 1920, 1922 and 1923 and although they won the majority of seats in the 1926 Parliament elections, the Populist-Social Democratic coalition formed the government. It should be pointed out that the National Party (*Tautininkai*) did not have popular support in this period.

43. Interview with Ona Ruzelyte, 27 November 1992. The right-wing parties are National and Liberal parties. See also: G. von Rauch (1974) *The Baltic States: the Years of Independence.* London: C. Hurst and Company, p.97.
44. S. Gringauz (1952), p.238. M. Friedman (1976), p.99 and p.101.
45. G. von Rauch (1974), p.98.
46. On 29 March 1920 the Ministry of Jewish Affairs issued instructions elaborating on the 'Provisional Law Granting the Jewish *kehillah* Boards the Right to Impose Taxes on the Jewish Population' (issued by the Cabinet on 10 January 1920) which stated that in any given place there could be only one local *kehillah*. M. Friedman (1976), p.87.
47. J. Lestchinsky (1946) 'The Economic Struggle of the Jews in Independent Lithuania', *Jewish Social Studies*, vol.8, no.4, p.269. M.M. Laserson (1941), p.275 and p.277.
48. M. Friedman (1976), p.99.
49. This point is discussed in all history books on Lithuania. A.E. Senn (1959) gives a short summary of Lithuanian nationalism on the eve of the First World War as well as the way the Lithuanian nation was perceived by various historians, pp.16–18. See also V.S. Vardys and J.B. Sedaitis (1997), p.31. The quotes are from E. Mendelsohn (1983), p.217 and M.M. Laserson (1941), p.273.
50. See also: E. Mendelsohn (1983), p.22. He argues that research on the Jews in more backward regions of East Central Europe points out that 'relations between Jews and non-Jews were often less tension-ridden than in rather more developed regions such as Slovakia and Poland', p.216. J. Lestchinsky (1946) argues that the Lithuanian intelligentsia was not patriotic but nationalistic, p.284.
51. The law meant that religious Jews did not work on the Sabbath and Sunday – two days a week and during winter even two and a half.
52. M. Wischnitzer (1955) *Die Juden in der Welt.* Berlin: Erich Reiss Verlag, p.188. M. Friedman (1976), p.101.
53. O.I. Janowsky (1938) *People at Bay: the Jewish Problem in East-Central Europe.* London: Victor Gollancz, pp.117–18. M. Wischnitzer (1955), p.186.
54. O.I. Janowsky (1938), p.83.
55. J. Lestchinsky (1946), pp.276–83.
56. O.I. Janowsky (1938), pp.82–3.
57. 'In the last 12 years 6,500 Lithuanian Jews left for Palestine.' M. Wischnitzer (1955), p.187. (This book was originally published in 1935.) '...the rate of Jewish emigration was relatively high; during the years 1928–1936, 12,690 Jews left the country (many going to South Africa, which had already become

an important center of Lithuanian Jewry in the "new world").' E. Mendelsohn (1983), p.225.
58. O.I. Janowsky (1938), p.103.
59. The most detailed account of the *Verslininkaj* I found in J. Lestchinsky (1946), pp.272–6. According to the 1923 Population Census the occupational structure of the Jews was as follows: 6 per cent in agriculture, 32 per cent in trade, 23 per cent in handicraft, 5 per cent in public service, 34 per cent in domestic labour and labour in general. M. Wischnitzer (1955), p.186. The Jews were mostly urban, 63 per cent lived in bigger cities, 32 per cent in small towns and 5 per cent in villages. p.185.
60. O.I. Janowsky (1938), pp.80–1.
61. John Hiden and Patrick Salmon argue that 'the indoctrination of youth in the schools' was carried out by the Nationalist Union. J. Hiden and P. Salmon (1994), p.55.
62. J. Lestchinsky (1946), p.285; M. Witschnitzer (1955), pp.188–9; M. Friedman (1976), p.86; *Jewish Social Studies: Supplement* (1946), vol.8, no.3, p.66.
63. J. Lestchinsky (1946), pp.270–1, pp.286–9; O.I. Janowsky (1938), pp.86–7; M.M. Laserson (1941), p.278.
64. 'The dominant Lithuanian majority laid exclusive claim not only to the more important and to the lower economic positions in the country, but even to the very humblest. The extent of the pressure to dislodge members of the minorities from the positions they had long filled, sometimes varied but the pressure itself was exerted everywhere. The spearhead of the offensive consisted of Lithuanian professional men and officials; both groups had scored early victories in obtaining the choicest government jobs. Following in their footsteps came the commercial and manufacturing elements, representing spheres in which Lithuanian co-operatives as well as private enterprise made very substantial progress. Finally came the new Lithuanian artisans, shouldering aside their Jewish colleagues and making every effort to replace them with recruits from the Lithuanian youth growing up in the villages. … the Jewish masses were almost completely shut out from these professions (labourers in industry and agriculture) as well.' J. Lestchinsky (1946), p.268.
65. A. Lieven (1994), p.145.
66. J. Hiden and Patrick Salmon (1994), p.89
67. O.I. Janowsky (1938), p.81; A. Lieven (1994), p.145.
68. D. Levin (1994) points out that there are documents of the German Foreign Ministry which indicate that at the end of 1930s Germans gave money to the supporters of Voldemaras to encourage pogroms in Lithuania, but refused to give them weapons. 'On the Relations Between the Baltic Peoples and their Jewish Neighbours Before, During and After World War II', p.380, in: *Baltic Jews Under the Soviets, 1940–1946*. Jerusalem: The Hebrew University of Jerusalem.
69. In 'The Authoritarian Personality' Adorno ascribed the following characteristics to an anti-Semite: stereotype, rigid adherence to middle-class values, the tendency to regard one's own group as morally pure in contrast to the immoral out-group, opposition to and exaggeration of prying and sensuality, extreme concern with dominance and power, fear of moral contamination,

fear of being overwhelmed and victimised, and the desire to erect social barriers in order to separate one group from another and to maintain the morality and dominance of one's own group. T.W. Adorno *et al.* (1950) *The Authoritarian Personality*. New York: Harper and Row, pp.744–83.

70. On 23 September 1992, the anniversary of the liquidation of the Vilnius Ghetto, which was named the 'Day of Genocide', Vytautas Landsbergis presented medals to the Lithuanians who helped the Jews (including one to his father) or to their families. A. Lieven (1994), p.157.

71. E. Mendelsohn (1983), p.213.

72. M. Tumin (1971) 'Anti-Semitism and Status Anxiety: a Hypothesis', *Jewish Social Studies*, vol.33, no.4, pp.307–16.

73. O.I. Janowsky (1938), p.117. A. Lieven (1994), pp.143–4.

74. C. Milosz (1981) *The Issa Valley*. London: Sidgwick and Jackson, p.6.

75. 'A Journey by Howard Jacobson', a programme on Channel 4, 26 March 1993.

76. M. Friedman (1976), p.84.

77. E. Mendelsohn (1983) points out that Jewish 'knowledge of Lithuanian … was far from impressive' (p.222). He then adds: 'Languages utterly unknown to the pre-war generation, such as Lithuanian and Latvian, were by the 1930s spoken by large numbers of Jews' (p.255).

78. However, one has to bear in mind that the written Lithuanian linguistic tradition appeared only in the late eighteenth century and the Jews were proudly pointing to their thousands-year-old literary tradition. Jonas Jablonskis, in the late nineteenth century, codified the Lithuanian grammar and vocabulary. Interview with A. Petrauskiene and S. Petrauskas, 28 October 1992. They were my landlords in Vilnius. Jablonskis is the maternal great-grandfather of Landsbergis and his paternal grandfather wrote the first plays in Lithuanian. Landsbergis' prestige was partly based on his family background as well as his knowledge of Lithuanian. Very often I was told: 'We are not without any tradition as we have been often portrayed. Our tradition is not only pagan or folk.'

79. L. Sabaliunas (1972) *Lithuania in Crisis: Nationalism to Communism, 1939–1940*. Bloomington: Indiana University Press, p.9.

80. In the 1938 Constitution Smetona's aim was finally reached – the President was given unlimited powers and the *Seimas* (Parliament) was only an advisory body.

81. 'The Nationalists particularly treasured qualities innate in the land and the people which distinguished one nation from another. However, the nationalist writers failed to identify any of these qualities. Instead, they merely placed emphasis on the need for individuality and hoped that ultimately, "in the process of our nation's life and work", this would produce a national culture which would make the country "an inimitable phenomenon of the universe", which would "justify" the nation's existence.' Ibid., p.27.

82. From Smetona's Spoken Written, 1927–1934, in Ibid., pp.27–8.

83. G. von Rauch (1974), pp.161–4, L. Sabaliunas (1972), p.39. N. Hope (1994), p.63.

84. J. Hiden and P. Salmon (1994), pp.53–6. A. Lieven (1994), pp.67–8. L. Sabaliunas (1972).

85. A. Smetona (1990) 'Collected Papers, Vilnius', p.464, in: M. Povilas Saulauskas (1994) *Revolution 1989: Farewell to Modernity? An Outline of Lithuanian Experience*. Vilnius: Independent Institute for Social Research, p.62, footnote 8.
86. D. Levin (1991) 'The Sovietization of the Baltics and the Jews, 1940–1941', *Soviet Jewish Affairs*, vol.21, no.1, p.53.
87. D. Levin (1994) *Baltic Jews Under the Soviets*. Jerusalem: The Hebrew University of Jerusalem, p.3.
88. See dithyrambs written by the Lithuanian authors when the Red Army entered Lithuania. 'Were the Jews in 1940 Guilty Before Lithuania?' *Jews and Jewish Topics in the Soviet Union and Eastern Europe*, vol.11, no.1, 1990, pp.63–5.
89. Z. Ivinskis (1965) 'Lithuania During the War: Resistance Against the Soviet and Nazi Occupation', in: V.S. Vardys, ed., *Lithuania Under the Soviets: Portrait of a Nation, 1940–1965*. London: Frederick A. Praeger, pp.68–76.
90. It is also reprinted in D. Levin (1994), pp.116–55.
91. D. Levin (1975) 'Participation of the Lithuanian Jews in the Second World War', *Journal of Baltic Studies*, vol.6, no.4, p.310, footnote 15. See also: A. Lieven (1994), pp.150–1. S. Ycikas (1990) 'Introduction to Lithuanian–Jewish Relations in the Shadow of the Holocaust', *Jews and Jewish Topics in the Soviet Union and Eastern Europe*, vol.11, no.1, p.35.
92. Among 986 industries which were nationalised, 560 (57 per cent) belonged to the Jews. D. Levin (1975), p.309, footnote 6. Y. Litvak (1991) 'The Plight of Refugees from the German-Occupied Territories', p.65, in: K. Sword, ed., *The Soviet Takeover of the Polish Eastern Provinces, 1939–1941*. London: Macmillan in association with the School of Slavonic and East European Studies, University of London.
93. D. Levin (1994), p.144.
94. M.M. Laserson (1941) 'The Jewish Minorities in the Baltic Countries', *Jewish Social Studies*, vol.3, pp.282–4.
95. This was not acknowledged in the official Soviet and even present day Lithuanian history (S. Atamukas (1990) *Jews in Lithuania*, pp.148–9). These Zionist groups which later formed a resistance movement were treated as 'antifascist fighting organizations' and not as independent non-communist organisations. 'New Lithuanian's Old Policy Toward the Holocaust', *Jews in Eastern Europe*, no.2, pp.20–1.
96. Interview with Harry (Herschel) Gordon, then a Jewish boy in Kaunas, in: A. Lieven (1994), p.149.
97. Ibid., pp.149–50. 'According to data of the Lithuanian Security Service, on the eve of the Second World War, the Communist party of Lithuania had only 600–650 members.' A. Terliackas (1990) 'No Justification for the Murder of the Lithuanian Jews', *Jews and Jewish Topics in the Soviet Union and Eastern Europe*, vol.11, no.1, p.48.
98. D. Levin (1975), p.310, footnote 15.
99. Under the Lithuanian Jews we understand not only the Jews from the territory of the inter-war independent Lithuania but also the Jews from the Vilnius region. In 1939 there were 55 000 Jews in Vilnius or 25 per cent of its population. *Jewish Social Studies: Supplement* (1946), vol.8, no.3, p.65.

100. A powerful and disturbing account of the Kaunas ghetto is given by a survivor A. Tory (1990) *Surviving the Holocaust: the Kovno Ghetto Diary*. Cambridge, Mass.: Harvard University Press. Another survivor gave an account from a historico-sociological point of view. S. Gringauz (1949) 'The Ghetto as an Experiment of Jewish Social Organization: Three Years of Kovno Ghetto', *Jewish Social Studies*, vol.11, no.1, pp.3–20.

101. D. Levin (1991), p.58. The LAF was established on 17 November 1940 in Berlin by the Lithuanian nationalist who had fled from the Soviet rule on the initiative of Kazys Skirpa, former Lithuanian Ambassador to Germany. See also: T. Venclova (1995) 'A Fifth Year of Independence: Lithuania, 1922 and 1994', *East European Politics and Society*, vol.9, no.2, pp.365–6. See more details about the charter itself in: I. Cohen (5704-1943) *Vilna*. Philadelphia: The Jewish Publication Society of America, pp.7–10.

102. The answer of Jonas Matulionis, Finance Minister in the Lithuanian Provisional Government, to the question by a Jewish representative why he could not do nothing to prevent the killings and why, therefore, the Jews should be moved to the ghetto. A. Lieven (1994), p.152.

103. In 1952 a new edition, critical and revised, was published in the United States clearly stating that this research employed falsified statistics and partial information. D. Levin (1994), p.353.

104. T.W. Adorno *et al.* (1950) *The Authoritarian Personality*. New York: Harper and Row, p.609.

105. He is the very same person who decided to receive and said to a delegation of Jews who came to ask him for help in late 1941: 'The Church cannot help you. I personally can only weep and pray.' D. Levin (1994), p.373.

106. Ibid., p.365.

107. Interview with M. Jakobas, 4 November 1992. 'Only occasionally Lithuanians would raise the issue of the Holocaust and say that they are sorry for what their nation did to mine.' He was President of the Jewish Community of Vilnius.

108. Interview with G. Kanovich, 5 November 1992. 'Only some people in Lithuania are anti-Semitic. Some of them are very influential.' He was President of the Lithuanian Jewish Community and a writer.

109. Interview with A. Ploksto, 5 November 1992. He was a member of the Union of Poles and its MP in the period 1992–6. In the 1996 elections he ran as an LDDP candidate and won a seat.

110. J. Hiden and P. Salmon (1994), p.56.

111. Interview with V. Jarmolenka, 15 December 1992. He was a Russian, a member of *Sajudis* and since 1993, the Homeland Union.

112. Interview with R. Zepkaite, 24 June 1993. She was a historian at the Institute of Lithuanian History.

113. R. Zepkaite pointed out that Vilnius University was closed down because it used only Polish while the Polish primary and secondary schools were left open as well as their cultural institutions. See also: D.M. Crowe (1993) *The Baltic States and the Great Powers: Foreign Relations, 1938–1940*. Boulder, Col.: Westview Press, p.143 and p.230, footnote 22.

114. See the more detailed account of the Old Believers' culture in V. Baranovskii (1989) 'Kitezh-Grad (Kitezh Town)'. *Vilnius*, no.8, pp.140–56.

115. A. Lieven (1994), p.182.

116. Interview with N. Medvedev, 26 November 1992. He was a Russian, a former member of *Sajudis*, and a member of the Social Democratic Party and its MP.
117. A. Lieven (1994), p.182. S. Vaitiekus (1992) 'National Minorities in Lithuania: Russians in Lithuania', *Galve*, 11 September 1992, p.3. (*Galve* is a newspaper in Russian of the Vilnius region.) Interview with I. Arefjeva, 10 December 1992. She was a President of the Russian orthodox organisation *Zhivoi kolos*.
118. H. Arendt (1950), pp.272–3. C.A. Macartney (1934), pp.276–7.

3 Opposition Movements and the Birth of the Lithuanian National Movement

1. Interview with V. Efremov, 9 November 1992. He was a member of *Sajudis*.
2. Interview with J. Marcinkevicius, 3 December 1992. He was a former member of *Sajudis*. Some people pointed out that 'he was expelled from *Sajudis* because he, *our* pride, was too honest'.
3. The exception were mostly the Lithuanian and Jewish émigré communities.
4. P. Kostloe (1995) *Russians in the Former Soviet Republics*. London: C. Hurst and Co., p.91.
5. In Lithuania, however, only a few minor party figures and academics were either dismissed or arrested and tried. Purges took place in Latvia and some Central Asian and Caucasian states. In 1959 Eduards Berklavs and nearly 2000 party and government officials were purged in Latvia because of the promotion of the Latvian language. J. Dreifelds (1989) 'Latvian National Rebirth', *Problems of Communism*, vol.38, no.4, p.78.
6. The Brezhnev era saw a tightening of centralist efforts while Lenin argued for self-administration of the state organs and the economy in federal republics. See: P. Kostloe (1995), p.91 and G. Simon (1991) *Nationalism and Policy Towards the Nationalities in the Soviet Union: From Totalitarian Dictatorship to Post-Stalinist Society*. Boulder, Col.: Westview Press, p.73.
7. G. Simon (1991), p.282. Lithuania is a land of poets. Poetry has always played a very important role in the process of national awakening. As Maironis was both a poet and symbol of national awakening in the last century, Marcinkevicius is a poet and symbol of national awakening today. He was the one who opened the First Congress of *Sajudis*, his poetry was published in the first *Sajudis* bulletin, his books of poetry have been bestsellers for the last 40 years.
8. This statement also shows that *Sajudis* was turning into a myth.
9. See detailed analyses of the Forest Brothers and the exile in Siberia in: R. Misiunas and R. Taagepera (1993) *The Baltic States: the Years of Dependence*. London: C. Hurst and Company, pp.39–43, pp.83–94 and pp.99–100. See also short but good summary in: A. Shtromas (1996) 'The Baltic States as Soviet Republics: Tensions and Contradictions', in: G. Smith, ed., *The Baltic States: National Self-determination of Estonia, Latvia and Lithuania*. Basingstoke: Macmillan, pp. 86–97.

10. R. Brubaker (1996) *Nationalism Reframed: Nationhood and the National Question in the New Europe*. Cambridge: Cambridge University Press, p.29 (italics by the author).
11. P. Kolstoe (1995), p.2.
12. Peter Reddaway argued in 1983 that different currents of dissent are 'the seedbeds of future political opposition'. P. Reddaway (1983) 'Dissent in the Soviet Union', *Problems of Communism*, vol.32, no.6, p.15.
13. H. Carrere d'Encausse (1995) *The Nationality Question in the Soviet Union*. Oslo: Scandinavian University Press, pp.34–5.
14. H. Carrere d'Encausse (1995), pp.31–48. J. Chinn and R. Kaiser (1996) *Russians as the New Minority: Ethnicity and Nationalism in the Soviet Successor States*. Boulder, Col.: Westview Press, pp.65–90.
15. Ch. Doersam (1977) 'Sovietization, Culture and Religion', in: E. Allworth, ed., *Nationality Group Survival in Multi-Ethnic States: Shifting Support Patterns in the Soviet Baltic Region*. London: Frederick A. Praeger Publishers, p.149.
16. N. Sadomskaia (1990) 'New Soviet Rituals and National Integration in the USSR', in: H.R. Huttenbach, ed., *Soviet Nationality Policies: Ruling Ethnic Groups in the USSR*. London: Mansell Publishing Ltd, pp.94–120.
17. Vardys states 'a "new communist men" … means a collectivist, atheistic Russophile, unreservedly loyal to the Party and to Moscow directed state'. V.S. Vardys (1965) *Lithuania Under the Soviets: Portrait of the Nation, 1940–1965*. London: Frederick A. Praeger Publishers, p.238.
18. The first experiments began in Latvia and Ukraine. 'Under Khrushchev the tendency of the rituals was more anti-religious; later, under Brezhnev, the struggle against separatist tendencies assumed primary importance.' In: N. Sadomskaia (1990), p.96.
19. 'Integration of various ethnic groups through common ceremonies has hardly been achieved. But if the aim was the destruction of old links, the atomisation of religious and ethnic communities that were at one time united, and the withdrawal of ritual life from the family, then here the plan has been more successful.' Ibid., p.116.
20. The national intelligentsia was quite hostile towards the new rituals (understood as ceremonies, festivals and holidays) either openly arguing against them (like the Ukrainian author, Valentin Moroz in 1968) or trying to prove that existing holidays are not linked with religion (as the Lithuanian intelligentsia did, drawing on the pre-Christian era).
21. R. Krooth and B. Vladimirovitz (pseudonym) (1993) *Quest for Freedom: the Transformation of Eastern Europe in the 1990s*. London: McFarland and Company, p.6.
22. 'Our studies of nationalities dissent and state response to it during the period 1965–81 is based on accounts of individuals who were active nationalities dissenters in this period.' T.C. Smith and T.A. Oleszczuk (1990) 'The Brezhnev Legacy: Nationalities and Gorbachev', in: Z. Gitelman, ed., *The Politics of Nationality and the Erosion of the USSR*. New York: St. Martin's Press, p.27. In footnote 10 they list 10 different sources of data, pp.47–8. Smith and Oleszczuk's file for the period 1965–81 consists of 594 cases. The validity of these data should be questioned from the point of view of sources, bias and representativeness as the author himself is doing. However, except for the 'purists', social scientists argued that these types of

data should have been used bearing in mind 'the limitations of coverage, bias and representativeness'. In: T.A. Oleszczuk (1988) *Political Justice in the USSR: Dissent and Repression in Lithuania, 1969–1987*. Boulder, Col.: Westview Press (East European Monographs), p.210. See also: T.A. Oleszczuk (1985) 'An Analysis of Bias in *Samizdat* Sources: a Lithuanian Case Study', *Soviet Studies*, vol.37, no.1, pp.131–7.

23. T.C. Smith and T.A. Oleszczuk (1990), pp.28–30.
24 A. Shtromas (1996), p.98.
25. T.C. Smith and T.A. Oleszczuk (1990), p.32. M. Feshbach (1982) 'The Soviet Union: Population Trends and Dilemmas', *Population Bulletin*, vol.37, no.2, p.10, quoted in: T.C. Smith and T.A. Oleszczuk (1990), p.34.
26. Ibid., pp.28–30. This finding also confirms the leading role of the intelligentsia discussed in Chapter 2 and above.
27. T.C. Smith and T.A. Oleszczuk (1990), pp.38–9.
28. T.A. Oleszczuk (1988), pp.33–68. D. Kowalewski (1979) 'Lithuanian Protest for Human Rights in the 1970s: Characteristics and Consequences', *Lituanus*, vol.25, no.2, pp.43–57. His research does not deal directly with reasons for discontent.
29. T.A. Oleszczuk (1988), p.56.
30. Doersam argues that through the *Chronicle of the Catholic Church in Lithuania* 'a connecting link between the nationality and religious dissatisfaction in Lithuania and the general Soviet human rights movement seems to be established'. Ch. Doersam (1977) 'Sovietization, Culture and Religion', in: E. Allworth, ed., *Nationality Group Survival in Multi-Ethnic States*. London: Praeger, p.182.

    The *Chronicle of the Catholic Church in Lithuania* was the most famous and major journal of the Lithuanian national movement (established in March 1972) in the Soviet period whose aim was to inform the world outside the former Soviet Union about the religious and national rights or lack of them in Lithuania.
31. Reddaway argues that Catholicism gave Lithuanian nationalism strength and, therefore, makes dissent endemic and ineradicable. P. Reddaway (1983), p.11.
32. Valancius encouraged and supported secret schools which educated children in catechism in native Lithuanian. He organised the printing of prayerbooks and other religious books in Latin characters. The books were printed in East Prussia (Lithuania Minor) and smuggled into Lithuania (Lithuania Major). He played an extremely important role in stimulating his fellow clerics to develop an interest in Lithuanian culture and he encouraged the use of the Lithuanian language within the Church.
33. D. Kowalewski (1979), p. 43.
34. Vardys stresses, 'The *Chronicle of the Catholic Church of Lithuania* quickly became not only the spokesman for religious interests and for the religious sector of society, but also an uncensored national voice for articulating a secular civil rights philosophy as well as national interests.' V.S. Vardys (1987) 'The Role of the Churches in the Baltic Republics', *Journal of Baltic Studies*, vol.28, no.3, p.295.
35. On 5 January 1975 Radio Liberty started to broadcast to Lithuania in Lithuanian. From March onwards there were daily broadcasts. G.H. Flanz

(1992) 'Lithuania', in: A.P. Blaustein and G.H. Flanz, eds, *Constitutions of the Countries of the World*. New York: Oceania Publications, p.13.

36. In 1976 *Ausra* (Dawn) and *Dievas ir tevyne* (God and Homeland), in 1977 *Varpas* (Bell), in 1978 *Ausrele* (Little Dawn) and *Perspectyvos* (Perspectives), in 1979 *Alma Mater* and *Vytis* (The Knight), in 1980 *Tautos Kelias* (The Nation's Path) were founded. G. Simon (1991), p.340.

37. T.A. Oleszczuk (1988), p.54. See also: 'Current Constitutional and Factual Condition of Religion in Lithuania (As Reflected in Official and *Samizdat* Documents)', *Lituanus*, 1979, vol.25, no.1, pp.46–72.

38. Interview with L. Bielinis, 6 November 1992. He was a member of the Party of Centre and works as a professional for the Party at its Department for Political Questions. He was a political scientist. Vytautas Landsbergis was the Leader of *Sajudis* and after 1993, the Leader of the Homeland Union.

39. A. Shtromas (1996), p.98 and p.114, footnote 30.

40. Ibid., p.101.

41. Ibid., p.99.

42. Interview with G. Kirkilas, 23 November 1992. He was a former member of the Communist Party of Lithuania, Vice-President of the LDDP, MP. His use of language should be noted in connection with his interpretation of history. In December 1989 the Communist Party reorganised itself. It declared itself to be a social-democratic party and changed its name to the Lithuanian Democratic Workers Party (LDDP).

43. Interview with J. Karosas, 28 October 1992. He was a former member of the Communist Party of Lithuania, a member of the LDDP, MP.

44. S. Bialer (1980) *Stalin's Successors: Leadership, Stability and Change in the Soviet Union*. Cambridge: Cambridge University Press, pp.216–17.

45. A. Shtromas (1978) 'Baltic Problems and Peace Studies', *Journal of Baltic Studies*, vol.9, no.1, p.5. R. Medvedev (1980) *On Soviet Dissent: Interviews with Piero Ostellino*. New York: Columbia University Press, p.124. One type of support was also financial. A. Solzhenitcin established the Russian Social Fund out of the profits from his book *Gulag Archipelago*. That fund gave some 2500 rubles to the families of Lithuanian political prisoners. D. Kowalewski (1979) 'Lithuanian Protest for Human Rights in the 1970s: Characteristics and Consequences', *Lituanus*, vol.25, no.2, p.54.

46. V.S. Vardys (1978) *The Catholic Church, Dissent and Nationality in Soviet Lithuania*. Boulder, Col.: Westview Press, p.154. However, he mentions 'Moscow's dissidents who helped the Lithuanians'. Ibid., p.184.

47. J. Chinn and R. Kaiser (1996), p.12. Misiunas also argues that most Balts assume 'a near-universal identification of all matters Soviet with Russia and Russians'. R.J. Misiunas (1994) 'National Identity and Foreign Policy in the Baltic States', in: S.F. Starr, ed., *The Legacy of History in Russia and the New States of Euroasia*. London: M.E. Sharpe, p.95.

48. A. Shtromas (1996), p.115, footnotes 38 and 40.

49. Originally Lithuania was not included in the Soviet sphere of influence but according to the agreement concluded on 28 September 1939 it was given to the Soviet Union when 'the Soviet Union renounced its claim to all Polish territory west of the 1919 Curzon Line in exchange for absolute control of Lithuania'. Georg von Rauch (1974) *The Baltic States: the Years of*

Independence. London: C. Hurst and Company, p.209. See also D. Kirby (1996) 'Incorporation: the Molotov–Ribbentrop Pact', in: G. Smith, ed., *The Baltic States: the National Self-Determination of Estonia, Latvia and Lithuania*. Basingstoke: Macmillan, pp.69–85.

50. FBIS-SOV-89-149, 4 August 1989, pp.68–9.

51. I understand Sovietisation as a process primarily connected with the development of the leading role of the Communist Party and its influence on all spheres of the social system and individual life. Russification is primarily connected with the role the Russian language played in implementing the policies of Sovietisation.

52. Interview with R. Ozolas, 27 November 1992. He was a founding member of *Sajudis*, deputy Chairman of its National Council responsible for ideology, deputy Prime Minister under Kazimiera Prunskiene, philosopher by education, book editor and editor of *Atgimimas* (Rebirth), a *Sajudis* newspaper. He was a member of the Communist Party and adviser to its Central Committee. He left *Sajudis* and founded the Party of Centre.

53. It should be noted that officers of the Soviet Army were allowed in retirement to choose their place of living. Furthemore, many people were happy to move to Lithuania, and the other two Baltic states, because of the higher standard of living.

54. V.S. Vardys (1981a) 'Human Rights Issues in Estonia, Latvia and Lithuania', *Journal of Baltic Studies*, vol.12, no.3, p.280.

55. Here two cases can be mentioned: the Simon Kudirka one and the Romas Kalanta one. Kudirka's attempt to defect to the USA triggered Jerzy Kosinski to write a play *Cockpit* which raised very interesting issues (especially in connection with dissidents) of individualism, self-reliance and no group affiliation. See: M. Kupcinskas Keshawarz, 'Simas Kudirka: a Literary Symbol of Democratic Individualism in Jerzy Kosinski's "Cockpit" ', *Lituanus*, 1979, vol.25, no.4, pp.38–42. Kalanta burnt himself to death in May 1972 demanding independence for Lithuania. A. Lieven (1994), p.104.

56. Interview with R. Ozolas, 27 November 1992 (emphasis by the respondent). The conference entitled 'The Russian Language is the Language of Friendship and Co-operation of the USSR Peoples' was held in May 1979 in Tashkent to propagandise the October 1978 Decree. According to that decree Russian was to be studied in smaller classes, permission was given to study Russian at the expense of other subjects in the curriculum, a right was granted to use Russian in higher educational institutions, different types of technical aid were to be introduced, proposals to encourage the training and retraining of Russian-language teachers and the creation of new faculties at higher educational institutions were made. J. Pennar (1981) 'Current Soviet Nationality Policies', *Journal of Baltic Studies*, vol.12, no.1, p.7.

57. P. Goble (1989) 'Ethnic Politics in the USSR', *Problems of Communism*, vol.38, no.4, p.9.

58. C. Thompson (1992), p.23. G. Hosking (1992) *A History of the Soviet Union, 1917–1991* (final edition). London: Fontana Press, pp.486–9.

59. E. Vilkas, 'Lithuania-Interlink of West Europe and Russia' (mimeograph) and 'Economic Reform in Lithuania' (mimeograph). Given to me by the author in 1992. Eduardas Vilkas, as a Secretary of the Lithuanian Academy

of Sciences, was in charge of the commission which was formed to propose changes in the Lithuanian Constitution in 1988 and when the commission met on 3 June 1988 the 'unintended result' of the meeting was the formation of *Sajudis*.

60. From a booklet given to me at *Sajudis* Headquarters in Vilnius in October 1992, p.33.

61. M. McAuley (1992) *Soviet Politics 1917–1991*. Oxford: Oxford University Press, p.94. See also: V.S. Vardys (1991) '*Sajudis*: National Revolution in Lithuania', in: J.A. Trapans, ed., *Towards Independence: the Baltic Popular Movements*. Boulder, Col.: Westview Press, pp.11–23.

62. As a young Latvian argued: 'A whole generation grew up in silence.' Finally, they were able to voice their opinion. C. Thompson (1992) *The Singing Revolution: a Political Journey through the Baltic States*. London: Michael Joseph, p.85.

63. Most of them grew up in the shadow of the Khrushchev 'airing' and were called 'the children of the 20th Party Congress'.

64. C. Thompson (1992) quotes one Estonian historian who said: '*Glasnost* means winning back *our* history of the war', p.51 (emphasis mine).

65. The best example is the reforms proposed by Gorbachev at the 19th Party Conference in July 1988. He argued for the reforms of the Soviet and governmental structures which would introduce the division of power. However, the Party was still to retain power and authority.

66. Brazauskas was elected as First Secretary (from the position of Central Committee Secretary for Industry) on 20 October 1988.

67. V.S. Vardys (1989) 'Lithuanian National Politics', *Problems of Communism*, vol.38, no.4, p.61.

68. The organisational structure of *Sajudis* is as follows: local committees (four different types: territorial, workplace, professional associations, operational/activity organisations), the Congress, the *Seimas* (Assembly) and the National Council.

69. T. Parming (1977) shows that the number of eponymous nationality in the Communist Party of Lithuania was rising: 1945 – 31.8 per cent, 1953 – 38.0 per cent, 1959 – 55.7 per cent, 1970 – 67.1 per cent, 1973 – 69.1 per cent ('Roots of Nationality Differences', in: E. Allworth (1990), p.51). Vardys (1990) argues that it was since the 1970s always around 70 per cent; in early 1989, 70.7 per cent ('Lithuanians', in: G. Smith, ed., *The Nationalities Question in the Soviet Union*. London: Longman, p. 77).

70. O. Norgaard *et al.* (1996) *The Baltic States After Independence*. Cheltenham: Edward Elgar, p.41. See also: S. Bialer (1980), pp.213–14; J. Dreifelds (1989) p.78; T. Rakowska-Harmstone (1985) 'Die Aktuelle Problematik sowjetischer Nationalitaetenpolitic', *Osteuropa*, vol.35, p.500.

71. Eduardas Esmuntas, in charge of the Lithuanian branch of the KGB, argues that between 1961 and 1985 there were actions taken against only 84 criminal acts in connection with anti-Soviet propaganda. After 1985 not a single one. *Lietuvos rytas*, 16–23 April 1993, p.5.

72. A. Shtromas (1996), p.101.

73. J. Rothschild (1981) argues that there is a general tendency toward the politisation of ethnicity. 'Politized ethnicity has become the crucial principle of political legitimation and delegitimation of systems, states, regimes, and

governments and at the same time has also become an effective instrument for pressing mundane interests in society's competition for power, status and wealth.' *Ethnopolitics: a Conceptual Framework*. New York: Columbia University Press, p.2.

74. A. Shtromas (1996), pp.98–9. Furthermore, a Lithuanian anthropologist told me that, according to prevalent ethnic stereotypes, Snieckus came from the region of book smugglers and therefore knew how to get his message across without making it too obvious. According to the conversation with Vitys Ciubrinskas, a cultural anthropologist from Vilnius, London, 28 October 1996. While it is difficult to assess the role of ethnic stereotypes in this context, they are certainly an important part of national ideology, simply because people produce them and believe in them.

75. This model is based upon research of the Crozier, Worms and Thoening school of organisational sociology which was carried out with the aim of understanding problems of personnel management and employee satisfaction within the organisation. See: M. Crozier (1966) *The Bureaucratic Phenomenon*. Chicago: Chicago University Press.

76. S. Tarrow (1977) *Between Centre and Periphery: Grassroot Politicians in Italy and France*. New Haven: Yale University Press, p.29.

77. T.H. Rigby (1986) 'Was Stalin a Disloyal Patron?', *Soviet Studies*, vol.38, no.3, p.315.

78. R. Karklins (1986) *Ethnic Relations in the USSR*. Boston: Allen and Unwin, pp.50–5.

79. R.J. Brym (1988) 'Soviet Jewish Emigration: a Statistical Test of Two Theories', *Soviet Jewish Affairs*, vol.18, no.3, p.16.

80. R. Dahrendorf (1959) argues that 'Within the frame of reference of this model, (1) the distribution of authority in associations is the ultimate "cause" of the formation of conflict groups, and (2) being dichotomous, it is, in any given association, the cause of the formation of two, and only two, conflict groups.' *Class and Class Conflict in Industrial Society*. London: Routledge and Kegan Paul, pp.172–3.

81. L.A. Coser (1956) concludes after analysing 16 propositions 'that conflict tends to be dysfunctional for a social structure in which there is no or insufficient toleration and institutionalisation of conflict. The intensity of a conflict which threatens to "tear apart", which attacks the consensual basis of a social system, is related to the rigidity of the structure.' *The Functions of Social Conflict*. London: Routledge and Kegan Paul, p.157.

82. T. Venclova (1995) 'A Fifth Year of Independence: Lithuania, 1922 and 1994', *East European Politics and Society*, vol.9, no.2, p.348. Venclova is borrowing the concept mandarin from Leonidas Donskis and it describes the new intelligentsia that mostly became political elite. Tomas Venclova was a Lithuanian émigré not by choice; his passport was withdrawn when he visited the USA. He is today a Lithuanian citizen, a poet living in USA.

83. G. Efremov (1990) *My ljudi drug drugu* (We See Each Other as Human Beings). Moscow: Progress, p.168.

84. On 22 October 1988 'Lithuanian authorities return St Kazimeras Church and allow the construction of a church in one of the new suburbs of Vilnius. ... Cardinal Sladkevicius states that in spite of the offer from Lithuanian authorities permitting the use of the cathedral for one day

(23 October) the Church will not be a guest in their own cathedral. Brazauskas reconsiders and announces that the cathedral will also be returned.' *Sajudis* Documents (1989). Vilnius, pp.53–4.

85. On 17–18 November 1988 '*Sajudis* accuses the Communist leadership of using crude procedural manoeuvres to block a vote on a statement of Lithuanian sovereignty. … 10,000 demonstrators show their displeasure with the deputies by spitting on them and calling them "traitors" and "boot lickers". … In an attempt to defuse the situation the authorities point to their final legalisation of the Lithuanian Flag, National Anthem, and the Lithuanian Language.' Ibid., p.55.

86. Viktoras Petkus, Father Sigitas Tamkevicius, a member of the Lithuanian Catholic Committee in Defence of Religious Rights, Gintautas Iesmantas, a former Marxist and national right activist and Balys Gajauskas. Ibid., p.55.

87. FBIS-SOV-89-246, 26 December 1989, p.33. It should be noted that those who supported the Law argued that it is needed as an instrument in 'the defence of human rights, particularly the rights of national minorities'. See also: P. Goble (1989), p.4.

88. A small group of Party members did not agree with this decision and stayed organised in a Communist Party loyal to the Union.

89. In 1990, 99 MPs were either *Sajudis* candidates or elected with the support of *Sajudis*. In the 1992 elections the LDDP won 73 seats out of 141. *Sajudis* won only 30 seats.

90. Interview with A. Juozaitis, 11 December 1992. He was a philosopher who left *Sajudis* in 1991 to form the Future Forum (together with other well-known former members of *Sajudis* such as, for example, Kazimiera Prunskiene), a political association which was vocal in its criticism of *Sajudis*. The so-called Kaunas faction in the struggle for independence against the Soviet rule, pushed for Kaunas to be given again the status of Lithuanian capital because it is 'the pure home of the race'. See: Chapter 2, section on anti-Semitism.

91. N. Lomaniene (1994), p.28.

92. That was seen as one significant cause for losing elections in 1992. Others were: it closed its ranks, was not critical enough towards those who dragged back into the past, a lack of co-operation between the central and regional, city and village offices, some members being connected with the KGB, some corrupted. FBIS-SOV-92-235, 7 December 1992, p.40.

93. Landsbergis argued that he did not have either the time or the ability to transform *Sajudis* into a political party. However, my impression during the interview was that he wanted to keep power. He accused people who formed political parties of not being able to accept that they were not leaders. Interview with V. Landsbergis, 24 November 1992. He was the Leader of *Sajudis* and after 1993, the Leader of the Homeland Union.

94. Interview with A. Kuliesius, 29 October 1992. He was the Leader of the Lithuanian Liberal Union.

95. See: *Basic Documents of the Second Congress of Sajudis*. Vilnius, 1990. Given to me at the *Sajudis* Headquarters in Vilnius.

96. Interview with L. Bielinis, 6 November 1992. According to my interviews 13 out of 35 members of the National Council elected in 1988 withdrew

from politics up to the period of the Second Congress of the *Sajudis* mostly because they were not satisfied with its nationalistic orientation.

97. It is difficult to judge if Landsbergis changed because of the pressure from the right or because he himself realised that the right-wing ideology could fulfil his ambitions. I would agree with Lieven that right-wing ideology could allow him to fulfil his ideal to be the Father of the Nation.

98. I base my analysis of these events on my interviews. See also: A. Lieven (1994), pp.214–63. V.S. Vardys and J.B. Sedaitis (1997) *Lithuania: the Rebel Nation*. Boulder, Col.: Westview Press, p.152.

98. FBIS-SOV-89-246, 26 December 1989, p.145–99.

99. The Soviet blockade was imposed on Lithuania in April 1990 as a result of the Lithuanian decision to declare independence. Lithuania was sealed off and its economy suffered. See: V.S. Vardys and J.B. Sedaitis (1997), p.166.

100. Ibid., p.195.

101. 'A Lithuanian Army officer grumbled: On Monday, you turn on the television – Landsbergis. On Tuesday, you turn on the radio – Landsbergis. On Wednesday, you open the newspaper – Landsbergis. On Thursday, you are afraid to open a tin of fish!' A. Lieven (1994), p.258.

102. FBIS-SOV-91-241, 17 December 1991, p.36.

103. *Golos Litvi: Zerkalo Litovskoi Presi*, 11–17 November 1992, p.4.

104. A. Lieven (1994), p.258.

105. According to V.S. Vardys (1965) it should be pointed out that the percentage of Russians in the Lithuanian Communist Party was, in the 1960s, two times higher (20 per cent) than the percentage of Russians in the population of Lithuania (9 per cent). In: *Lithuania Under the Soviets: Portrait of the Nation, 1940–1965*. London: Frederick A. Praeger Publishers, p.243. In 1989 30 per cent of the members of the Lithuanian Communist Party were non-Lithuanians. V.S. Vardys (1990), p.77.

106. Interview with L. Bielinis, 6 November 1992.

107. Interview with A. Juozaitis, 11 December 1992.

108. Interview with G. Kirkilas, 23 November 1992.

109. A. Lieven (1994), p.239. V.S. Vardys and J.B. Sedaitis (1997), p.155.

110. Interview with R. Ozolas, 27 November 1992.

111. In the 1992–6 Lithuanian Parliament there were six Poles, three Russians and one Jew. From a document 'Breakdown of Deputies by Nationality', given to me in November 1992 in the Lithuanian Parliament.

112. Landsbergis saw himself as a representative of a Lithuanian nation and thought that, therefore, he should stay in power. Interview with A. Juozaitis, 11 December 1992.

113. R. Brubaker (1996), pp.83–4.

4 The Issue of Citizenship in Lithuania: Legislation and the Ways it was Perceived

1. According to D.J. Harris (1979) *Cases and Material on International Law*. London: Sweet and Maxwell, p.499.

2. It is a well-known fact that minority rights were swept under the carpet in the light of the Third Reich's aggression against Czechoslovakia and Poland. Both countries were unable and unwilling to give up concessions under the constant pressure of their German minorities and therefore, enabled the Reich to start the Second World War.

3. The International Bill of Human Rights is based on the four instruments: Universal Declaration of Human Rights (1948), International Covenant of Economic, Social and Cultural Rights (1966), the International Covenant on Civil and Political Rights (1966) and its two Optional Protocols (1966 and 1989). Sometimes a fifth instrument is added, the International Convention on the Elimination of All Forms of Racial Discrimination. E. Lawson (1996) *Encyclopaedia of Human Rights*, second edition. London: Taylor and Francis, p.806.

4. T. Lindholm (1992a) 'Multi-ethnic Societies and Human Rights'. Paper for the Conference on 'Democracy and Ethnopolitics', Riga, Latvia, 19–21 May 1992, p.3.

5. E. Nekrasas (1993) 'Lithuania and Her Neighbours', in: N. Petersen, ed., *The Baltic States in International Politics*. Copenhagen: The Danish Institute of International Studies, p.48.

6. Interview with R. Ozolas, 27 November 1992. He was a founding member of *Sajudis*. He left *Sajudis* and founded the Party of Centre. The Russian military forces left Lithuania, as agreed, on 31 August 1993.

7. All of these laws are published by the publishing house of the Lithuanian Parliament in English translation in the *Selected Anthology of Institutional, Economic and Financial Legislation* or in different issues of the Parliamentary Record.

8. The Provisional Basic Law of the Republic of Lithuania, in: *Selected Anthology of Institutional, Economic and Financial Legislation* (1991), p.7.

9. Ibid., Article 16, p.8.

10. Ibid., Article 23, p.9.

11. Ibid., Article 30, p.10.

12. Ibid., Article 44, p.12.

13. *The Draft Constitution of the Republic of Lithuania* (1992). Vilnius: Publishing House of the Supreme Council of the Republic of Lithuania, Article 29, p.8.

14. Ibid., p.10.

15. Ibid., Article 45, p.11. This Constitution was approved on 25 October 1992 by 75.4 per cent of the votes or 56.8 per cent of the electorate. V.S. Vardys and J.B. Sedaitis (1997) *Lithuania: the Rebel Nation*. Boulder, Col.: Westview Press, p.206.

16. 'Article 38. The family shall be the basis of society and the State.' *The Draft Constitution of the Republic of Lithuania* (1992), p.10. A. Lieven (1994) *The Baltic Revolution: Estonia, Latvia, Lithuania and the Path to Independence*. New Haven: Yale University Press, p.265.

17. Interview with R. Ozolas, 27 November 1992.

18. Interview with V. Cepaitis, 1 December 1992. He was a former member of *Sajudis* and its first National Council with responsibility towards national minorities issues. He had to resign because of his connections with the KGB.

19. *The Draft Constitution of the Republic of Lithuania* (1992), Article 43, p.10.
20. Ibid., Article 36, p.9.
21. The Sociological Laboratory of Vilnius University conducted in September 1991 the research on citizenship among Russians and Poles. The results showed that 55 per cent of Russians and 52 per cent of Poles had made up their mind to become Lithuanian citizens, 35 per cent of Russians and 39 per cent of Poles were undecided and 9 per cent of Russians and 7 per cent of Poles decided not to acquire Lithuanian citizenship. When it comes to undecided Russians and Poles, 42 per cent of Russians and 67 per cent of Poles decided to stay in Lithuania, 15 per cent of Russians and 7 per cent of Poles decided to leave Lithuania and 43 per cent of Russians and 26 per cent of Poles were still considering the options. FBIS-SOV-91-198, 11 October 1991, p.39. Rasa Alisauskiene, Director of the Sociological Laboratory, argued that the research showed that the majority of national minorities decided to acquire Lithuanian citizenship. The major problem was that the people, especially Poles, 'mixed up nationality and citizenship'. She continued: 'one has also to bear in mind the role of the uprising for autonomy in the South-East of Lithuania' (as is discussed in Chapter 7). Interview with R. Alisauskiene, 24 June 1993. This requirement of the draft Law was contested by some public organisations in Lithuania who argued that a referendum should be held 'on the legitimacy of granting citizenship to people who have arrived in Lithuania after 15 June 1940'. FBIS-SOV-91-232, 3 December 1991, p.59.
22. Parliamentary Record, 1/1992. Vilnius: Supreme Council of the Republic of Lithuania, Article 1, p.2.
23. Ibid., Article 12, p.4.
24. L. Barrington (1995) 'The Domestic and International Consequences of Citizenship in the Soviet Successor States', *Europe–Asia Studies*, vol.47, no.5, p.734.
25. Parliamentary Record, 1/1992, Article 16, p.5.
26. *Selected Anthology of Institutional, Economic and Financial Legislation*, p.63. Parliamentary Record, 1/1992, p.4.
27. In this number are also included 40 000 Russians who acquired Lithuanian citizenship according to the Lithuanian–Russian Agreement which excluded them from meeting the language and ten years' residency requirements. O. Norgaard *et al.* (1996) *The Baltic States After Independence*. Cheltenham, UK: Edward Elgar, p.183.
28. R. Bernhardt and H. Schermers (1992) 'Lithuanian Law and International Human Rights Standards', *Human Rights Law Journal*, vol.13, no.5–6, p.253.
29. *Eho Litvi*, 11 June 1993, p.3. See also: L. Barrington (1995), p.734.
30. R. Bernhardt and H. Schermers (1992), p.252.
31. Interview with N. Kasatkina, 24 June 1993. She was a Russian sociologist at the Institute for Sociology, Philosophy and Law. See also: A. Lieven (1994), p.168.
32. Among Russians it was argued that there were already quite a lot of people with dual citizenship but they were Americans who got Lithuanian citizenship. Therefore, Russians addressed the dual citizenship argument as 'dual morality'.
33. However, at that point in time they were not aware that Russia would come up with the law which did not allow dual citizenship. The representative

of the Russian Embassy pointed out that in the Russian Citizenship Law there is a paragraph which states that this issue could be a part of a bilateral agreement between two states. Meeting organised by the Russian Society, 11 December 1992. *Lietuvos rytas*, 19–26 March 1993, p.8.

34. *Lietuvos rytas*, 28 May–4 June 1993, p.6.
35. L. Barrington (1995), p.735.
36. Before leaving for the United Nations Conference on Human Rights, Halina Kobeckaite argued that the Lithuanian government would not go along with such changes. Interview with H. Kobeckaite, 22 June 1993. She was the Director of the Department of National Minorities of the Government of the Republic of Lithuania.
37. R. Bernhardt and H. Schermers (1992), p.253.
38. E. Lawson (1996), p.1401.
39. *Eho Litvi*, 10 June 1993, p.3. *Selected Anthology of Institutional, Economic and Financial Legislation*, p.61.
40. Parliamentary Record, 1/1992, p.13.
41. The first Law on National Minorities became law on 23 November 1989.
42. It is in accordance with Article 27 of the International Covenant on Civil and Political Rights. E. Lawson (1996), p.816.
43. See: *National Minorities in Lithuania*. Vilnius: Department of Nationalities of the Government of the Republic of Lithuania, 1992, pp.29–31.
44. This is not legal language and, therefore, it could be interpreted in different ways and misused.
45. A. Lieven (1994), p.169.
46. Decree on Language, in *Selected Anthology of Institutional, Economic and Financial Legislation*, p.70.
47. Ibid., p.72.
48. Cepaitis points out that the Decree on Language is a good example of showing that *Sajudis* was less radical than the Supreme Council of *Seimas*. *Sajudis* was against introducing a time period to learn the language. 'I do not remember the details just the surprise when I heard about the Supreme Council decision.' Interview with V. Cepaitis, 1 December 1992.
49. Decree on Language, ibid., p.71.
50. See also: V.S. Vardys and J.B. Sedaitis (1997), p.209.
51. Lituanus Data Bank (1990). *Lituanus*, vol.36, no.1, p.91.
52. Law on Immigration. Parliamentary Record, 5/1992, p.11. This Law was ratified on 4 September 1991.
53. Interview with E. Raisuotis, 21 June 1993. He was a member of the Committee on Human Rights and National Minorities in the Lithuanian government. Credit should be given to Raisuotis who openly spelled out that the quota was related to the immigration coming from the former Soviet Union.
54. See: Appendix: Demographic Data, Tables A1.3c and A1.3d.
55. For the first time I found the quota for 1998. It was 1000. *The Baltic Times*, 22–28 January 1998, p.7.
56. Law on the Employment of the Population, Parliamentary Record, 10/1992, p.2.
57. Law on the Legal Status of the Foreigners in the Republic of Lithuania, Parliamentary Record 5/1992, p.8.
58. R. Bernhardt and H. Schermers (1992), p.256.

59. Ibid., p.256.
60. See: J.B. Marie (1993) 'International Instruments Relating to Human Rights: Classification and Status of Ratifications as of 1 January 1993', *Human Rights Law Journal*, vol.14, no.1–2, pp.57–73.
61. R. Bernhardt and H. Schermers (1992), p.256.
62. Ibid., p.251.
63. Letter to the Minister of Foreign Affairs of Lithuania, HE Mr Povilas Gylys. *Human Rights Law Journal*, 1993, vol.14, no.5–6, p.221.
64. FBIS-SOV-93-031, 18 February 1993, p.75.
65. V.S. Vardys and J.B. Sedaitis (1997), p.209.
66. Those people were members of *Sajudis*, the Lithuanian Christian Democratic Party, the Centre Movement of Lithuania and the Lithuanian Independence Party. For the 1992 elections 17 parties, movements and party coalitions put forward their candidates for election.
67. Interview with M. Cobot(as), 2 December 1992. He was a Pole, a member of the Christian Democratic Party, MP and a doctor.
68. Interview with R. Ozolas, 27 November 1992.
69. Interview with V. Cepaitis, 1 December 1992.
70. Those members came from the Lithuanian Democratic Labour Party, the Lithuanian Social Democratic Party, the Lithuanian Liberal Union and the Union of Poles.
71. Interview with A. Plokszto, 15 June 1993. He was the Leader of the Union of Poles and MP. Interview with E. Raisuotis, 21 June 1993.
72. Interview with M. Stakvilevicius, 17 June 1993. He was a Chairperson of the Human Rights and National Minorities Committee at the Lithuanian Parliament. A large number of Lithuanians I interviewed agreed with his statement.
73. Interview with V. Jarmolenka, 15 December 1992. He was a Russian, MP, a member of *Sajudis* and after 1993 of the Homeland Union.
74. Interview with N. Sokolov, 18 June 1993. He was the Russian Vice-Ambassador to Lithuania.
75. Algirdas Kuliesius argued that after the introduction of the Law on Public Services in 1990 the people were chosen by *Sajudis* for all vital positions. Interview with A. Kuliesius, 29 October 1992. He was the Leader of the Lithuanian Liberal Union.
76. Interview with G. Kirkilas, 23 November 1992. He was the Deputy-Leader of the LDDP.
77. My own experience is the same. I was in a tram in Vilnius reading a Russian newspaper. I was addressed as 'These Russians who do not know Lithuanian,' and asked to show a ticket. I was shocked and first said in English: 'What!' and then continued in Russian. The person (man) realised that I was not Russian and jumped off the tram (which was fortunately still on the tram stop). Author's diary, 2 November 1992.
78. Interview with N. Medvedev, 26 November 1992. He was a Russian, a former member of *Sajudis*, a member of the Social Democratic Party and its MP.
79. Interview with G. Kirkilas, 22 June 1993.
80. Interview with J. Karosas, 28 October 1992. He was a member of LDDP and its MP.
81. Interview with N. Medvedev, 26 November 1992.

5   Introduction to Part II

1. E. Hobsbawn (1996) 'Language, Culture and National Identity', *Social Research*, vol.63, no.4, p.1067. See also L. Coley (1996) *Britons: Forging the Nation 1707–1837*. London: Vintage, p.6.
2. I recall spending quite a few nights listening to 'explanations' why a person was a good director – 'Of course, he is from Suvalkai' – or why he was stubborn – being from Zemaiciai – or why he was open-hearted – being from Dzukai. In these conversations ethnic stereotypes were accepted as a reality in their own right, not as constructs. See also: J. Kudirka (1991) *The Lithuanians: an Ethnic Portrait*. Vilnius: Lithuanian Folk Culture Centre.
3. VILMORUS in Lithuania, EMOR in Estonia and LASOPEC in Latvia.
4. Interview with Rasa Alisauskiene, 24 June 1993. She was a sociologist, in charge of the Sociological Laboratory at the University of Vilnius. She pointed out that according to the 'opinion polls the main basis to understand different answers was nationality.' Interview with J. Lakis, 3 November 1992. He was Head of the Centre for National Minorities, Teachers' Training College in Vilnius.
5. R. Rose and W. Maley (1994) *Nationalities in the Baltic States: a Survey Study*. Centre for the Study of Public Policy, University of Strathclyde, p.iv (italics by the author).
6. A. Aasland (1992) 'Russians in Latvia'. A paper presented at the conference 'The New Russian Diaspora'. Jurmala, Latvia, 12–15 November 1992.
7. See also: P. Kostlo (1996) 'The New Russian Diaspora – an Identity of its own? Possible Identity Trajectories for Russians in the former Soviet Republics', *Ethnic and Racial Studies*, vol.19, no.3, pp.609–39. V. Shlapentokh and M. Sendich (1994) Preface, in: V. Shlapentokh *et al.*, *The New Russian Diaspora: Russian Minorities in the Former Soviet Republics*. New York: M.E. Sharpe, p.xii.
8. V.S. Vardys (1975), pp.32–48.
9. A. Prazauskas (1994) 'The Influence of Ethnicity on the Foreign Policies of the Western Littoral States', in: R. Szporluk, ed., *National Identity and Ethnicity in Russia and the New States of Euroasia*. New York: M.E. Sharpe, p.160.

6   Russian Responses

1. R. Brubaker (1995) 'Aftermaths of Empire and the Unmixing of Peoples: Historical and Comparative Perspectives', *Ethnic and Racial Studies*, vol.18, no.2, pp.189–218.
2. *Collins English Dictionary* (1991) Glasgow: HarperCollins Publishers, p.10.
3. H. Pilkington (1998) *Migration, Displacement and Identity in Post-Soviet Russia*. London: Routledge, p.10.
4. During the seventeenth century the reforms in the Russian Orthodox Church pushed by Patriarch Nikon caused a schism which resulted in the foundation of a new sect: the Old Believers. The Patriarch was also ready to resort to their persecution. As a result there was an Orthodox migration to Lithuania (as well as to Latvia). According to my interview with an Old Believer his predecessors moved to Livonia because it was tolerant of different religions and

sects. At the beginning of the eighteenth century Peter the Great in the Great Northern War conquered Estland (north Estonia) and Livonia (southern Estonia and eastern Latvia) and established *de facto* control over the Duchy of Courland (present western Latvia). Although he followed the reformist rite in the Church he curtailed the power of the Patriarch and some of the Old Believers stayed in Livonia while a smaller number settled in the districts of Zarasai, Rokiskis and Kaunas (in present-day Lithuania). 'In all these places they were accepted in a civilised way.' Interview with V. Baranovskii, 15 December 1992. He was a Russian Old Believer and writer. His well-known novel about the Old Believers is *Kitezh-gorad* (Kitezh town).

5. J. Chinn and R. Kaiser (1996) 'Lithuanians', in: J. Chinn and R. Kaiser, *Russians as the New Minority: Ethnicity and Nationalism in the Soviet Successor States*. Boulder, Col.: Westview Press, p.117.
6. See: Appendix: Demographic Data, Tables 6, 7, 8a, 8b, 8c; and Education, Table 1.
7. Juozas Lakis argued that 'political point of view is a very important indicator in differentiating among different Russian groups'. Interview with J. Lakis, 3 November 1992. He was a sociologist, the Head of the Centre for National Minorities, Teachers' Training College, Vilnius.
8. See also: N. Melvin (1995) *Russians Beyond Russia: the Politics of National Identity*. London: Royal Institute of International Affairs, p.126.
9. This term was used by Eugenij(us) Petrov(as) during my four interviews with him. He was a Russian, a member of *Sajudis* and MP in the period 1990–2 who lost his seat in the 1992 elections.
10. Interview with E. Petrov(as), 4 December 1992. It should be noted that Eugenij(us) Petrov(as) is using his first name and surname with a Lithuanian ending. I would argue that this is a public way to show where he belongs. This type of statement was during a national reawakening period often (felt) required by members of national minorities.
11. *Lietuvos rytas*, 18–25 December 1992, p.6.
12. Interview with N. Medvedev, 26 November 1992. A Russian born in Lithuania between the two World Wars, he was a member of the Social Democratic Party and its MP, and a former member of *Sajudis*.
13. Interview with V. Efremov, 9 November 1992. A Russian actor and member of *Sajudis*.
14. Interview with J. Lakis, 3 November 1992.
15. The 4.1 per cent of Russians who consider Lithuanian their mother tongue should be regarded as belonging to the category of 'Lithuanian Russians'. See: Appendix: Demographic Data, Table A1.4.
16. See: C. Thomas (1992) who argues that these Russians are assimilated in the local culture, p.128.
17. Interview with N. Kasatkina, 24 June 1993. She is a sociologist at the Institute for Philosophy, Sociology and Law, working on the Russian intelligentsia between the two World Wars.
18. A comment very often given in relation to well-known members of this group and also Old Believers.
19. Natalija Kasatkina, 'Russians in Lithuania', *Eho Litvi*, 12 December 1992, p.3.
20. Interview with V. Baranovskii, 15 December 1992.
21. Natalija Kasatkina, 'Russians in Lithuania', *Eho Litvi*, 12 December 1992, p.3.

22. He disagreed with the official figure of 75 000 which was given at the Conference on Russian National Minority and its Problems, Vilnius, 11 June 1993.
23. I personally have not met anybody who was a descendant from this community.
24. Interview with N. Kasatkina, 24 June 1993.
25. N. Kasatkina (1996) 'Russians in the Lithuanian State: the Historical Perspective of the National Identity', in: *Changes of Identity in Modern Lithuania*. Vilnius: Institute of Philosophy and Sociology, Republic of Lithuania and Centre for Russian and East European Studies, University of Goteborg, Sweden, pp.127–8.
26. Interview with N. Medvedev, 29 November 1992.
27. Interview with T. Pogozhilskaia, 11 December 1992. She was the President of the Russian Society (*Ruskoe Obshchestvo*).
28. C. Thompson (1992) *The Singing Revolution: a Political Journey through the Baltic States*. London: Michael Joseph, p.128. Interview with A. Kubilius, 23 November 1992. He was the President of the *Sajudis* branch in the city of Vilnius.
29. Interview with T. Muzhnjova, 8 December 1992. She was the co-President of the Russian Cultural Centre.
30. From the discussion during the meeting organised by the Russian Society with the representatives from the Russian Embassy in Lithuania, 11 December 1992. See also: V. Gaidys (1994) 'Russians in Lithuania', in: V. Shlapentokh *et al.*, *The New Russian Diaspora: Russian Minorities in the Former Soviet Republics*. New York: M.E. Sharpe, pp.98–9.
31. See: R. Service (1997) *A History of Twentieth Century Russia*. Harmondsworth: Penguin, pp.448–66. Eduardas Vilkas argued that *perestroika* did not have a chance because it unleashed national movements. Interview with E. Vilkas, 28 October 1992. He was an economist and one of the founding fathers of *Sajudis*.
32. Interview with V. Asovskii, 16 December 1992. He was a Russian who moved to Lithuania when he was seven years old. He is a member of the editorial board of the journal *Vilnius*, journal of the Association of Writers of Lithuania, published in Russian, and a poet himself.
33. Interview with P. Lavrinec, 16 June 1993.
34. Interview with E. Raisuotis, 21 June 1993. He was a member of the Committee on Human Rights and National Minorities in the Lithuanian government. See also: *Opozicija*, no.2, November 1992, p.1. (*Opozicija* is a weekly, established in November 1991 (Lithuanian edition) and in October 1992 a Russian edition.) *Lietuvos rytas*, 19–26 February 1993, p.1.
35. Interview with T. Iasinskaia, 18 June 1993. She was a co-President of the Russian Cultural Centre. One example was the removal of the Pushkin monument from the park in the centre of Vilnius to the hill in the suburbs. See: a letter by T. Iasinskaia in: *Nasza Gazeta*, 28 June 1992, p.3.
36. In 1992 each ethnic community received 20 000 rubles or roughly 100 pounds. P. Kolstoe (1995), p.141.
37. The only exception was a request for a paper to be presented at the Conference on Russian Minority (June 1993) organised by the Department of National Minorities before the United Nations Conference in Vienna. But that

conference was organised in a Soviet tradition, reading out previously written papers without leaving enough time to have a dialogue. It was seen by the majority of Russians as a means to show to the world that Lithuania respects its Russians. According to Iasinskaia their (the Russian Cultural Centre) paper presented at the conference was turned down by a few Lithuanian newspapers which demanded that it be edited before being published.
38. Interview with J. Lakis, 3 November 1992.
39. Interview with I. Arefjeva, 10 December 1992. She is a Russian, who came to Lithuania when she was three years old. She was the President of the Association of Orthodox Enlightenment (*Zhivoi kolos*). Interview with N. Medvedev, 26 November 1992.
40. From the discussion of the Russian Embassy representatives organised by the Russian Society with the representatives from the Russian Embassy, 11 December 1992.
41. Interview with T. Iasinskaia, 18 June 1993.
42. A.E. Senn (1990) *Lithuanian Awakening*. Berkeley: University of California Press, p.240.
43. Interview with E. Petrov(as), 4 and 11 November 1992.
44. After the January events two Russian communists barricaded themselves inside the Vilnius television tower to send 'a message to all people, in the whole world fascism will not pass'. They argued that the Soviet Army was invited to storm the tower 'to allow the opinions of the working-class people' to be broadcast. FBIS-SOV-91-023, 4 February 1991, pp.67–8.
45. A. Zinov'ev (1985) *Homo Sovieticus*. London: Gollancz, p.12.
46. The group demanded that the plans to make Lithuanian the official language of the republic should be delayed.
47. See also: A. Lieven (1994) *The Baltic Revolution: Estonia, Latvia, Lithuania and the Path to Independence*. New Haven: Yale University Press, pp.199–200.
48. Interview with N. Medvedev, 26 November 1992.
49. Interview with I. Melianas, 30 October 1992. He was a Lithuanian, Secretary of the Lithuanian Liberal Union, and manager of a technical unit within an industrial factory.
50. As was already pointed out in Chapter 1, I mostly interviewed members of the Russian intelligentsia. I interviewed 20 men and 10 women. The majority of them were professionals with a university degree, nearly equally divided between science, social sciences and humanities. I also interviewed four so-called working-class people, two unemployed, one who left for Belarus and one (woman) who was retired. One-third of them were between 20 and 40 years old and two-thirds were between 41 and 60 years old. All of them lived in privately owned flats. Only two of them moved to Lithuania in the 1980s. The rest were either born in Lithuania or came there as children with their parents.
51. After the United Nations World Conference on Human Rights held in Vienna between 14 and 25 June 1993 the Lithuanian Parliament *Seimas* passed in July 1993 an amendment which allowed for naturalisation without a language test for those aged 65 and older or those with certain disabilities (blindness, deafness, etc.). See also: L. Barrington (1995), p.735.
52. A report from Visaginas (formerly Snieckus) informed us that two main issues raised by the Russians were that there were not enough teachers and

not enough rooms to perform teaching. *Lietuvos rytas*, 19–26 March 1993, p.8 and p.12. Research presented by A. Steen confirms the low level of confidence in political institutions in the Baltic states. A. Steen (1996) 'Consolidations and Competence: Research on the Politics of Recruiting Political Elites in the Baltic States', *Journal of Baltic Studies*, vol.27, no.2, pp.154–5.

53. Interview with M. Stakvilevicius, 17 June 1993. He was a Chairperson of the Human Rights and National Minorities Committee at the Lithuanian Parliament.

54. Interview with E. Krukauskiene, 3 December 1992. She was a sociologist at the Institute of Sociology, Philosophy and Law.

55. Interview with V. Jarmolenka, 15 December 1992. He was a Russian, MP, a founding member of *Sajudis* from Kaunas and, after 1993, of the Homeland Union.

56. Interview with E. Petrov(as), 4 December 1992.

57. Interview with Sergei Ietuhov, an unemployed Russian worker, 27 November 1992.

58. During the interview with T. Pogozhilskaia this was said by a member of the Russian Society, 11 December 1992.

59. Statement of the Supreme Council of the Republic of Lithuania on the Status of the Soviet Armed Forces in Lithuania. G.H. Flanz (1992), p.179.

60. Interview with V. Gruzalis, 15 June 1993. He was the Director of the Department on Migration, Ministry of Social Security, and President of the Commission on National Minorities of the City of Vilnius. Interview with M. Stakvilevicius, 17 June 1993. However, he was not able to specify how many officers of the Soviet Army had left Lithuania and how many stayed there. According to Sokolov there were 9000 military pensioners in Lithuania. Interview with N. Sokolov, 18 June 1993. He was the Russian Vice-Ambassador to Lithuania.

61. Interview with P. Frolov, 25 June 1993. He was a co-President of the Russian Community (*Ruskaia Obshchina*).

62. Interview with K. Skrebys, 25 November 1992. He was MP and a member of the Independence Union. Interview with E. Raisuotis, 21 June 1993.

63. FBIS-SOV-91-118, 19 June 1991, pp.63–4. A. Lieven (1994), p.341.

64. Interview with E. Gruzas, 16 June 1993. He was the Director of the Migration Department of the Republic of Lithuania.

65. Interview with T. Muzhnjova, 8 December 1992. She was a Russian, a co-President of the Russian Cultural Centre.

66. Seven in Vilnius and five in Kaunas – according to the Open Letter to the President of the Republic of Lithuania, Algidras Brazauskas (15 March 1993) given to me by Piotr Frolov on 25 June 1993.

67. Interview with P. Frolov, 25 June 1993.

68. From the Open Letter to the President of the Republic of Lithuania, Algidras Brazauskas, 15 March 1993.

69. See also: R. Bernhardt and H. Schermers (1992), p.251.

70. Interview with Khrizostom, 18 June 1993. He was Archbishop of the Russian Orthodox Church in Lithuania.

71. Interview with V. Gruzalis, 15 June 1993.

72. V.S. Vardys and J.B. Sedaitis (1997), p.29.

73. Interview with V. Gruzalis, 24 June 1993. He showed me a list of the buildings returned until April 1991. The majority of buildings are listed in Vilnius: Department of Nationalities of the Government of the Republic of Lithuania, 1992, Vilnius: Department of Nationalities of the Government of the Republic of Lithuania, 1992, pp.27–31.
74. Interview with V. Gruzalis, 15 June 1993.
75. Interview with S. Ietuhov, 27 November 1992.
76. Interview with B. Gruzevskis, 25 June 1993. He was a sociologist at the Institute of Social Policy at the Ministry for Social Security.
77. Interview with T. Iasinskaia, 18 June 1993. She was a co-President of the Russian Cultural Centre.
78. From her discussion at the Conference on Russian National Minority and its Problems, Vilnius, 11 June 1993. This was also argued by the Russian Vice-Ambassador to Lithuania, N. Sokolov, 18 June 1993.
79. See: Appendix: Education, Tables 4 and 5. However, research carried out in Vilnius showed that the number of Russian children going to Russian schools was falling but not in favour of Lithuanian schools. However, there was no attempt to explain this trend. E. Krukauskiene (1996) 'State and National Identity', in: *Changes of Identity in Modern Lithuania*. Vilnius: Institute of Philosophy and Sociology, Republic of Lithuania, Centre for Russian and East European Studies, University of Goteborg, pp.260–1.
80. See Appendix: Education, Tables A2.2, A2.3 and A2.6.
81. From the speech given by E. Barkauskaite, a member of the Ministry of Culture and Education, at the Conference on Russian National Minority and its Problems, Vilnius, 11 June 1993.
82. From the speech given by E. Barkauskaite at the Conference on Russian National Minority and its Problems, Vilnius, 11 June 1993. Each book cost 500 talonas. The average salary was 1700 talonas.
83. Argued by Sergei Ietuhov's wife who in 1992 was a teacher in a Russian secondary school, after being made redundant due to the closure of departments where lectures were delivered in Russian at the Teacher Training College in Vilnius. Only the Russian Language and Literature stayed open. Pointed out during the interview with S. Ietuhov, 27 November 1992.
84. From the speech by P. Lavrinec at the Conference on Russian National Minority and its Problems, Vilnius, 11 June 1993. Pavel Lavrinec is a member of the editorial board of *Lad* and the Russian Cultural Centre.
85. See: Appendix: Education, Table 2.
86. Interview with N. Makeeva, 25 June 1993. She was a Russian and the Director of the Lithuanian Centre of the Russian Open University.
87. Interview with E. Petrov(as), 25 June 1993.
88. Interview with S. Temchin, 27 November 1992. He was a Russian and a lecturer in Slavonic languages at the University of Vilnius. See also: An interview with the Dean of the Language Department of the Teachers' Training College in Siauliu, in: *Eho Litvi*, 17 June 1993, p.3. *Eho Litvi*, 11 December 1992, p.3. *Eho Litvi*, 30 April 1993, p.3.
89. Interview with J. Karosas, 28 October 1992. He was a member of the LDDP and MP.
90. *Lietuvos rytas*, 11–18 December 1992, p.1.

91. Argued by the representatives of the Russian Embassy during the meeting organised by the Russian Society, 11 December 1992.
92. See: Chapter 4, note 21.
93. As discussed in Chapter 1 'polyethnic rights' are understood as legal protection and financial support for cultural and educational purposes.
94. Between 1990 and 1995 the formulation of international standards regulating state conduct towards national minorities was a priority for European organisations. They agreed that minority rights should be based in an individual. The only exception was the 1992 Council of Europe Charter for Regional and Minority Languages. See: J.J. Preece (1997) 'National Minority Rights vs State Sovereignty in Europe: Changing Norms in International Relations', *Nations and Nationalism*, vol.3, no.3, pp.345–64.
95. Interview with E. Petrov(as), 25 June 1993.
96. Interview with N. Kasatkina, 24 June 1993.
97. Interview with V. Asovskii, 16 December 1992.
98. Interview with Archbishop Khrizostom, 18 June 1993.
99. Interview with V. Efremov, 9 November 1992.
100. Interview with J. Lakis, 3 November 1992.
101. Interview with P. Lavrinec, 8 December 1992.
102. See: Appendix: Mass Media, Table A3.1.
103. Interview with P. Lavrinec, 16 June 1993.
104. *Vilnius* is a journal published by the Writers' Union of Lithuania. *Lad* is a journal published by the Ministry of Culture and Education and the Department of National Minorities.
105. Interview with E. Matvekas, 23 June 1993.
106. See: Appendix: Mass Media, Table 2. From the speech by P. Lavrinec at the Conference on Russian National Minority and its Problems, Vilnius, 11 June 1993.
107. Interview with V. Asovskii, 21 June 1993. The Lithuanian population was 'hooked' on a Mexican soap opera, *Even Rich People Cry*.
108. E. Staneika argued that it was impossible to give the exact number of cultural organisations of different minorities because they appear and disappear very quickly. Interview with E. Staneika, 2 November 1992. He was the Head of the Sociological Research Group at the House of National Minorities of the Government of the Republic of Lithuania. The same was argued by S. Vaitiekus, a member of the Department of National Minorities at the Government of the Republic of Lithuania. Interview with S. Vaitiekus, 8 December 1992.
109. Kitchens were meeting points in family life which was a result of the housing problem in Eastern Europe. They were also the places where different organisations had been founded as is pointed out in Barbara Einhorn's book *Cinderella Goes to Market* (1993). London: Verso, pp.182–215.
110. When in 1992 and 1993 I asked for the above documents from different Russian organisations I was not given a single one. See: R.J. Dalton and M. Kuechler, eds (1990) *Challenging the Political Order*. Cambridge: Polity Press, pp.10–16.
111. Interview with I. Arefjeva, 10 December 1992.

112. Interview with P. Frolov, 25 June 1993.
113. Their Presidents were surprised when they heard in 1993 that they could be constituent members, together with the Russian Community and the Russian Society, of a Russian political party.
114. Interview with T. Muzhnjova, 8 December 1992.
115. Interview with T. Iasinskaia, 18 June 1993.
116. Kostloe argues that, in general, Russians were culturally and linguistically privileged over other national groups in non-Russian republics but not over the indigenous population. P. Kostloe (1995), pp.102–3.
117. Interview with T. Iasinskaia, 18 June 1993.
118. Lakis argued that this point was confirmed by his research. Interview with J. Lakis, 3 November 1992.
119. Rasa Alisauskiene pointed out that mostly the Russian technical intelligentsia left and, nevertheless, Russians still had a higher number of people with higher education than Lithuanians. Interview with R. Alisauskiene, 24 June 1993. She is the Director of the Sociological Laboratory at the Faculty of Philosophy, University of Vilnius.
120. New Unity Group's Declaration, in: FBIS-SOV-88-234, 6 December 1988, p.96.
121. Ibid., p.96.
122. G. Efremov (1990) *My ljudi drug drugu* (We See Each Other as Human Beings). Moscow, pp. 212–13. V. Ivanov (1996) *Litovskaia Tiur'ma* (Lithuanian Prison). Moscow: Paleia, p.34 and p.72. A.E. Senn (1990), p.240.
123. R. Szporluk (1989) 'Dilemmas of Russian Nationalism', *Problems of Communism*, vol.38, no.4, p.33.
124. Interview with E. Petrov(as), 11 December 1992.
125. V. Ivanov (1996), p.26, p.40, p.79, p.83, p.156. On a more personal level about this connection see: 'Children of the Russian Military', *Respublika*, 22 June 1993, p.3. Vitalii Asovskii argued that the leaders of the *Edinstvo* were definitely 'connected with the Communist Party of the Soviet Union'. Interview with V. Asovskii, 10 December 1992.
126. FBIS-SOV-91-001, 2 January 1991, pp. 65–6.
127. FBIS-SOV-90-179, 14 September 1990, p.60. FBIS-SOV-91-013, 18 January 1991, pp.52–5. FBIS-SOV-91-016, 24 January 1991, p.47. A. Lieven (1994), p.190.
128. A.E. Senn (1990), p.239.
129. C. Thompson (1992), p.128. Interview with V. Cepaitis, 1 December 1992. He was a former member of *Sajudis* and its first National Council with responsibility towards national minorities issues. He had to resign because of his connections with the KGB.
130. See also: C. Thompson (1992), p.35 and p.140.
131. He was editor of the Russian version of *Atmoda* (Awakening), the Popular Front newspaper in Latvia. C. Thompson (1992), p.131.
132. Interview with T. Pogozhilskaia, 11 December 1992.
133. One example is the anecdote about a conversation between a Lithuanian and Russian: Lithuanian: Why don't you speak Lithuanian? Russian: We made you free in 1945. Lithuanian: But you forgot to leave.
134. V. Gaidys, mimeograph, pp.10–11. 'The attitudes of Russians towards it (*Sajudis*) were positive at the beginning. Later the attitudes changed to negative…(1989–90). Russians could have interpreted *Sajudis* as

Gorbachev's *perestroika* movement in the beginning but later they understood that this movement was dangerous for the stability of their life.'

135. Interview with V. Asovskii, 10 December 1992. Interview with T. Pogozhilskaia, 11 December 1992.

136. Interview with Archbishop Khrizostom, 18 June 1993.

137. A.E. Senn (1992) 'The Political Culture of Independent Lithuania: a Review Essay', *Journal of Baltic Studies*, vol.23, no.3, p.308.

138. See also N. Lomaniene (1994) 'On Lithuanian Nationalism: the Movement and the Concept', in: *Social Change*, vol.1. Vilnius: Independent Institute for Social Research, p.29 and p.30, footnote 14 which reads, 'It was a real and very symptomatic case with Antanas Terleckas, the chief of the Lithuanian Freedom League. Today it will sound like an anecdote. It was in 1990 that he pointed out the necessity to replace disguised "enemies of nation" from the official positions and to employ instead the "true patriots". The TV interviewer wondered how could one recognise both of them. Terleckas answered: "Oh, it can be easily seen! According to their faces! Can't you? For me it's not a problem."'

139. FBIS-SOV-89-116, 19 June, p.82.

140. Vilkas argued that *Edinstvo* fought for communism not for the Russian people. Interview with E. Vilkas, 28 October 1992. He was an economist and a founding member of *Sajudis*.

141. Interview with R. Alisauskiene, 24 June 1993. See also: A. Lieven (1994), p.199.

142. Interview with S. Temchin, 27 November 1992.

143. Interview with P. Frolov, 25 June 1993.

144. Interview with N. Kasatkina, 24 June 1993.

145. Interview with E. Petrov(as), 25 June 1993.

146. Will Kymlicka argues that if 'cultural diversity arises from individual or familial immigration' such immigrants should be called 'ethnic groups' not 'national minorities' where 'cultural diversity arises from the incorporation of the previously self-govering, territorially concentrated cultures into a larger state'. The problem with this distinction is that quite a few Russians did not perceive themselves as immigrants. Half of them were born in Lithuania. But more importantly, the majority of them (especially 'Russians of Lithuania') saw themselves as moving within their own country which fell apart. However, they wanted to integrate into Lithuanian state and society (a characteristic of 'ethnic group' according to Kymlicka) but 'Russians of Lithuania' in particular argued that the only way would be through cultural autonomy defined in terms of collective rights (a characteristic of 'national minority' according to Kymlicka). W. Kymlicka (1995) *Multicultural Citizenship*. Oxford: Clarendon Press, pp.10–11.

147. Interview with N. Kasatkina, 24 June 1993.

148. R. Szporluk (1989) 'Dilemmas of Russian Nationalism', *Problems of Communism*, vol.38, no.4, p.32.

149. If I compare my field-work notes I can see the clear difference between autumn 1992 and the late spring 1993 when the representatives of the Russian Embassy argued that they could take care only of Russian citizens in Lithuania and later stressing that 'we have to take care of all Russians in

Lithuania'. This is confirmed by the meeting held on 11 December 1992 with the representatives of the Russian Embassy and interview with N. Sokolov on 18 June 1993.

150. Interview with E. Petrov, 4 and 11 November 1992.

151. Stated during the discussion at the meeting with the represen-tatives of the Russian Embassy organised by the Russian Society, 11 December 1992.

152. Interview with N. Kasatkina, 24 June 1993.

153. Reports like the following one, according to the Russians, could be heard (too) often: 'several young men are visiting people's residences and demanding that people of other nationalities leave Lithuania within 24 hours...' FBIS-SOV-91-014, 22 January 1991, p.60.

154. A. Juozaitis (1992) 'New Beginning and Lithuanian Self-understanding', *Respublika*, 24–30 November 1992, p.4.

155. See: Appendix: Demographic Data, Tables A1.3a and A1.3b.

156. See: Appendix: Demographic Data, Table A1.3e. In the period between 1988 and 1993 net migration for Russians was −31765.

157. See: Appendix: Demographic Data, Tables A1.3c and A1.3d.

158. See: Appendix: Demographic Data, Table A1.3e.

159. Interview with V. Grazulis, 15 June 1993. He was the Director of the Migration Department at the Ministry of Social Security and the President of the Commission on National Minorities of Vilnius city.

160. See documents collected in: *The Road to Negotiations with the USSR*. Vilnius: State Publishing House, 1991.

161. This could not be said for the issues concerning the withdrawal of the Army. See documents collected in: *Negotiation with the Russian Federation Concerning the Withdrawal of Russian Military Forces from the Territory of the Republic of Lithuania*. Vilnius: Supreme Council of the Republic of Lithuania, 1992.

162. It was signed in Moscow on 29 July 1991 and ratified by the Supreme Council of Lithuania on 19 August 1991. *Respublika*, 13–19 October 1992, p.3.

163. In 1992 an agreement was signed between Russia and Lithuania allowing the Russians who moved to Lithuania between 3 November 1989 and 29 July 1991 to get Lithuanian citizenship according to the 'zero option' if they applied before 23 January 1993. *Lietuvos rytas*, 11–18 December 1992, p.1.

164. One has to bear in mind that a certain number of them stayed, not only retired Army officers but also active ones who were married to Lithuanians or people who obtained Lithuanian citizenship and, therefore, they were as spouses granted Lithuanian citizenship as argued in Chapter 4.

165. Interview with M. Stakvilevicius, 17 June 1993.

166. Interview with V. Jarmolenka, 15 December 1992. He was on the Lithuanian delegation negotiating the withdrawal of the Soviet Army from Lithuania.

167. Interview with S. Etuhov, 27 November 1992. During this interview I also talked to his friend Sergei who left in 1990 for Belarus. Interview with J. Karosas, 28 October 1992.

168. From the reseach data collected by V. Gruzalis. In 1991, a large group of Russians left Mazeikiai oil refinery for the Saint Petersburg region. An article from *Sovetskaia Rosiia*, quoted in: FBIS-SOV-91-072, 15 April 1991, pp.36–7.

169. From an article on Visaginas stating that young people were leaving Lithuania. 'They are – engineers, teachers, doctors, cultural workers.' *Lietuvos rytas*, 19–26 March 1993, p.8.
170. Interview with T. Iasinskaia, 18 June 1993. According to the research done in Vilnius in 1993 people who wanted to leave for the CIS countries were mostly aged 40–49 years old. Vida Kasparaviciene (1996) 'Ethnic Composition of Vilnius Residents, National Relations and Estimations', in: M. Taljunaite, ed., *Changes of Identity in Modern Lithuania*. Vilnius: Institute of Philosophy and Sociology, Republic of Lithuania, Centre for Russian and East European Studies, University of Goteborg, p.268.
171. See: Appendix: Demographic Data, Table A1.3c.
172. FBIS-SOV-91-227, 25 November 1991, p.63. The same percentage was given to me in the interview with J. Karosas, 28 October 1992. He also stated they are mostly Army officers and blue-collar workers.
173. From the speech by V. Grazalis on social security issues at the conference Russian National Minority and its Problems, organised by the Committee for Human Rights and National Issues of the Lithuanian Parliament and the Department of National Minorities, Vilnius, 11 June 1993.
174. Interview with E. Sviklas, 2 November 1992. He was a sociologist at the Sociological Research Group at the House of National Minorities of the Government of the Republic of Lithuania. See also: *Tautiniu mazumu socialines savijautos tyrimai (Lietuvos Rusai)*. Vilnius: Tautybiu departamentas prie Lietuvos Respublikos vyriausybes, 1991, p.23.
175. See: Appendix: Demographic Data, Table A1.3c.
176. In a survey carried out by the Ministry for Social Security and Department of Migration in 1991–2, 7852 people or 3015 families were interviewed, which means nearly one-third of all people who left Lithuania in 1991 and 1992 for CIS countries. Among them 57.4 per cent answered repatriation, 19.4 family reunion, 8.7 national tensions, 3.3 changes in labour market and 11.2 gave some other answers. A. Sipaviciene, 'Migration Policy in the Baltic States', mimeograph, p.21.
177. Interview with N. Kasatkina, 24 June 1993.
178. Quoted in V.S. Vardys and J.B. Sedaitis (1997) *Lithuania: the Rebel Nation*. Boulder, Col.: Westview Press, p.213.
179. From the discussion organised by the Russian Society with the representatives from the Russian Embassy, 11 December 1992.
180. One has to bear in mind that the prices of apartments in Russia were higher than in Lithuania. From the discussion at the meeting organised by the Russian Society, 11 December 1992.
181. Nikolai Sokolov argued that Russia did not have a big enough budget to support Russians who wanted to return to Russia. He also pointed out, 'Russians still hope that Russia will be able to do something as it is doing at the moment in Tajikistan and Abhazija.' Interview with N. Sokolov, 18 June 1993.
182. From the paper by E. Gruzas at the Conference on Russian National Minority and its Problems, Vilnius, 11 June 1993. He was the Director of the Migration Department of the Vilnius Region.
183. From the material given to me by V. Gruzalis on 24 June 1993.

184. This was confirmed by the results of Kasatkina's interviews with the Russian minority in Visaginas. Interview with N. Kasatkina, 24 June 1993.
185. 'I spoke with the Department of National Minorities and they told me that Russians are first to be made redundant.' Interview with N. Sokolov, 18 June 1993.
186. H. Pilkington (1998), p.138.
187. N. Kasatkina and T. Muzhnjova quoted in their interviews research done by the Swedes on Russian business in Lithuania which was pointing out that Russians are the richest businessmen in Lithuania. P. Frolov argued that these businessmen to his knowledge prefer to employ Russians, 'their own fellow-nationals'.
188. From Ziukas's speech at the Conference on Russian National Minority and its Problems, Vilnius, 11 June 1993. According to the data published by the European Bank for Reconstruction and Development, unemployment in Lithuania has been constantly on rise since 1991. *Transition Report* (1997) London: EBRD, p. 229. This report relies on the official Lithuanian statistical data.
189. Adolfas Slezevicius, Prime Minister, said that 'there are currently 26 000 registered unemployed (1 per cent of working-age residents), although hidden unemployment in industry and transport alone affect about 200 000 potential workers.' *Baltic News*, May 1993, 17–18 (34–35), p.8.
190. Interview with B. Gruzevskis, 25 June 1993.
191. Quoted in G. Smith (1998) 'Post-colonialism and Borderland Identities', in: G. Smith *et al.*, *Nation-building in the Post-Soviet Borderlands: the Politics of National Identities*. Cambridge: Cambridge University Press, p.12.
192. For example the Soviet Army withdrew as scheduled. FBIS-SOV-93-166, 30 August 1993, p.61. Eltsin argued that national minorities in Lithuania did not need support. *Panorama*, Lithuanian TV, 2 November 1992, 8.30 p.m.
193. Interview with E. Vilkas, 28 October 1992.

7 Polish Demands

1. See: Appendix: Demographic Data, Table A1.6.
2. See: Appendix: Education, Table A2.1.
3. See: Appendix: Demographic Data, Table A1.2b.
4. See also: A. Lieven (1994) *The Baltic Revolution: Estonia, Latvia, Lithuania and the Path to Independence*. New Haven: Yale University Press, pp.161–2.
5. The reaction to such statements was not always pain, anger and fear but it also trigged a number of jokes. Here is one: 'A linguist came to a polish village and after a long discussion about their language (in their own language) concluded that they were Lithuanians. An old grandmother responded: "But last year somebody came and told us that our predecessors were monkeys."'
6. 'The Poles who have last names like Gaidelis, Petrulis, etc. are probably of Lithuanian origin', in: *The Congress Bulletin*, no.2, 22 October 1988, in: Lituanus Data Bank (1990), *Lituanus*, vol.36, no.1, p.92. A. Budreckis (1985) argues that Poles are Polonised Lithuanians and Belorussians are Slavophone Lithuanians. 'Demographic Problems of Vilnius Province',

pp.312–15, in: A. Budreckis, ed., *Eastern Lithuania: a Collection of Historical and Ethnographic Studies*. Chicago: Lithuanian Association of the Vilnius Region. 'The people of Vilnius and Salcininkai Regions feel that they are Poles. Let them be. These people are Polonised. But the most important thing is that they are citizens of Lithuania.' Interview with V. Jarmolenka, 15 December 1992. He was a Russian, MP and a member of *Sajudis* and since 1993, the Homeland Union. Exactly the same was argued by A. Kubilius, 23 November 1992. He was the President of the *Sajudis* branch in Vilnius. 'Some of those Poles who consider themselves Poles are not Poles but Belorussians. Very often their logic is: I am a Slav, I am a Catholic and therefore, I must be Pole.' Interview with V. Cepaitis, 1 December 1992. He was a former member of *Sajudis* and its first National Council with responsibility towards national minorities issues. He had to resign because of his connections with the KGB.

7. Interview with E. Krukauskiene, 3 December 1992. She was a sociologist at the Institute for Philosophy, Sociology and Law, Lithuanian Academy of Sciences. In 1989 she carried out research 'Culture and You' (*Kul'tura i vy*), in the Salcininkai region. In 1990, 'Your Life' (*Vasha zhizn'*) in the Vilnius and Svencionys regions and in 1991 'Life Beside the Capital' (*Zhizn' vozle stolicy*) in the Vilnius and Trakai regions.

8. Krukauskiene argued that according to her research carried out in 1991 90 per cent of Poles in the Salcininkai region felt that they were Poles, 93 per cent in the Vilnius region and 84 per cent in the city of Vilnius. She argued that choosing nationality was a political decision, especially after independence. Interview with E. Krukauskiene, 3 December 1992.

9. Interview with A. Kulakauskas, 2 December 1992. He was a historian, teaching at Vilnius University, a member of the committee formed by the Lithuanian Parliament (1990–2) to write a report on the Polish minority in Lithuania.

10. Sometimes this language is not acknowledged as a separate one and it is called the Polish language. Ellen J. Gordon (1996) 'The Revival of Polish National Consciousness: a Comparative Study of Lithuania, Belarus and Ukraine', *Nationalities Papers*, vol.24, no.2, pp.218–22.

11. Before the Second World War, in 1939, Halina Turska published a study on the Polish language in the Vilnius, Kaunas and Smalvos regions, *O powstaniu polskich obszarow jezykowych na Wilenszczyznie*. The same study was reprinted in Polish and Russian with an introductory chapter (in Russian and Lithuanian) by V. Cekmonas in 1995 (Vilnius: Mintis). According to Zofia Kurzowa between 1982 and 1990 there were 33 studies published in Poland on the Polish language in Lithuania, Belorussia and the Ukraine. Z. Kurzowa (1992) 'Jezyk polski na kresach wschodnich po II wojnie swiatowej', in: Hieronim Kubiak *et al.*, *Mniejszosci Polskie i Polonia w ZSRR*. Wroclaw, Warszawa, Krakow: Zaklad Narodowy imienia Ossolinskich, p.131.

12. H. Turska (1995), p.115.

13. Ibid., p.117.

14. Ibid., p.123, footnote 42.

15. Ibid., p.169.

16. *Lietuvos respublikos pagrindiniu tautytibiu gyventojai* (1991) Vilnius: Statistikos departamentas prie Lietuvos respublikos vyriausybes, p.7.

V. Cekmonas argues that since the fourteenth century the Lithuanians of the South-East were undergoing belorussification, and after the Third Partition of Poland (1795) both Lithuanians and Belorussians in the light of Russification and Polish national reawakening started to consider themselves as Polish because being Catholic meant being Polish. V. Cekmonas (1995) Introductory chapter in H. Turska, pp.24–6.

17. Iryda Grek-Pabisowa and Irena Maryniakowa argued that Poles in Lithuania are divided into the three communities according to their knowledge of Polish: those who speak Polish, a community where only the older generation speak Polish and a community where Polish is not spoken. The last two communities use '*mowa prosta*'. They also pointed out that all these communities have a Polish identity, they call themselves Poles, sing Polish songs and their memory draws upon Polish history. I. Grek-Pabisowa and I. Maryniakowa (1992) 'Wspolczesne gwary polskie na Litwie i Bialorusi' (Contemporary Polish Dialects in Lithuania and Belorussia), in: Hieronim Kubiak *et al.*, op. cit., p.151.

18. Interview with Z. Siemenowicz, 3 December 1992. He was a Pole, a member of the Union of Poles, MP and a doctor.

19. Interview with M. Cobot(as), 2 December 1992. He was a Pole, a member of the Lithuanian Christian Democratic Party, MP and a doctor.

20. *The Lithuanians in Poland – The Poles in Lithuania*, 1994. Warsaw-Vilnius, 1995, p.85.

21. Interview with M. Cobot(as), 2 December 1992.

22. Interview with A. Kulakauskas, 2 December 1992. Kulakauskas was a historian at the University of Vilnius. Raisuotis showed me a letter which he received from a Lithuanian living in Australia arguing against the Polish Department at the University of Vilnius. Interview with E. Raisuotis, 21 June 1993. Interview with A. Skakowska, 5 December 1992. She was in charge of the department of Culture of the Union of Poles. One could study the Polish language at the Teachers' Training College in Vilnius which had, according to the Poles, a bad reputation.

23. *Respublika*, 20–26 October 1992, p.3.

24. S.R. Burant (1997) 'Belarus and the "Belarusian Irredenta" in Lithuania', *Nationalities Papers*, vol.25, no.4, p.651. T. Snyder (1998) 'The Polish-Lithuanian Commonwealth Since 1989: National Narratives in Relations among Poland, Lithuania, Belarus and Ukraine', *Nationalism and Ethnic Politics*, vol.4, no.3, p.9. I could not find data on how many Vilnius Poles left Lithuania between 1955 and 1957.

25. In my interviews the 'Poles of Lithuania' used the word 'rule' (*vlast* in Russian). In Kymlicka's terms they asked for 'special representation rights'.

26. Vardys pointed out that in the Soviet Lithuania 'the percentage of Polish representatives in the local Communist Party or in the government is considerably smaller than their share of the population'. V.S. Vardys (1983) 'Polish Echoes in the Baltics', *Problems of Communism*, vol.32, no.4, p.24.

27. V.S. Vardys (1990) 'Die Entwicklung der Republic Litauen', in: Boris Meissner, Hrsg., *Die baltische Nationen: Esland, Lettland, Litauen*. Koeln: Markus, p.76.

28. S.R. Burant (1997), p.651.

29. S.R. Burant (1991) 'Polish–Lithuanian Relations: Past, Present and Future', *Problems of Communism*, vol.40, no.3, p.79. According to the data the number of students who studied in Polish (as well as in Russian) slowly declined as more students began to study in Lithuanian. However, the number of pupils taught in primary and secondary schools in Polish was growing. See: Appendix: Education, Tables A2.2, A2.3, A2.4 and A2.5.
30. In my interviews they would point out that in the inter-war period their grandparents were able to get good education and were thought proper Polish.
31. Interview with A. Plokszto, 5 November 1992. He was the Leader of the Union of Poles, MP and a physicist.
32. Quoted in S.R. Burant (1997), p.652.
33. I understand Sovietisation as a process primarily connected with the development of the leading role of the Communist Party and its influence on all spheres of the social system and individual life. Russification is primarily connected with the role the Russian language played in implementing the policies of Sovietisation.
34. A. Lieven (1994), p.170.
35. Ibid., p.165.
36. K. Sword (1994) pointed out in his research on the deportation of the Poles to the Soviet Union that *tutejszy* should be understood as people who 'did not feel a particularly strong pull to either Polish or Belorussian communities. They were more attached to their homes and their land.' But he also pointed out that all the Poles living in that region cannot be described in these terms. *Deportation and Exile: Poles in the Soviet Union, 1939–48*. London: Macmillan in association with School of Slavonic and East European Studies, University of London, p.181.
37. Marion Grydziuszko sent a letter to *Nasza Gazeta* pointing out that it was 'easy' to change the Lithuanian version of his name into Polish, simply waiting for three months and paying 380 roubles. *Nasza Gazeta*, 29 September 1992, p.3.
38. I interviewed 15 Poles, 14 men and one woman. Seven of them were between 20 and 40 years old, another seven between 41 and 60 years old and one person was 64 years old. All of them were professionals with a university degree. All men had a science degree and the woman a degree in Polish Language and Literature. They lived in privately owned flats which four of them (and their families) shared with their parents.
39. FBIS-SOV-92-062, 31 March 1992, p.72.
40. Law on Land Reform. Parliamentary Record 4/1992.
41. Interview with M. Stakvilevicius, 17 June 1993. He was a Chairperson of the Human Rights and National Minorities Committee at the Lithuanian Parliament.
42. Interview with A. Eigirdas, 4 December 1992. He was a Deputy-Chairperson of the State Committee to Investigate the Problems of Eastern Lithuania founded by the Presidium of the Supreme Council on 6 July 1990. He is a sociologist.
43. Interview with E. Raisuotis, 21 June 1993. He was a member of the Committee on Human Rights and National Minorities at the Lithuanian Government.

44. Interview with Z. Mackiewicz, 2 December 1992. He was the Head of the Institute of Polish Culture and Chairman of the Senate of the State Institute of Experimental and Clinical Medicine.
45. Interview with G. Kirkilas, 23 November 1992. The same was argued by Eduardas Vilkas. Interview with E. Vilkas, 28 October 1992. Vilkas was an economist and a founding member of *Sajudis*. See also: V.S. Vardys and J.B. Sedaitis (1997), pp.202–3.
46. Interview with A. Plokszto, 15 June 1993.
47. Interview with Z. Mackiewicz, 2 December 1992. See: Appendix: Education, Tables A2.2 and A2.3.
48. Interview with A. Skakowska, 5 December 1992. She was in charge of the Cultural Department of the Union of Poles.
49. Severinas Vaitekus pointed out that around 300 Poles studied in Poland. 'National Minorities in Lithuania', *Galve*, 15 September 1992, p.3.
50. V.S. Vardys and J.B. Sedaitis (1997), p.215.
51. Interview with A. Skakowska, 5 December 1992.
52. Interview with M. Stakvilevicius, 17 June 1993.
53. Interview with M. Cobot(as), 2 December 1992.
54. Interview with Z. Mackiewicz, 2 December 1992.
55. Interview with A. Plokszto, 15 June 1993.
56. Interview with A. Plokszto, 15 June 1993.
57. Interview with V. Gruzalis, 15 June 1993.
58. Interview with T. Muzhnjova, 8 December 1992. She was a Russian, a co-president of the Russian Cultural Centre.
59. Interview with A. Skakowska, 5 December 1992.
60. Interview with A. Plokszto, 15 June 1993.
61. Interview with Z. Siemenowicz, 3 December 1992.
62. Interview with A. Plokszto, 15 June 1993. See also: *Nasza Gazeta*, 4 July 1992, p.1. *Nasza Gazeta* is the official newspaper of the Union of Poles.
63. Interview with M. Stakvilevicius, 17 June 1993.
64. See also: A. Lieven (1994), p.168.
65. Interview with A. Skakowska, 5 December 1992.
66. See: Appendix: Education, Tables A2.4 and A2.5.
67. This law was changed for the 1996 elections and the threshold of 5 per cent was introduced for all political parties. See: K. Henderson and N. Robinson (1997) *Post-communist Politics: an Introduction*. Hemel Hempstead: Prentice Hall, p.330.
68. A. Lieven (1994), p.168.
69. According to Will Kymlicka's typology mentioned in Chapter 6 (footnote 146) the Poles are a national minority because 'cultural diversity arises from the incorporation of previous self-governing, territorially concentrated cultures into a larger state'. According to my interviews the Poles did not question the issue of being a national minority as especially 'Russians of Lithuania' and 'Soviet Russians' did. After all, they had that status for the previous 50 years (since the end of the Second World War). What they questioned, as pointed out above, were the rights they were denied. W. Kymlicka (1995) *Multicultural Citizenship*. Oxford: Clarendon Press, p.10.
70. *Nasza Gazeta*, 15 September 1992, p.2.

71. *Lithuanian Political Parties, Political Movements and Political Organisations*. A Document given to me in October 1992 in the Lithuanian Parliament by its Press Office, p.8.
72. Interview with Z. Siemenowicz, 3 December 1992. Krukauskiene pointed out that in comparison with 1989 the research carried out in 1993 showed that the number of Poles who consider Lithuania their motherland is slowly growing. E. Krukauskiene (1996) 'State and National Identity', in: *Changes of Identity in Modern Lithuania*. Institute of Philosophy and Sociology, Republic of Lithuania and Centre for Russian and East European Studies, University of Goteborg, p.251.
73. Interview with A. Plokszto, 5 November 1992.
74. They felt like the Pole in a cartoon, surrounded by knives which all aim towards him. Shown to me by Artur Plokszto during the interview on 5 November 1992.
75. From the Programme of the Union of Poles adopted at their Third Convention, 14 December 1991. From the Documents compiled by the Lithuanian Parliament, given to me by A. Eigirdas in December 1992, Appendix V: Document 3.
76. One has to bear in mind that according to the Statute of the Union of Poles the organisation acknowledged the territorial integrity of Lithuania through the decision to obey its Constitution.
77. Plokszto argued that in the 1990–2 Parliament there were eight Union of Poles' MPs (see footnote 79). From this statement it could be concluded that the Union was collaborating with the Communist Party loyal to the Soviet Union. Interview with A. Plokszto, 5 November 1992.
78. Interview with A. Plokszto, 5 November 1992.
79. However, in the 1990–2 Parliament out of 141 MPs there were ten Polish MPs, six were members of the Communist Party loyal to the Soviet Union, one of the Christian Democratic Party and three of the Union of Poles. A. Lieven (1994), p.167. In the 1992–6 Parliament out of 141 MPs there were six Polish MPs, one member of the Christian Democratic Party, one of the LDDP and four of the Union of Poles.
80. *The Baltic Independent*, 13–19 November 1992, p.9.
81. S. Girnius (1993) 'Lithuania's Foreign Policy', *RFE/RL Research Report*, vol.12, no.35, 3 September 1993, p.32.
82. From a press release distributed during the press conference on 4 December 1992 in the *Seimas*. See also: *Eho Litvi*, 5 December 1992, p.2.
83. See also: *The Baltic Independent*, 30 October–5 November 1992, p.9.
84. From a leaflet given to me in November 1992 in Vilnius. See: Appendix: Leaflet.
85. *The Baltic Independent*, 13–19 November 1992, p.9.
86. Antanas Kulakauskas pointed out that Lithuanian schools were opened after the Second World War but they were very quickly closed down and turned into Polish schools. Interview with A. Kulakauskas, 2 December 1992. See also: V.S. Vardys and J.B. Sedaitis (1997) *Lithuania: the Rebel Nation*. Boulder, Col.: Westview Press, p.214.
87. Interview with A. Skakowska, 5 December 1992. It is a fact that the Polish schools were reduced from more than 260 in the 1950s to 85 in 1987/9 but in the same period two-thirds of the schools in the whole of Lithuania were closed down. K. Sword (1993) 'Ethnic Poles in Ukraine, Belorus and

Lithuania', in: *Minorities in Central and Eastern Europe: an MRG International Report*. London: Minority Rights Group, p.21 and p.43, footnote 35. It is important to add that this was due to the merging of the schools and decline of the number of pupils. S.R. Burant (1997), p.651.

88. Some of my interviewees pointed out that sometimes Polish teachers in mixed schools could scarcely speak Polish.

89. See: *Lietuvos respublikos pangrindiniu tautybiu gyventojai* (1991) Vilnius: Statistikos departamentas prie Lietuvos respublikos vyriausybes, p.26.

90. E. Krukauskiene (1990) 'The Survey of Notions about the Independence of Lithuania in its Diverse Language Speaking Regions', in: *Sociological Research in the Baltic States*. Vilnius: Lithuanian Sociological Association, Latvian Sociological Association, Estonian Academic Union of Sociologists, Institute of Philosophy, Sociology and Law of Lithuanian Academy of Sciences, p.21.

91. See: Appendix: Mass Media, Table A3.2.

92. Interview with A. Skakowska, 5 December 1992.

93. Okinczyc was a member of the Social Democratic Party who lost his seat in the 1992 general elections.

94. *Vechernie Novosti*, 29 October 1992, p.3.

95. *National Minorities in Lithuania*. Vilnius: Department of Nationalities of the Government of the Republic of Lithuania, 1992, p.24.

96. The Vilnius Question addresses not only the city of Vilnius but Eastern Provinces of Lithuania which were part of Poland between 1920 and 1939.

97. T. Snyder (1998), p.9.

98. See: J. Maceevski, 'Lithuania–Poland: a Knot Which Could be Undone Only by Both Sides', *Lietuvos rytas*, 14–21 May 1993, p.5. T. Snyder (1998), p.9.

99. A.S. Byatt, 'Memory and the Making of Fiction', Eleventh Annual Darwin College Lecture 1996, Lady Mitchell Hall, Cambridge, 8 March 1996.

100. A.D. Smith, 'The Resurgence of Nationalism?', Lecture at the Post-Soviet States Seminar, Sidney Sussex College, Cambridge, 6 March 1996.

101. When A.D. Smith (1996) analyses 'the other side of the coin'; the influence of ethnic origins and culture on politics and state formation he points out the territorialisation of memory (together with the purification of culture and the universalisation of chosenness). 'Culture, Community and Territory: the Politics of Ethnicity and Nationalism', *International Affairs*, vol.72, no.3, pp.445–58.

102. Interview with A. Kulakauskas, 22 June 1993.

103. See: footnote 119. See: Appendix: Demographic Data, Table 5b.

104. T. Venclova (1995) 'A Fifth Year of Independence: Lithuania 1922 and 1994', *East European Politics and Society*, vol.9, no.2, p.355.

105. Interview with A. Eigirdas, 3 and 4 December 1992.

106. S.R. Burant (1991), p.81.

107. T. Snyder (1995) 'National Myths and International Relations: Poland and Lithuania, 1989–1994', *East European Politics and Society*, vol.9, no.2, p.323.

108. Ibid., p.327. FBIS-SOV-92-011, p.85.

109. T. Snyder (1995), pp. 322–3.

110. Poland's underground organisations issued a statement on 16 December 1984, arguing that 'The present boundaries must remain, because we understand that to be in the best interest of our nations and such is our

common will.' 'To Our Brother Ukrainians, Belorussians, and Lithuanians: an offer to Adopt a Common Position Regarding the Borders of Poland-Ukraine, Poland-Belorussia, Poland-Lithuania', in: Lituanus Data Bank (1988), *Lituanus*, vol.34, no.3, pp.92–4. However, at that time only the Lithuanian World Community responded to the statement arguing 'that the historical boundary that existed before the last partition of the Commonwealth of Two Nations in 1795, remains the valid border between Lithuania and Poland except in those sectors where it has been changed by treaties'. 'Reply to the Four Polish Underground Organisations'. Ibid., p.95.

111. Interview with Jan Widacki, Polish Ambassador to Lithuania. *Nasza Gazeta*, June 1992, p.1. See also: *Respublika*, 13 April 1993.

112. This was the last treaty, out of seven, which Poland signed with its neighbouring countries.

113. FBIS-SOV-94-036, 23 February 1994, p.61.

114. Article 1 of the Treaty on Friendly Relations and Good-Neighbourly Cooperation Between the Republic of Lithuania and the Republic of Poland, FBIS-SOV-94-093, 13 May 1994, p.69.

115. Interview with E. Vilkas, 28 October 1992.

116. The Decree on Language was passed on 18 November 1988 and the follow-up legislation was passed on 25 January 1989. The first law established Lithuanian as the official language of the country and the second one put a requirement on the state officials to acquire a basic knowledge of Lithuanian by 1 January 1991.

117. S.R. Burant (1991), p.80.

118. FBIS-SOV-89-173, 8 September 1989, p.41.

119. Before briefly analysing events, it should be pointed out that territorial autonomy was understood as a right to rule or self-government in a territorially defined district. M.A. Vachudova and T. Snyder (1997) 'Are Transitions Transitory? Two Types of Political Change in Eastern Europe Since 1989', *East European Politics and Society*, vol.11, no.1, pp.18–19. It should also be noted that territorial autonomy often leads towards the self-inflicted marginalisation of a minority. The majority of the Lithuanian population, especially ethnic Lithuanians, saw a demand for territorial autonomy as a threat to their independence and sovereignty and labelled the Polish minority as traitors.

120. See also: footnote 144.

121. Interview with E. Petrov(as), 18 December 1992. He was appointed by the Parliament of the Republic of Lithuania on 25 May 1990 (together with M. Laurinkus, and from 6 June 1990 K. Motieka) to accumulate and analyse information concerning the situation in Eastern Lithuania and to suggest possible solutions. On 28 August 1991 he was appointed as chairperson of the Committee to Investigate the Unconstitutional Activity of Municipal Councils, their Organs and Employees in the Region of Salcininkai and the Settlement of Snieckus of the Region of Ignalina. In the 1992 elections he lost his seat.

122. FBIS-SOV-89-150, 7 August 1989, p.94, S.R. Burant (1991), p.80. and V.S. Vardys (1989) 'Lithuanian National Politics', *Problems of Communism*, vol.38, no.4, p.60.

123. FBIS-SOV-89-150, 7 August 1989, p.94.

124. Prunskiene argued, 'At the present a certain destabilising role in our repub-lic is played not so much by the Polish population in Lithuania but by the attempts to use the Polish population … in the interest of Moscow.' FBIS-SOV-90-060, 28 March 1990, p.97.
125. *National Minorities in Lithuania*. Ministry of Foreign Affairs of the Republic of Lithuania, Department of Nationalities of the Government of the Republic of Lithuania. Vilnius, 1992, p.6.
126. FBIS-SOV-89-179, 18 September 1989, p.67.
127. FBIS-SOV-89-183, 22 September 1989, p.69.
128. Interview with V. Cepaitis, 1 December 1992.
129. Interview with A. Kulakauskas, 2 December 1992.
130. R. Ozolas was elected as Chairperson of the State Committee to Investigate the Problems of Eastern Lithuania by the Parliament on 6 July 1990. He was already Deputy Prime Minister which shows that the Polish question was taken very seriously.
131. The Polish faction within the Parliament did not vote in favour of inde-pendence but also did not vote against it. Interview with E. Petrov(as), 18 December 1992.
132. FBIS-SOV-90-101, 24 May 1990, p.93.
133. Interview with E. Petrov(as), 18 December 1992. See also: T. Snyder (1995), p.321.
134. FBIS-SOV-90-179, 14 September 1990, p.60. According to my interviews, in those days 'Soviet Poles' kept reminding Lithuanians in Lithuanian, *Vilnius musu, Lietuva Rusu* (Vilnius is ours, Lithuania is Russian). They wanted to highlight that Stalin returned Vilnius to Lithuania.
135. That resolution states that the regions of Vilnius and Salcininkai, the city of Pabrade and the municipalities of Pabrade and Magunai of the Svencionys region, the municipalities of Poluknys, Trakai, Old Trakai, Kariotiskes of the Trakai region, and the municipality of Jauniunai of the Sirvintos region create the Polish National Territory. From the Documents compiled by the Lithuanian Parliament given to me by A. Eigirdas in December 1992. Appendix III: Document 8.
136. FBIS-SOV-90-195, 9 October 1990, p.86.
137. In a new administrative-territorial division Vilnius and Salcininkai regions were to constitute the Vilnius territorial district. This administrative-territorial division was introduced on 19 July 1994. *Lietuvos statistikos metrastis, 1996*. Vilnius: Metodinis leidybinis centras, p.26.
138. FBIS-SOV-90-249, 27 December 1990, p.59.
139. In August 1991, there was an attempt by the conservative communist lead-ership of the Soviet Union to prevent economic and, more importantly, political changes.
140. When the Vilnius Regional Council adopted a resolution to go ahead with the Union referendum on 17 March 1991 41 people supported it, 15 voted against and 20 abstained. From the Documents compiled by the Lithuanian Parliament, given to me by A. Eigirdas in December 1992, Chronology, p.13.
141. For example, although there was not a quorum at the extraordinary meet-ing of the Parliament on 4 September 1991 (the very day Poland recog-nised Lithuania) to discuss a draft decision on direct rule in both regions

for the period of six months, four days later the Deputy Prime Minister, Vytautas Pakalniskis, appointed government representatives who had unlimited powers. According to Petrov(as) the Lithuanian government was afraid that OMON, a special police unit which defected from the Lithuanian Interior Ministry in January 1991, could get involved. OMON staged attacks on Lithuanian frontier posts. Interview with E. Petrov(as), 18 December 1992. See also: A. Lieven (1994), p.169.

142. From the Documents compiled by the Lithuanian Parliament, Appendix I: Document 16. The General Procurator, A. Paulauskas, based his decision on the material showing that the Salcininkai and Vilnius Regional Councils took an active part in supporting unconstitutional formations, attempting to overthrow the Russian Federation as well as Lithuania.

143. Interview with A. Juozaitis, 11 December 1992. He was a member of *Sajudis* but left the movement being disappointed with its nationalistic policies. He founded in April 1992 the Future Forum.

144. This was argued by Okinczyc, a member of the Polish faction within the Lithuanian Parliament who in the same interview was critical of this group of communists. He is a member of the Social Democratic Party. FBIS-SOV-91-172, 5 September 1991, p.62.

145. FBIS-SOV-92-018, 28 January 1992, p.86. As a result of this decision Maciejkaniec, leader of the Polish faction in the Parliament, announced that he was starting a hunger strike. FBIS-SOV-91-242, 17 December 1991, p.42.

146. From the Documents compiled by the Lithuanian Parliament, given to me by A. Eigirdas in December 1992, Chronology, p.20.

147. On 24 March 1992 the Parliament adopted a decision to extend direct administration in the regions of Salcininkai and Vilnius until 12 September 1992.

148. FBIS-SOV-92-057, 24 March 1992, pp.83–4. According to that law the members of the Communist Party loyal to Moscow could not be employed.

149. S. Girnius (1993) 'Lithuania's Foreign Policy', *RFE/RL Research Report*, vol.12, no.35, 3 September 1993, p.32. He continues, 'Even today, not all members of these local councils have been elected. An example of the difficulties in filling the posts was provided by the Vilnius Region elections on 17 July, when only five of the 14 vacancies could be filled after the counting of absentee ballots.'

150. Interview with E. Petrov(as), 18 December 1992.

151. A summary of different opinion polls was given by A. Plokszto in *Nasza Gazeta*, 22 September 1992, p.3.

8   Jewish Answers

1. According to the Jewish Museum in Vilnius 94 per cent of Lithuanian Jews were killed during the Second World War.

2. See: Appendix: Education, Table A2.1.

3. See: Appendix: Demographic Data, Tables A1.5c and A1.6 and Map 8.1.

4. In 1989 the average age of Jews was 43.5 years old, while for Lithuanians it was 34.9, for Russians 34 and Poles 36.5. Jews are the only national minority

whose mortality rate is higher than birth rate and as a result the natural increase in 1989, measured as 'the average data per 1000 people', was −11.2. Natural increase for Lithuanians was: 5.1, Russians 3.1 and Poles 3.3. *National Minorities in Lithuania*. Vilnius: Department of Nationalities of the Government of the Republic of Lithuania, 1992, p.10 and p.15.

5. I interviewed ten Jews and one Russian of Jewish descent who did not consider himself a Jew any longer. They were all men. Two people were between 20 and 40, four between 41 and 60 and four over 60 years old. They were all professionals with a university degree, two in science and the rest in social sciences and humanities. They were all Jews born in Lithuania. See: Appendix: Demographic Data, Table A1.2b.

6. See: Appendix: Demographic Data, Tables A1.1c and A1.1d.

7. See: Appendix: Demographic Data, Table A1.4.

8. G. Kanovich (1989) 'Evropeiskaia Romaneshka' (Jewish Flower-Petal Game), *Jews and Jewish Topics in the Soviet Union and Eastern Europe*, vol.10, no.3, p.68.

9. Interview with G. Kanovich, 5 November 1992. According to the statistical data which he was referring to only 39 babies were born of Jewish mothers in 1991. The data for 1989 are 90, for 1990 76 and for 1992 35. *Statisticheskii Ezhegodnik Litvi, 1992*. Vilnius: Department Statistiki Litvi, 1993, p.21.

10. Interview with G. Kanovich, 5 November 1992.

11. Interview with G. Kanovich, 5 November 1992. 'Only some people in Lithuania are anti-Semitic. Some of them are very influential.'

12. Interview with M. Jakobas, 4 November 1992. He was the President of the City of Vilnius Jewish Community (founded in 1991).

13. S. Rapoport (1992) *Litovskoe evreistvo v epohu obshchestvenii peremen* (Lithuanian Jews in the Age of Social Changes), p.7. The last sentence is what S. Rapoport calls 'usual formula' – very often cited.

14. Interview with S. Rapoport, 14 December 1992. He was a sociologist at the Institute for Philosophy, Sociology and Law at the Academy of Sciences in Vilnius.

15. H. Zukier (1996) 'The Essential "Other" and the Jews: from Antisemitism to Genocide', *Social Research*, vol.63, no.4, p.1151.

16. J. Weber (1997) 'Jews and Judaism in Contemporary Europe: Religion or Ethnic Group', *Ethnic and Racial Studies*, vol.20, no.2, p.274.

17. When it comes to our sphere of research interest it has to be pointed out that only in Lithuania the number of deputies parallels the percentage of Jews in the population (three out of 209, or 1.44 per cent). W. Korey (1968) 'The Legal Position of the Jewish Community of the Soviet Union', p.338, in: E. Goldhagen, ed., *National Minorities in the Soviet Union*. New York: Frederick A. Praeger. However, the data on Jewish representation in local soviets was the complete opposite. E.M. Jacobs (1976) 'Jewish Representation in Local Soviets', *Soviet Jewish Affairs*, vol.6, no.1, pp.21–3.

18. Interview with D. Golinsky, 23 June 1993. He was the President of the Vilnius Jewish Religious Community.

19. See also: A. Lieven (1994) *The Baltic Revolution: Estonia, Latvia, Lithuania and the Path to Independence*. New Haven: Yale University Press, p.141.

20. D. Romanovsky (1993) 'Judaism and Other Religions Towards the End of the Soviet Period', *Jews in Eastern Europe*, vol.20, no.1, p.65.

21. See: Appendix: Demographic Data, Table A1.9.
22. J. Weber (1997), p.262.
23. This sentence points out clearly the Soviet heritage because it is high-lighting collective responsibility versus an individual one. The whole Lithuanian nation cannot be blamed (as the Jews themselves pointed out) but the newly independent Lithuanian state could be blamed because it was not firmly and clearly trying to deal with its own history.
24. D. Levin (1994), pp.15–18, pp.343–68.
25. Haimas Finkelsteinas argues that the killing took place on 27 June 1941 and that it was known in Kaunas as 'Bloody Friday'. 'Pogroms in Kaunas: another Version', *Jews and Jewish Topics in the Soviet Union and Eastern Europe*, vol.11, no.1, 1990, p.58.
26. A. Bendinskas (1990) 'Pogrom in Kaunas: One Version', *Jews and Jewish Topics in the Soviet Union and Eastern Europe*, vol.11, no.1, p.57. Originally published in *Gimtasis krastas*, a weekly published by the *Teviske* (Homeland) Association for Cultural Ties With Countrymen Abroad, no.32, 10–16 August 1989.
27. Quoted in: D. Levin (1994), p.17, footnote 8.
28. D. Levin (1994), p.23, p.347. 'In the last war the Germans did not even succeed in setting up an SS battalion of Lithuanians. The Germans were forced to make use of criminals to get anything done to the country's Jews'. The words of Audrius Butkevicius, Defence Minister. FBIS-SOV-91-234, 5 December 1991, p.40.
29. The estimates are that fewer than 1000 Lithuanian Jews were saved by Lithuanians, Poles and Russians. D. Levin (1994), p.374.
30. D. Levin (1994), pp.343–68. V.S. Vardys (1965) 'Soviet Social Engineering in Lithuania: an Appraisal', in V.S. Vardys, ed., *Lithuania Under the Soviets: Portrait of a Nation, 1940–65*. London: Frederick A. Praeger, p.241. *National Minorities in Lithuania*. Vilnius: Department of Nationalities of the Government of the Republic of Lithuania, 1992, p.4.
31. The Declaration of the Supreme Council of the Republic of Lithuania on the Genocide of the Jewish Nation in Lithuania During the Period of Nazi Occupation. Given to me by the Office of Emanuelis Zingeris, December 1992.
32. S. Vaitiekus (1992) 'National Minorities in Lithuania: 5. Jews of Lithuania', *Galve*, 6 October 1992, p.3. He is a sociologist and adviser in the Department of National Minorities of the Lithuanian government.
33. A. Lieven (1994), p.140.
34. Ibid., p.157.
35. Op. cit.
36. '2. To state that the heads of local governments of the districts of Akmene, Anyksciai, Birzai, Lazdijai, Panevezys, Salcininkai, Silale, Sirvintos, and the towns of Klaipeda and Marijampole have not ensured the implementation of the 7 November 1990 Presidium of the Supreme Council of the Republic of Lithuania resolution No. 1-763 "On Putting in Order the Graves and Cemeteries of the Victims of Genocide of the Jewish People and the Marking of the Heritage".' Given to me by the Office of Emanuelis Zingeris, December 1992.
37. S. Vaitiekus (1992), p.3.

38. On 2 May 1990 the Supreme Council of the Republic of Lithuania introduced the Law on Rehabilitation of Persons Repressed for Resistance to the Occupying Regime. Six days later the Supreme Council issued an Appeal Concerning the Genocide of the Jewish Nation in Lithuania During the Period of the Nazi Occupation.
39. Interview with M. Jakobas, 4 November 1992.
40. On 8 May 1990 the Supreme Council of the Republic of Lithuania adopted the Declaration on the Genocide of the Jewish Nation During the Period of Nazi Occupation.
41. From the Declaration given to me by the Office of Emanuelis Zingeris, December 1992.
42. Interview with S. Alperovich, 14 December 1992. He was a member of the governing body of the Lithuanian Jewish Community (founded in 1988) and a lawyer.
43. A. Lieven (1994), p.156.
44. A Statement Concerning the Working Groups Between the Republic of Lithuania and the State of Israel by the Presidium of the Supreme Council of the Republic of Lithuania. 9 September 1991. Given to me by the Office of Emanuelis Zingeris in December 1992.
45. 'Lithuania has rather reluctantly agreed to reopen some of those cases but claims that it cannot afford such a massive research effort without funding.' N. Lane (1995) 'Estonia and its Jews', *East European Jewish Affairs*, vol.25, no.1, p.3.
46. R. Bernhardt and H. Schermers (1992) 'Lithuanian Law and International Human Rights Standards', *Human Rights Law Journal*, vol.13, no.5–6, p.256 and p.251.
47. A. Lieven (1993), p.156. D. Levin (1994), p.20.
48. Quoted in: N. Levin (1990) *The Jews in the Soviet Union Since 1917: Paradox of Survival*. London: I.B. Tauris, vol.1, p.430.
49. T. Venclova (1990) 'Some Lithuanians Saved Jews from the Nazis', *Jews and Jewish Topics in the Soviet Union and Eastern Europe*, vol.11, no.1, p.40. Originally published in 1976 and reprinted in 1989 in Lithuania in *Literatura I Menas*. In the same issue of the journal Haimas Finkelsteinas on page 60, footnote 43, points that the wording was changed in 1989.
50. A. Lieven (1994), pp.153–4. D. Levin (1994), p.22. L. Dymerskaya-Tsigelman (1986) 'M.S. Gorbachev Answers *L'Humanite's* Questions', *Jews and Jewish Topics in Soviet and East-European Publications*, no.2–3, p.3. In the latter article see also a photo documentation of the vandalised Jewish cemeteries all over the Soviet Union, among them in Vilnius and Kaunas.
51. Z. Katz, ed. (1975) *Handbook of Major Soviet Nationalities*. New York: The Free Press, p.364, p.370, p.381. V. Konstantinov (1991) 'Jewish Population of the USSR on the Eve of the Great Exodus', *Jews and Jewish Topics in the Soviet Union and Eastern Europe*, vol.16, no.3, pp.15–21.
52. N. Levin (1990), vol.2, p.577.
53. Like the case of Irene Versaite or the book in Yiddish, published in the Soviet Union by Genrikas Zimanas (1984) *Soviet Jews: Patriots of their Socialist Homeland*. Moscow: Socialist Writer. He was editor-in-chief of *Tiesa* and *Kommunist* in the SSR of Lithuania. The books published in Israel are often an important source like a case described by Sigitas Bleda in: S. Bleda

(1990) 'Some Lithuanians Saved Jews From the Nazis', *Jews and Jewish Topics in the Soviet Union and Eastern Europe*, vol.11, no.1, pp.65–6. Originally published in *Tiesa*, 25 October 1989.

54. Although between 1989 and 1991 Israel was the most popular destination for Lithuanian Jewry, in 1992 and 1993 more emigrated to the United States. Y. Floersheim (1992) 'Immigration to Israel from the Soviet Union in 1991', *Jews and Jewish Topics in the Soviet Union and Eastern Europe*, vol.19, no.3, p.6; Y. Floersheim (1993) 'Jewish Emigration to Israel and the United States from the Former Soviet Union, 1992', *Jews in Eastern Europe*, vol.22, no.3, p.37; Y. Floersheim (1995) 'Jewish Emigration from the Former Soviet Union in 1993', *Jews in Eastern Europe*, vol.26, no.1, p.26 and p.31.

55. J.A. Ross (1978) 'Interethnic Relations and Jewish Marginality in the Soviet Baltic', *Journal of Baltic Studies*, vol.9, no.4, pp.354–66.

56. See: Appendix: Demographic Data, Table 4.

57. My impression was that the Jews themselves do not like to 'dwell' on it in conversation because of the traditional ethnic stereotype of Jews as economically involved and doing well or better than the rest of the population. Furthermore, in the time of reawakening the search for identity and the importance of independence are of primary importance and any hardship is worth going through, so mentioning economic reasons is considered non-ethical.

58. These non-Jewish friends were not analysed according to their ethnic background. However, we have to bear in mind that Jews, according to the same research, had more friends among Russians than the native population. J.A. Ross (1978), p.359.

59. From the greeting of the Council of the *Seimas* of *Sajudis*, 1 May 1989. Published in 'Lithuanian–Jewish Relations in the Shadow of the Holocaust', *Jews and Jewish Topics in the Soviet Union and Eastern Europe*, vol.11, no.1, p.49.

60. D. Levin (1994), p.376.

61. As Isaac Detscher argues, 'Jews do not have roots, they have legs.' S. Schama (1995) *Landscape and Memory*. London: HarperCollins Publishers, p.36.

62. See: Appendix: Demographic Data, Table A1.1c.

63. T. Sawyer (1979) *The Jewish Minority in the Soviet Union*. Colorado: Westview Press, pp.34–8, pp.205–10.

64. *Lietuvos rytas*, 26 March–2 April 1993, p.2.

65. M. Altshuler (1988) 'Who Are the "Refuseniks"? A Statistical and Demographic Analysis', *Soviet Jewish Affairs*, vol.18, no.1, pp.3–15. However, the article does not offer enough data to understand why Lithuania had the highest number of *refuseniks*.

66. See: Appendix: Demographic Data, Tables A1.3c, A1.3d and A1.3e.

67. See: Appendix: Demographic Data, Table A1.1c.

68. According to Agranovskii and Guzenberg there were only 4000 Jews in Vilnius. G. Agranovskii and I. Guzenberg (1992) *Litovskii Erusalim* (Lithuanian Jerusalem). Vilnius: Lituanus, p.7. In my interviews the Jews would agree with that and would add that in the whole of Lithuania there are no more than 5000 Jews.

69. Interview with A. Juozaitis, 11 December 1992. He was a member of *Sajudis* but left the movement being disappointed with its nationalistic policies.
70. T. Venclova (1990), p.41.
71. A. Lieven (1993), pp.146–8. Interview with R. Ozolas, 27 November 1992. He left *Sajudis* to form the Party of the Centre.
72. H. Arendt (1958, second, enlarged edition) *The Origins of Totalitarianism*. London: George Allen and Unwin Ltd, p.54.
73. A. Terliackas (1990), p.48.
74. Lieven agrees with their conclusion. 'Given the present rate of emigration however, they will soon all be gone.' A. Lieven (1994), p.132.
75. See a review of the newspaper by D. Levin (1989) 'Once Again a Yiddish Newspaper in Vilna, the *Jerusalem of Lithuania*', *Jews and Jewish Topics in the Soviet Union and Eastern Europe*, vol.10, no.3, pp.96–9.
76. Interview with S. Alperovich, 14 December 1992.
77. He pointed out that the two anti-Semitic newspapers from Russia were banned (*Molodaia Guardia* and *Sovremenik*).
78. Interview with S. Alperovich, 14 December 1992.
79. Interview with S. Rapoport, 14 December 1992.

9 Postscript

1. M.P. Saulauskas (1994) 'Revolution 1989: Farewell to Modernity? An Outline of Lithuanian Experience', in: N. Lomaniene and M.P. Salauskas, eds., *Social Change*, vol.1. Vilnius: Independent Institute for Social Research, p.63, footnote 12.
2. Interview with R. Ozolas, 27 November 1992. He left *Sajudis* to establish the Party of the Centre.
3. O. Norgaard *et al.* (1996) *The Baltic States After Independence*. Cheltenham: Edward Elgar, p.187.
4. *The Lithuanian Policy on National Minorities* (November 1996). Vilnius: Governmental Information Centre, p.21.
5. Ibid., p.25.
6. Ibid., p.25.
7. See: Appendix: Demographic Data, Tables A1.1c, A1.1d and A1.3c.
8. See: Appendix: Demographic Data, Tables A1.1c, A1.1d, A1.3d and A1.3e.
9. See: Appendix: Demographic Data, Tables A1.1c and A1.1d.
10. Interview with Halina Kobeckaite, 30 October 1992. She was the Director of the Department of National Minorities of the Government of the Republic of Lithuania.
11. According to a document provided by the Lithuanian Embassy in London in January 1999, *Tauten mazumu organizaciju sarasas*.
12. *The Baltic Times*, 15–21 January 1998, p.6.
13. Interview with P. Frolov, 25 June 1993. He was a co-President of the Russian Community of Lithuania.
14. *The Baltic Independent*, 2–8 November 1995.
15. *The Baltic Times*, 19–25 September 1996, p.6.
16. O. Norgaard *et al.* (1996), p.186.
17. FBIS-SOV-95-161-21 August, p.90.

18. *The Baltic Times*, 29 January–4 February 1998, p.6.
19. See: Appendix: Education, Table A2.4.
20. *The Baltic Times*, 29 January–4 February 1998, p.6.
21. E-mail message from Professor Brazis, 9 June 1998.
22. *The Baltic Times*, 22–28 January 1998, p.6.
23. *The Baltic Times*, 16–22 October 1997, p.6.
24. Although the Vilnius province took the Vilnius region to court the case has still not been decided. According to the 19 July 1994 law ten provinces were formed in Lithuania. *Lietuvos statistikos metrastis, 1996*. Vilnius: Metodinis leidybinis centras, p.26.
25. *Financial Times* Survey, Lithuania. 25 November 1998, p.iv.
26. *The Baltic Times*, 6–12 June 1996, p.6. See also: *The Baltic Times*, 2–8 May 1996, p.1 and p.6.
27. *Financial Times* Survey, Lithuania. 25 November 1998, p.iv.
28. N. Lane (1995) 'Estonia and its Jews', *East European Jewish Affairs*, vol.25, no.1, p.4.
29. Ibid., p.16.
30. *The Baltic Times*, 6–12 February 1997, p.6. See: Chapter 2, note 29.
31. *The Baltic Times*, 25 September–1 October 1997, p.6.
32. *The Baltic Times*, 2–8 October 1997, p.6.
33. *The Baltic Times*, 28 June–2 July 1998, p.6.

Bibliography

Aasland, A. (1992) 'Russians in Latvia'. A paper presented at the conference 'The New Russian Diaspora'. Jurmala, Latvia, 12–15 November 1992.

Adorno, Th.W. *et al.* (1950) *The Authoritarian Personality*. New York: Harper and Row.

Agranovskii, G. and Guzenberg, I. (1992) *Litovskii Ierusalim* (Lithuanian Jerusalem). Vilnius: Lituanus.

Alfredsson, G. and De Zayas, A. (1993) 'Minority Rights: Protection by the United Nations', *Human Rights Law Journal*, vol.14, no.1–2.

Allworth, E. (1990) 'A Theory of Soviet Nationality Policies', in: H.R. Huttenbach, ed., *Soviet Nationality Policies: Ruling Ethnic Groups in the USSR*. London: Mansell.

Altshuler, M. (1988) 'Who Are the "Refuseniks"? A Statistical and Demographic Analysis', *Soviet Jewish Affairs*, vol.18, no.1.

Anderson, B. (1983) *Imagined Communities*. London: Verso.

Anderson, B. and Silver, B. (1990) 'Some Factors in Linguistic and Ethnic Russification of Soviet Nationalities', in: L. Hajda and M. Beissinger, eds., *The Nationalities Factor in the Soviet Politics and Society*. Boulder, Col.: Westview Press.

Arato, A. (1991) 'Revolution, Civil Society, and Democracy', in: Z. Rau, ed., *The Reemergence of Civil Society in Eastern Europe and the Soviet Union*. Boulder, Col.: Westview Press.

Arendt, H. (1946) Book Review: O. Janowsky, *Nationalities and National Minorities, Jewish Social Studies*, vol.8, no.2.

Arendt, H. (1950, second, enlarged edition) *The Origins of Totalitarianism*. London: George Allen and Unwin.

Arendt, H. (1963) *On Revolution*. London: Faber and Faber.

Arendt, H. (1970) *On Violence*. London: Allen Lane and Penguin Books.

Arutiunian, Iu. *et al.* (1980) *Opyt etnosotciologicheskogo issledovaniya obraza zhizni* (An Ethno-Sociological Approach Towards the Way of Life). Moscow: Nauka.

Atamukas, S. (1990) *Jews in Lithuania: 14th–20th Century*. Vilnius: Lituanus.

de Azcarate, P. (1945) *League of Nations and National Minorities: an Experiment*. Washington, DC: Carnegie Endowment for International Peace.

The Baltic States. Oxford: Oxford University Press, 1938.

Banton, M. (1977) *Rational Choice: a Theory of Racial and Ethnic Relations*, SSRC Research Unit on Ethnic Relations, University of Bristol.

Baranovskii, V. (1989) 'Kitezh-Grad' (Kitezh Town), *Vilnius*, no.8.

Barbalet, J.M. (1988) *Citizenship: Rights, Struggle and Class Inequality*. Milton Keynes: Open University Press.

Barrington, L. (1995) 'The Domestic and International Consequences of Citizenship in the Soviet Successor States', *Europe–Asia Studies*, vol.47, no.5.

Bendinskas, A. (1990) 'Pogrom in Kaunas: One Version', *Jews and Jewish Topics in the Soviet Union and Eastern Europe*, vol.11, no.1.

Berdichievsky, N. (1992) 'The Baltic Revival and Zionism', *Lituanus*, vol.38, no.1.

Bernhardt, R. and Schermers, H. (1992) 'Lithuanian Law and International Human Rights Standards', *Human Rights Law Journal*, vol.13, no.5–6.

Bialer, S. (1980) *Stalin's Successors: Leadership, Stability, and Change in the Soviet Union*. Cambridge: Cambridge University Press.

Blaustein, A.P. and Flanz, G.H., eds. (1992) *Constitutions of the Countries of the World: Lithuania*, by G.H. Flanz. New York: Oceana Publications, Dobbs Ferry.

Bleda, S. (1990) 'Some Lithuanians Saved Jews from the Nazis', *Jews and Jewish Topics in the Soviet Union and Eastern Europe*, vol.11, no.1.

Bromley, Iu. (1977) 'Internatsionalnoe and natsionalnoe v stroitelystve social-isma' (The International and National Building of Socialism), *Sovetskaia etno-grafiia*, no.5.

Brubaker, R. (1992) *Citizenship and Nationhood in France and Germany*. Cambridge, Mass.: Harvard University Press.

Brubaker, R. (1992) 'Citizenship Struggles in the Soviet Successor States', *International Migration Review*, vol.26, no.2.

Brubaker, R. (1995) 'Aftermaths of Empire and the Unmixing of Peoples: Historical and Comparative Perspectives', *Ethnic and Racial Studies*, vol.18, no.2.

Brym, R.J. (1988) 'Soviet Jewish Emigration: a Statistical Test of Two Theories', *Soviet Jewish Affairs*, vol.18, no.3.

Budreckis, A., ed. (1985) *Eastern Lithuania: a Collection of Historical and Ethnographic Studies*. Chicago: Lithuanian Association of the Vilnius Region.

Burant, S.R. (1991) 'Polish–Lithuanian Relations: Past, Present and Future', *Problems of Communism*, vol.40, no.3.

Burant, S.R. (1997) 'Belarus and the "Belarusian Irredenta" in Lithuania', *Nationalities Papers*, vol.25, no.4.

Byatt, A.S. (1996) 'Memory and the Making of Fiction', Eleventh Annual Darwin College Lecture, Lady Mitchell Hall, Cambridge, 8 March 1996.

Carrere d'Encausse, H. (1995) *The Nationality Question in the Soviet Union*. Oslo: Scandinavian University Press.

Chinn, J. and Kaiser, R. (1996) 'Lithuanians', in: J. Chinn and R. Kaiser, *Russians as the New Minority: Ethnicity and Nationalism in the Soviet Successor States*. Boulder, Col.: Westview Press.

Cohen, I. (5704-1943) *Jewish Community Series: Vilna*. Philadelphia: The Jewish Publication Society in America.

Cohen, J. (1995) 'Interpreting the Notion of Civil Society', in: M. Waltzer, ed., *Towards a Global Civil Society*. Oxford: Berghahn Books.

Coley, L. (1996) *Britons: Forging the Nation 1707–1837*. London: Vintage.

Connor, W. (1984) *The National Question in Marxist-Leninist Theory and Strategy*. Princeton: Princeton University Press.

Coser, L.A. (1956) *The Functions of Social Conflict*. London: Routledge and Kegan Paul.

Crozier, M. (1966) *The Bureaucratic Phenomenon*. Chicago: Chicago University Press.

'Current Constitutional and Factual Condition of Religion in Lithuania (As Reflected in Official and *Samizdat* Documents)', *Lituanus*, 1979, vol.25, no.1.

Dahrendorf, R. (1959) *Class and Class Conflict in Industrial Society*. London: Routledge and Kegan Paul.

Dahrendorf, R. (1979) *Life Chances: Approach to Social and Political Theory*. London: Weidenfeld and Nicolson.

Dahrendorf, R. (1980) *After Social Democracy*. London: Liberal Publication Department.

Dahrendorf, R. (1990) *Reflections on the Revolution in Europe*. London: Chatto and Windus.

Dalton, R.J., Kuechler, M. and Buerklin, W. (1990) 'The Challenge of New Movements', in: R.J. Dalton and M. Kuechler eds., *Challenging the Political Order*. Cambridge: Polity Press.

Dawson, J.I. (1996) *Eco-nationalism: Anti-nuclear Activism and National Identity in Russia, Lithuania and Ukraine*. Durham and London: Duke University Press.

Declaration on the Rights of Persons Belonging to National or Ethnic, Religious or Linguistic Minorities (1993), *Human Rights Law Journal*, vol.14, no.1–2.

Doersam, Ch. (1977) 'Sovietization, Culture and Religion', in: E. Allworth, ed., *Nationality Group Survival in Multi-Ethnic States*. London: Praeger.

The Draft Constitution of the Republic of Lithuania (1992). Vilnius: Supreme Council of the Republic of Lithuania.

Dreifelds, J. (1989) 'Latvian National Rebirth', *Problems of Communism*, vol.38, no.4.

Duncan, S. and Goodwin, M. (1987) *The Local State and Uneven Development*. New York: St. Martin's Press.

Duverger, M. (1964) *Political Parties: their Organization and Activity in the Modern State* (second edition, rev.). London: Methuen.

Dymerskaya-Tsigelman, L. (1986) 'M.S. Gorbachev Answers *L'Humanite's* Questions', *Jews and Jewish Topics in Soviet and East-European Publications*, no.2–3.

Efremov, G. (1990) *My ljudi drug drugu* (We See Each Other as Human Beings). Moscow: Progress.

Faulks, K. (1998) *Citizenship in Modern Britain*. Edinburgh: Edinburgh University Press.

Finkelsteinas, H. (1990) 'Pogroms in Kaunas: Another Version', *Jews and Jewish Topics in the Soviet Union and Eastern Europe*, vol.11, no.1.

Flanz, G.H. (1992) 'Lithuania', in: A.P. Blaustein and G.H. Flanz, eds., *Constitutions of the Countries of the World*. New York: Oceania Publications.

Fleming, J. (1977) 'Political Leaders', in: E. Allworth, ed., *Nationality Group Survival in Multi-Ethnic States*. London: Praeger.

Floersheim, Y. (1992) 'Immigration to Israel from the Soviet Union in 1991', *Jews and Jewish Topics in the Soviet Union and Eastern Europe*, vol.19, no.3.

Floersheim, Y. (1993) 'Jewish Emigration to Israel and the United States from the Former Soviet Union, 1992', *Jews in Eastern Europe*, vol.22, no.3.

Floersheim, Y. (1995) 'Jewish Emigration from the former Soviet Union in 1993', *Jews in Eastern Europe*, vol.26, no.1.

Freedman, R.O. (1988) 'Relations Between the USSR and Israel Since the Accession of Gorbachev', *Soviet Jewish Affairs*, vol.18, no.2.

Friedgut, Th.F. (1990) 'Rejection and Rebellion: Jews and Other National Minorities Under Perestroika', *Jews and Jewish Topics in the Soviet Union and Eastern Europe*, vol.11, no.1.

Friedgut, Th.F. (1991) '*Perestroyka* and the Nationalities', *Soviet Jewish Affairs*, vol.21, no.1.

Friedman, M. (1976) 'The Kehillah in Lithuania 1919–1926: a Study Based on Panevezys and Ukmerge (Vilkomer)', *Soviet Jewish Affairs*, vol.6, no.2.

Gaidys, V. (1994) 'Russians in Lithuania', in: V. Shlapentokh, M. Sendich and E. Payin, eds., *The New Russian Diaspora: Russian Minorities in the Former Soviet Republics*. London: M.E. Sharpe.

Gellner, E. (1983) *Nations and Nationalism*. Oxford: Basil Blackwell.

Gellner, E. (1994) *Conditions of Liberty: Civil Society and its Rivals*. Harmondsworth: Penguin.

'General Comments No.23 (50) on Article 27 of the Draft Protocol of Minority Rights (1994)', *Human Rights Law Journal*, vol.15, no.4–6.

Giddens, A. (1985) 'Class, Sovereignty and Citizenship', in: A. Giddens, *The Nation State and Violence*. Cambridge: Polity Press.

Giddens, A. (1989) 'Citizenship and Authority', in: D. Held and J.B. Thompson, eds., *Social Theory of Modern Societies*. Cambridge: Cambridge University Press.

Girnius, K.K. (1982) 'The Opposition Movement in Postwar Lithuania', *Journal of Baltic Studies*, vol.13, no.1.

Girnius, K.S. (1985) 'Lithuania', in: V. Mastny, ed., *Soviet/East European Survey, 1983–1984: Selected Research and Analysis from Radio Free Europe/Radio Liberty*. Durham: Duke University Press.

Girnius, S. (1993) 'Lithuania's Foreign Policy', *RFE/RL Research Report*, vol.2, no.35, 3 September.

Gitelman, Z. (1980) 'Moscow and the Soviet Jews: a Parting of the Ways', *Problems of Communism*, vol.29, no.1.

Gitelman, Z. (1983) 'Are Nations Merging in the USSR?', *Problems of Communism*, vol.32, no.5.

Gleason, G. (1990a) *Federalism and Nationalism*. Boulder, Col.: Westview Press.

Gleason, G. (1990b) 'Leninist Nationality Policy: its Source and Style', in: H.R. Huttenbach, ed., *Soviet Nationality Policies: Ruling Ethnic Groups in the USSR*. London: Mansell.

Gordon, E.J. (1996) 'The Revival of Polish National Consciousness: a Comparative Study of Lithuania, Belarus and Ukraine', *Nationalities Papers*, vol.24, no.2.

Gray, J. (1991) 'Post-Totalitarianism, Civil Society, and the Limits of the Western Model', in: Z. Rau, ed., *The Reemergence of Civil Society in Eastern Europe and the Soviet Union*. Boulder, Col.: Westview Press.

Greene, V. (1975) *For God and Country: the Rise of Polish and Lithuanian Ethnic Consciousness in America, 1860–1910*. Madison, Wi.: The State Historical Society of Wisconsin.

Grek-Pabisowa, I. and Maryniakowa, I. (1992) 'Wspolczesne gwary polskie na Litwie i Bialorusi' (Contemporary Polish Dialects in Lithuania and Belorussia), in: H. Kubiak *et al.*, *Mniejszosci Polskie i Polonia w ZSRR*. Wroclaw, Warszawa, Krakow: Zaklad Narodowy imienia Ossolinskich.

Gringauz, S. (1949) 'The Ghetto as an Experiment of Jewish Social Organization: Three Years of Kovno Ghetto', *Jewish Social Studies*, vol.11, no.1.

Gringauz, S. (1952) 'Jewish National Autonomy in Lithuania (1918–1925)', *Jewish Social Studies*, vol.14, no.3.

Guinier, L. (1991) *The Triumph of Tokenism*, cited in: A. Phillips (1993).

van Gunsteren, H.R. (1998) *A Theory of Citizenship: Organizing Plurality in Contemporary Democracies*. Boulder, Col.: Westview Press.

Habermas, J. (1983) 'Hannah Arendt: on the Concept of Power', in: J. Habermas, *Philosophical-Political Profiles*. London: Heinemann.

Hall, J.A. (1995) 'In Search of Civil Society', in: J.A. Hall, ed., *Civil Society: Theory, History, Comparison*. Cambridge: Polity Press.

Hall, S. and Held, D. (1989) 'Citizens and Citizenship', in: S. Hall and M. Jacques, eds., *New Times*. London: Lawrence and Wishart.

Hammersley, M. and Atkinson, P. (1996) *Ethnography: Principles in Practice*. London: Routledge.

Harris, D.J. (1979) *Cases and Material on International Law*. London: Sweet and Maxwell.

Harvey, D. (1993) 'Class Relations, Social Justice and the Politics of Difference', in: J. Squire, ed., *Principled Positions: Postmodernism and the Rediscovery of Value*. London: Lawrence and Wishart.

Heather, D.B. (1990) *Citizenship: the Civic Idea in World History, Politics and Education*. London: Longman.

Heitman, S. (1988) 'The Third Soviet Emigration', *Soviet Jewish Affairs*, vol.18, no.2.

Heitman, S. (1989) 'A Soviet Draft Law on Emigration', *Soviet Jewish Affairs*, vol.19, no.3.

Heitman, S. (1990) 'Soviet Emigration Policies towards Germans and Armenians', in: H.R. Huttenbach, ed., *Soviet Nationality Policies: Ruling Ethnic Groups in the USSR*. London: Mansell.

Heitman, S. (1991) 'Soviet Emigration in 1990: a New "Fourth Wave"?, *Soviet Jewish Affairs*, vol.21, no.2.

Held, D. (1987) *Models of Democracy*. Cambridge: Polity Press.

Held, D. (1989) 'Citizenship and Authority', in: D. Held and J.B. Thompson, eds., *Social Theory of Modern Societies*. Cambridge: Cambridge University Press.

Heller, A. and Feher, F. (1989) *The Postmodern Political Conditions*. Cambridge: Polity Press.

Heltai, P.A. and Rau, Z. (1991) 'From Nationalism to Civil Society and Tolerance', in: Z. Rau, ed., *The Reemergence of Civil Society in Eastern Europe and the Soviet Union*. Boulder, Col.: Westview Press.

Henderson, K. and Robinson, N. (1997) *Post-communist Politics: an Introduction*. Hemel Hempstead: Prentice Hall.

Hiden, J. and Salmon, P. (1991) *The Baltic Nations and Europe: Estonia, Latvia and Lithuania in the Twentieth Century*. London: Longman.

Hirszowicz, L. (1988) 'Breaking the Mould: the Changing Face of Jewish Culture Under Gorbachev', *Soviet Jewish Affairs*, vol.18, no.3.

Hobsbawm, E.J. (1990) *Nations and Nationalism since 1780*. Cambridge: Cambridge University Press.

Hobsbawm, E. (1996) 'Language, Culture and National Identity', *Social Research*, vol.63, no.4.

Hroch, M. (1985) *Social Preconditions of National Revival in Europe*. Cambridge: Cambridge University Press.

Hroch, M. (1993) 'From National Movements to Fully-Fledged Nations', *New Left Review*, March/April.

Inkeles, A. (1968) *Social Change in Soviet Russia*. Cambridge, Mass.: Harvard University Press.

Irwin, Z. (1990) 'Soviet-Jewish Emigration Policy: Anti-Zionism and Philo-Semitism', in: H.R. Huttenbach, ed., *Soviet Nationality Policies: Ruling Ethnic Groups in the USSR*. London: Mansell.

Ivinskis, Z. (1965) 'Lithuania During the War: Resistance Against the Soviet and Nazi Occupation', in: V.S. Vardys, ed., *Lithuania Under the Soviets: Portrait of a Nation, 1940–1965*. London: Frederick A. Praeger.

Jacobs, E.M. (1976) 'Jewish Representation in Local Soviets', *Soviet Jewish Affairs*, vol.6, no.1.

Janowsky, O.I. (1938) *People at Bay: the Jewish Problem in East-Central Europe*. London: Victor Gollancz.

Jewish Social Studies: Supplement (1946), vol.8, no.3.

Jews and Jewish Topics in the Soviet Union and Eastern Europe, vol.11, no.1, 1990.

Johnson, R.J., Knight, D.B. and Kofman, E., eds. (1988) *Nationalism, Self-Determination and Political Geography*. London: Croom Helm.

Kanovich, G. (1989) 'Evropeiskaia Romaneshka' (Jewish Flower-Petal Game), *Jews and Jewish Topics in the Soviet Union and Eastern Europe*, vol.10, no.3.

Karklins, R. (1986) *Ethnic Relations in the USSR*. Boston: Allen and Unwin.

Kasatkina, N. (1996) 'Russians in the Lithuanian State: the Historical Perspective of the National Identity', in: M. Taljunaite, ed., *Changes of Identity in Modern Lithuania*. Vilnius: Institute of Philosophy and Sociology, Republic of Lithuania and Centre for Russian and East European Studies, University of Goteborg, Sweden.

Kasparaviciene, V. (1996) 'Ethnic Composition of Vilnius Residents, National Relations and Estimations', in: M. Taljunaite, ed., *Changes of Identity in Modern Lithuania*. Vilnius: Institute of Philosophy and Sociology, Republic of Lithuania and Centre for Russian and East European Studies, University of Goteborg.

Katz, Z., ed. (1975) *Handbook of Major Soviet Nationalities*. New York: The Free Press.

Keane, J. (1988) *Democracy and Civil Society*. London: Verso.

Kellas, J.G. (1991) *The Politics of Nationalism and Ethnicity*. London: Macmillan.

Kelner, V. (1994) 'Jewish Culture in Russia, 1991–1994: a Survey', *East European Jewish Affairs*, vol.24, no.2.

King, G.J. (1970) 'Comments on the Current State of Baltic Demographic Research', *Bulletin of Baltic Studies*, no.4.

Kirby, D. (1995) *The Baltic World, 1772–1993: Europe's Northern Periphery in an Age of Change*. London: Longman.

Kirby, D. (1996) 'Incorporation: the Molotov–Ribbentrop Pact', in: G. Smith, ed., *The Baltic States: the National Self-Determination of Estonia, Latvia and Lithuania*. Basingstoke: Macmillan.

Klebes, H. (1993) 'Draft Protocol on Minority Rights to the ECHR: Introduction', *Human Rights Law Journal*, vol.14, no.3–4.

Koch, K. (1993) 'The International Community and Forms of Intervention in the Field of Minority Rights Protection', in: I.M. Cuthbertson and J. Leibowitz, eds., *Minorities: the New Europe's Old Issue*. Boulder, Col.: Westview Press for the Institute for East–West Studies.

Konstantinov, V. (1991) 'Jewish Population of the USSR on the Eve of the Great Exodus', *Jews and Jewish Topics in the Soviet Union and Eastern Europe*, vol.16, no.3.

Korey, W. (1968) 'The Legal Position of the Jewish Community of the Soviet Union', in: E. Goldhagen, ed., *National Minorities in the Soviet Union*. New York: Frederick A. Praeger.

Korey, W. (1978) '*Anti-Zionism in the USSR* (book review)', *Problems of Communism*, vol.27, no.6.

Kostloe, P. (1992) 'The New Russian Diaspora: an Identity of its Own', A paper presented at the conference 'New Russian Diaspora', Riga, 13–15 November 1992.

Kostloe, P. (1995) *Russians in the Former Soviet Republics*. London: C. Hurst.

Kowalewski, D. (1979) 'Lithuanian Protest for Human Rights in the 1970s: Characteristics and Consequences', *Lituanus*, vol.25, no.2, p.52.

Krickus, R. (1993) 'Lithuania: Nationalism in the Modern Era', in: I. Bremmer and R. Taras, eds., *Nations and Politics in the Soviet Successor States*. Cambridge: Cambridge University Press.

Kritzman, L.D., ed. (1988) *Michel Foucault: Politics, Philosophy, Culture: Interviews and Other Writings 1977–1984*. New York: Routledge.

Krooth, R. and Vladimirovitz, B. (pseudonym) (1993) *Quest for Freedom: the Transformation of Eastern Europe in the 1990s*. London: McFarland.

Krukauskiene, E. (1990) 'The Survey of Notions about the Independence of Lithuania in its Diverse Language Speaking Regions', in: *Sociological Research in the Baltic States*. Vilnius: Lithuanian Sociological Association, Latvian Sociological Association, Estonian Academic Union of Sociologists, Institute of Philosophy, Sociology and Law of Lithuanian Academy of Sciences.

Krukauskiene, E. (1996) 'State and National Identity', in: *Changes of Identity in Modern Lithuania*. Vilnius: Institute of Philosophy and Sociology, Republic of Lithuania, Centre for Russian and East European Studies, University of Goteborg.

Kuchinskas, L. (1991) 'Lithuania's Independence: the Litmus Test for Democracy', *Lituanus*, vol.37, no.3.

Kudirka, J. (1991) *The Lithuanians: an Ethnic Portrait*. Vilnius: Lithuanian Folk Culture Centre.

Kudirka, S. and Eichel, L. (1977) *For Those Still at Sea: the Defection of a Lithuanian Sailor*. New York: The Dial Press.

Kupcinskas Keshawarz, M. (1979) 'Simas Kudirka: a Literary Symbol of Democratic Individualism in Jirzy Kosinski's "Cockpit"', *Lituanus*, vol.25, no.4, pp.38–42.

Kurzowa, Z. (1992) 'Jezyk polski na kresach wschodnich po II wojnie swiatowej', in: Hieronim Kubiak *et al.*, *Mniejszosci Polskie i Polonia w ZSRR*. Wroclaw, Warszawa, Krakow: Zaklad Narodowy imienia Ossolinskich.

Laserson, M.M. (1941) 'The Jewish Minorities in the Baltic Countries', *Jewish Social Studies*, vol.3.

Lawson, E. (1996) *Encyclopedia of Human Rights*, second edition. London: Taylor and Francis.

Lestchinsky, J. (1946) 'The Economic Struggle of the Jews in Independent Lithuania', *Jewish Social Studies*, vol.8, no.4.

Levin, D. (1975) 'Participation of the Lithuanian Jews in the Second World War', *Journal of Baltic Studies*, vol.6, no.4.

Levin, D. (1989) 'Once Again a Yiddish Newspaper in Vilna, the *Jerusalem of Lithuania*', *Jews and Jewish Topics in the Soviet Union and Eastern Europe*, vol.10, no.3.

Levin, D. (1991) 'The Sovietization of the Baltics and the Jews, 1940–1941', *Soviet Jewish Affairs*, vol.21, no.1.

Levin, D. (1994) *Baltic Jews Under the Soviets, 1940–1946*. Jerusalem: The Hebrew University of Jerusalem.

Levin, N. (1990) *The Jews in the Soviet Union Since 1917: Paradox of Survival*. London: I.B. Tauris and Co.

Lieven, A. (1994) *The Baltic Revolution: Estonia, Latvia, Lithuania and the Path to Independence*. New Haven: Yale University Press.

Lindholm, T. (1992a) 'Multi-ethnic Societies and Human Rights'. Paper for the Conference on 'Democracy and Ethnopolitics', Riga, 19–21 May 1992.

Lindholm, T. (1992b) 'The New Russian Diaspora and International Human Rights'. Paper for the Conference on the New Russian Diaspora, Riga, 13–15 November 1992.

Litvak, Y. (1991) 'The Plight of Refugees from the German-Occupied Territories', in: K. Sword, ed., *The Soviet Takeover of the Polish Eastern Provinces, 1939–1941*. London: Macmillan in association with School of Slavonic and East European Studies, University of London.

Lomaniene, N. (1994) 'On Lithuanian Nationalism: the Movement and the Concept', in: N. Lomaniene and M.P. Saulauskas, eds., *Social Change*, vol.1. Vilnius: Independent Institute for Social Research.

Luik, J. (1991) 'Intellectuals and their Two Paths to Restoring Civil Society in Estonia', in: Z. Rau, ed., *The Reemergence of Civil Society in Eastern Europe and the Soviet Union*. Boulder, Col.: Westview Press.

Lyman, S.M. and Douglass, W.A. (1973) 'Ethnicity: Strategies of Collective and Individual Impression Management', *Social Research*, vol.40, no.2.

Macartney, C.A. (1934) *National States and National Minorities*. Oxford: Oxford University Press.

McAuley, M. (1992) *Soviet Politics 1917–1991*. Oxford: Oxford University Press.

Maceevski, J. (1993) 'Lithuania–Poland: a Knot which could be Undone only by Both Sides', *Lietuvos rytas*, 14–21 May.

'Manifesto for New Times', in: S. Hall and M. Jacques, eds. (1989) *New Times*. London: Lawrence and Wishart.

Marie, J-B. (1993) 'International Instruments Relating to Human Rights: Classification and Status of Ratifications as of 1 January 1993', *Human Rights Law Journal*, vol.14, no.1–2.

Marshall, T.H. (1950) *Citizenship and Social Class*. Cambridge: Cambridge University Press.

Marston, S.A. and Staeheli, L.A. (1994) 'Citizenship, Struggle and Political and Economic Restructuring', *Environment and Planning* A, vol.26, no.6.

May, T. (1997, second edition) *Social Research: Issues, Methods and Process*. Buckingham: Open University Press.

Medvedev, R. (1980) *On Soviet Dissent: Interviews with Piero Ostellino*. New York: Columbia University Press.

Melucci, A. (1989) *Nomads of the Present*. London: Hutchinson Radious.

Melvin, N. (1995) *Russians Beyond Russia: the Politics of National Identity*. London: Royal Institute of International Affairs.

Mendelsohn, E. (1983) *The Jews of East Central Europe: Between the World Wars*. Bloomington: Indiana University Press.

Milosz, Cz. (1981) *The Issa Valley*. London: Sidgwick and Jackson.

Misiunas, R.J. (1994) 'National Identity and Foreign Policy in the Baltic States', in: S.F. Starr, ed., *The Legacy of History in Russia and the New States of Euroasia*. London: M.E. Sharpe.

Misiunas, R. and Taagepera, R. (1993) *The Baltic States: the Years of Dependence.* London: Hurst.

Mouffe, Ch., ed. (1992) *Dimensions of Radical Democracy: Pluralism, Citizenship, Community.* London: Verso.

Mouffe, Ch. (1995) 'Pluralism and the Left Identity', in: M. Waltzer, ed., *Towards a Global Civil Society.* Oxford: Berghahn Books.

National Minorities in Lithuania. Vilnius: Department of Nationalities of the Government of the Republic of Lithuania.

Nekrasas, E. (1993) 'Lithuania and her Neighbours', in: N. Petersen, ed., *The Baltic States in International Politics.* Copenhagen: The Danish Institute of International Studies.

'The New Soviet Emigration Law Revisited: Implementation and Compliance with Other Laws' (1988), *Soviet Jewish Affairs*, vol.18, no.1.

Norgaard, O. *et al.* (1996) *The Baltic States after Independence.* Cheltenham: Edward Elgar.

The Non-Estonian Population Today and Tomorrow (1992) Talinn: The Institute of Philosophy, Sociology and Law of the Estonian Academy of Sciences.

O'Connell, D.P. (1971) *International Law for Students.* London: Sterens and Sons.

Oleszczuk, T.A. (1985) 'An Analysis of Bias in *Samizdat* Sources: a Lithuanian Case Study', *Soviet Studies*, vol.37, no.1.

Oleszczuk, T.A. (1988) *Political Justice in the USSR: Dissent and Repression in Lithuania, 1969–1987.* Boulder, Col.: Westview Press (East European Monographs).

Olzak, S. (1998) 'Ethnic Protest in Core and Periphery States', *Ethnic and Racial Studies*, vol.21, no.2.

Parming, T. (1977) 'Roots of Nationality Differences', in: E. Allworth, ed., *Nationality Group Survival in Multi-Ethnic States: Shifting Support Patterns in the Soviet Baltic Region.* London: Praeger Publishers.

Phillips, A. (1993) *Democracy and Difference.* Cambridge: Polity Press.

Pilkington, H. (1998) *Migration, Displacement and Identity in Post-Soviet Russia.* London: Routledge.

Pospielovsky, D.V. (1976) 'Russian Nationalist Thought and the Jewish Question', *Soviet Jewish Affairs*, vol.6, no.1.

Povilas Saulauskas, M. (1994) *Revolution 1989: Farewell to Modernity? An Outline of Lithuanian Experience.* Vilnius: Independent Institute for Social Research.

Prazauskas, A. (1994) 'The Influence of Ethnicity on the Foreign Policies of the Western Littoral States', in: R. Szporluk, ed., *National Identity and Ethnicity in Russia and the New States of Euroasia.* New York: M.E. Sharpe.

Preece, J.J. (1997) 'National Minority Rights vs State Sovereignty in Europe: Changing Norms in International Relations', *Nations and Nationalism*, vol.3, no.3.

'Proposal for an Additional Protocol to the ECHR Concerning Persons Belonging to National Minorities' (1993), *Human Rights Law Journal*, vol.14, no.3–4.

Rakowska-Harmstone, T. (1985) 'Die Aktuelle Problematik sowjetischer Nationalitaetenpolitic', *Osteuropa*, vol.35.

Ramet, S.P. (1997) *Whose Democracy?: Nationalism, Religion and the Doctrine of Collective Rights in Post-1989 Eastern Europe.* Lanham, Maryland: Rowman and Littlefield.

Rau, Z. (1991) 'Introduction', in: Z. Rau, ed., *The Reemergence of Civil Society in Eastern Europe and the Soviet Union.* Boulder, Col.: Westview Press.

Rauch, von G. (1974) *The Baltic States: the Years of Independence*. London: C. Hurst.

Reddaway, P. (1983) 'Dissent in the Soviet Union', *Problems of Communism*, vol.32, no.6.

Resler, T.J. (1997) 'Dilemmas of Democratisation: Safeguarding Minorities in Russia, Ukraine and Lithuania', *Europe–Asia Studies*, vol.49, no.1.

Rigby, T.H. (1986) 'Was Stalin a Disloyal Patron?', *Soviet Studies*, vol.38, no.3.

Roche, M. (1992) *Rethinking Citizenship: Welfare, Ideology and Change in Modern Society*. Cambridge: Polity Press.

Romanovsky, D. (1993) 'Judaism and Other Religions Towards the End of the Soviet Period', *Jews in Eastern Europe*, vol.20, no.1.

Rose, R. and Maley, W. (1994) *Nationalities in the Baltic States: a Survey Study*. Centre for the Study of Public Policy, University of Strathclyde.

Ross, J.A. (1978) 'Interethnic Relations and Jewish Marginality in the Soviet Baltic', *Journal of Baltic Studies*, vol.9, no.4.

Rothschild, J. (1981) *Ethnopolitics*. New York: Columbia University Press.

Rubenstein, J. (1985) *Soviet Dissidents: their Struggle for Human Rights*, 2nd edition. Boston: Beacon Press.

Rutherford, L. and Bone, S., eds. (1993) *Osborn's Concise Law Dictionary*, eighth edition. London: Sweet and Maxwell.

Ryabchuk, M. (1991) 'Civil Society and National Emancipation: the Ukrainian Case', in: Z. Rau, ed., *The Reemergence of Civil Society in Eastern Europe and the Soviet Union*. Boulder, Col.: Westview Press.

Sabaliunas, L. (1972) *Lithuania in Crisis: Nationalism to Communism, 1939–1940*. Bloomington: Indiana University Press.

Sadomskaia, N. (1990) 'New Soviet Rituals and National Integration in the USSR', in: H.R. Huttenbach, ed., *Soviet Nationality Policies: Ruling Ethnic Groups in the USSR*. London: Mansell.

Saunders, G., ed. (1974) Samizdat: *Voices of the Soviet Opposition*. New York: Monad Press.

Sawyer, T.E. (1979) *The Jewish Minority in the Soviet Union*. Boulder, Col.: Westview Press.

Schama, S. (1995) *Landscape and Memory*. London: HarperCollins Publishers.

Schwartz, L. (1990) 'Regional Population Distribution and National Homelands in the USSR', in: H.R. Huttenbach, ed., *Soviet Nationality Policies: Ruling Ethnic Groups in the USSR*. London: Mansell.

Scott, A. (1990) *Ideology and the New Social Movements*. London: Unwin Hyman.

Selected Bibliography of Institutional, Economic and Financial Legislation (1991) Vilnius: State Publishing Centre.

Senn, A.E. (1959) *The Emergence of Modern Lithuania*. New York: Columbia University Press.

Senn, A.E. (1990) *Lithuania Awakening*. Berkeley: University of California Press.

Senn, A.E. (1992) 'The Political Culture of Independent Lithuania: a Review Essay', *Journal of Baltic Studies*, vol.23, no.3.

Senn, A.E. (1997) 'Lithuania: Rights and Responsibilities of Independence', in: I. Bremmer and R. Taras, eds., *New States, New Politics*. Cambridge: Cambridge University Press.

Service, R. (1997) *A History of Twentieth Century Russia*. Harmondsworth: Penguin.

Shtromas, A. (1978) 'Baltic Problems and Peace Studies', *Journal of Baltic Studies*, vol.9, no.1.

Shtromas, A. (1994) 'The Baltic States as Soviet Republics: Tensions and Contradictions', in G. Smith, ed., *The Baltic States: National Self-determination of Estonia, Latvia and Lithuania*. Basingstoke: Macmillan Press.

Silbajoris, R. (1989) 'Some Recent Baltic Poets: the Civic Duty to be Yourself', *Journal of Baltic Studies*, vol.20, no.3.

Simon, G. (1991) *Nationalism and Policy Towards the Nationalities in the Soviet Union: from Totalitarian Dictatorship to Post-Stalinist Society*. Boulder, Col.: Westview Press.

Smith, A.D. (1979) *Nationalism in the Twentieth Century*. Oxford: Martin Robertson.

Smith, A.D. (1983) *Theories of Nationalism*. London: Duckworth.

Smith, A.D. (1986) *The Ethnic Origins of Nations*. Oxford: Basil Blackwell.

Smith, A.D. (1991) *National Identity*. Harmondsworth: Penguin.

Smith, A.D. (1996) 'Culture, Community and Territory: the Politics of Ethnicity and Nationalism', *International Affairs*, vol.72, no.3.

Smith, A.D. (1996) 'The Resurgence of Nationalism?' Lecture at the Post-Soviet States Seminar, Sidney Sussex College, Cambridge, 6 March.

Smith, G. (1989) 'Administering Ethnoregional Stability', in: C.H. Williams and E. Kofman, eds., *Community Conflict, Partition and Nationalism*. London: Routledge.

Smith, G., ed. (1990) *The Nationalities Question in the Soviet Union*. London: Longman.

Smith, G. (1990) 'The Soviet Federation', in: M. Chisholm and D.M. Smith, eds., *Shared Space: Divided Space*. London: Unwin Hyman.

Smith, G. (1990) 'Nationalities Policies from Lenin to Gorbachev', in: G. Smith, ed., *The Nationalities Question in the Soviet Union*. London: Longman.

Smith, G. (1991) 'The State, Nationalism and the Nationalities Question in the Soviet Republics', in: C. Merridale and C. Ward, eds., *Perestroika*. London: E. Arnold.

Smith, G. (1995) 'Federation, Defederation and Refederation: from the Soviet Union to Russian Statehood', in: G. Smith, ed., *Federation: the Multiethnic Challenge*. London: Longman.

Smith, G. (1996a) 'The Nationalist Reawakening in the Baltic States of Estonia, Latvia and Lithuania', in: G. Smith, ed., *The Baltic States: the National Self-Determination of Estonia, Latvia and Lithuania*. Basingstoke: Macmillan.

Smith, G. (1996b) 'The Resurgence of Nationalism', in: G. Smith, ed., *The Baltic States: the National Self-Determination of Estonia, Latvia and Lithuania*. Basingstoke: Macmillan.

Smith, G. (1998) 'Nation Re-building and Political Discourses of Identity Politics in the Baltic States', in: G. Smith *et al.*, *Nation-building in the Post-Soviet Borderlands*. Cambridge: Cambridge University Press.

Smith, G. (1998) 'Post-colonialism and Borderland Identities', in: G. Smith *et al.*, *Nation-building in the Post-Soviet Borderlands: the Politics of National Identities*. Cambridge: Cambridge University Press.

Smith, G., Aasland, A. and Mole, R. (1996) 'Statehood, Ethnic Relations and Citizenship', in: G. Smith, ed., *The Baltic States: the National Self-Determination of Estonia, Latvia and Lithuania*. Basingstoke: Macmillan.

Smith, S.J. (1989) 'Society, Space and Citizenship: a Human Geography for the "New Times"?', *Transactions*, XIV, no.2.

Smith, T.C. and Oleszczuk, T.A. (1990) 'The Brezhnev Legacy: Nationalities and Gorbachev', p.32 in: Z. Gitelman, ed., *The Politics of Nationality and the Erosion of the USSR*. New York: St. Martin's Press.

Snyder, T. (1995) 'National Myths and International Relations: Poland and Lithuania: 1898–1994', *East European Politics and Society*, vol.9, no.2.

Snyder, T. (1998) 'The Polish-Lithuanian Commonwealth since 1989: National Narratives in Relations among Poland, Lithuania, Belarus and Ukraine', *Nationalism and Ethnic Politics*, vol.4, no.3.

Solchanyk, R. (1985) 'The "Merger" of Soviet Nationalities', in: V. Mastny, ed., *Soviet/East European Survey, 1983–1984: Selected Research and Analysis from Radio Free Europe/Radio Liberty*. Durham and London: Duke University Press.

Statement of the Supreme Council of the Republic of Lithuania on the Status of the Soviet Armed Forces in Lithuania, in: G.H. Flanz (1992) 'Lithuania', in: A.P. Blaustein and G.H. Flanz, eds., *Constitutions of the Countries of the World*. New York: Oceania Publications.

Statkus, N. (1997) 'Formation and Durability of Ethnic Identity: the Case of the Poles in Lithuania'. MA Dissertation, School of Slavonic and East European Studies, University of London.

Steen, A. (1996) 'Consolidations and Competence: Research on the Politics of Recruiting Political Elites in the Baltic States', *Journal of Baltic Studies*, vol.27, no.2.

Steiman, L.B. (1998) *Paths to Genocide*. Basingstoke: Macmillan.

Stepanovas, A. (1989) 'Who are the *Tutejszy*?', *Atgimimas*, 20 January.

van der Stoel, M. (1993) Letter to the Minister of Foreign Affairs of Lithuania, HE Mr Povilas Gylys, *Human Rights Law Journal*, vol.14, no.5–6.

Sword, K. (1993) 'Ethnic Poles in Ukraine, Belorus and Lithuania', in: *Minorities in Central and Eastern Europe*: An MRG International Report. London: Minority Rights Group.

Sword, K. (1994) *Deportation and Exile: Poles in the Soviet Union, 1939–48*. London: Macmillan in association with School of Slavonic and East European Studies, University of London.

Szporluk, R. (1989) 'Dilemmas of Russian Nationalism', *Problems of Communism*, vol.38, no.4.

Tarrow, S. (1977) *Between Centre and Periphery: Grassroot Politicians in Italy and France*. New Haven: Yale University Press.

Tarrow, S. (1994) *Power in Movement: Social Movements, Collective Action and Politics*. Cambridge: Cambridge University Press.

Tartakower, A. (1971) 'The Jewish Problem in the Soviet Union', *Jewish Social Studies*, vol.33, no.4.

Terliackas, A. (1990) 'No Justification for the Murder of the Lithuanian Jews', *Jews and Jewish Topics in the Soviet Union and Eastern Europe*, vol.11, no.1.

Thompson, C. (1992) *The Singing Revolution: a Political Journey through the Baltic States*. London: Michael Joseph.

Thompson, E.P. (1971) 'The Moral Economy of the English Crowd in the Eighteenth Century', *Past and Present*, vol.50.

Thornberry, P. (1994) 'International and European Standards on Minority Rights', in: H. Miall, ed., *Minority Rights in Europe: the Scope for a Transnational Regime*. London: Pinter Publishers for the RIIA.

Tolts, M. (1992) 'The Balance of Births and Deaths among the Soviet Jewry', *Jews and Jewish Topics in the Soviet Union and Eastern Europe*, vol.18, no.2.

Touraine, A. (1981) *The Voice and the Eye: an Analysis of Social Movements.* Cambridge: Cambridge University Press.

Touraine, A. *et al.* (1983) *Solidarity: the Analysis of a Social Movement: Poland 1980–1981.* Cambridge: Cambridge University Press.

Tumin, M. (1971) 'Anti-semitism and Status Anxiety: a Hypothesis', *Jewish Social Studies*, vol.33, no.4.

Turner, B.S., ed. (1993) *Citizenship and Social Theory.* London: Sage.

Turska, H. (1939–1995) *O powstaniu polskich obszarow jezykowych na Wilenszczyznie.* Vilnius: Mintis.

Vachudova, M.A. and Snyder, T. (1997) 'Are Transitions Transitory? Two Types of Political Change in Eastern Europe since 1989', *East European Politics and Society*, vol.11, no.1.

Vaitiekus, S. (1992) *National Minorities in Lithuania.* Galve, September, October, November 1992.

Vardys, V.S. (1965) 'Soviet Social Engineering in Lithuania: an Appraisal', in: V.S. Vardys, ed., *Lithuania Under the Soviets: Portrait of a Nation, 1940–65.* London: Frederick A. Praeger.

Vardys, V.S. (1975) 'Modernization and Baltic Nationalism', *Problems of Communism*, vol.24, no.5.

Vardys, V.S. (1978) *The Catholic Church, Dissent and Nationality in Soviet Lithuania.* Boulder, Col.: Westview Press.

Vardys, V.S. (1981a) 'Human Rights Issues in Estonia, Latvia and Lithuania', *Journal of Baltic Studies*, vol.12, no.3.

Vardys, V.S. (1981b) 'Introduction', in: N. Grazulis, ed., *The Chronicle of the Catholic Church in Lithuania*, vol.1. Chicago: Loyola University Press.

Vardys, V.S. (1987) 'The Role of the Churches in the Baltic Republics', *Journal of Baltic Studies*, vol.28, no.3.

Vardys, V.S. (1989) 'Lithuanian National Politics', *Problems of Communism*, vol.38, no.4.

Vardys, V.S. (1990) 'Die Entwicklung der Republic Litauen, S.76', in: Boris Meissner, Hrsg., *Die baltische Nationen: Esland, Lettland, Litauen.* Koeln: Markus.

Vardys, V.S. (1990) 'Lithuanians', in: G. Smith, ed., *The Nationalities Question in the Soviet Union.* London: Longman.

Vardys, V.S. (1991) '*Sajudis*: National Revolution in Lithuania', in: J.A. Trapans, ed., *Towards Independence: the Baltic Popular Movements.* Boulder, Col.: Westview Press.

Vardys, V.S. and Sedaitis, J.B. (1997) *Lithuania: the Rebel Nation.* Boulder, Col.: Westview Press.

Venclova, T. (1995) 'A Fifth Year of Independence: Lithuania, 1922 and 1994', *East European Politics and Society*, vol.9, no.2.

Venclova, T. (1990) 'Some Lithuanians Saved Jews from the Nazis', *Jews and Jewish Topics in the Soviet Union and Eastern Europe*, vol.11, no.1.

Watson, M. (1990) *Contemporary Minority Nationalism.* London: Routledge.

Weber, J. (1997) 'Jews and Judaism in Contemporary Europe: Religion or Ethnic Group', *Ethnic and Racial Studies*, vol.20, no.2.

White, J.D. (1996) 'The Origins of the National Movements in Russia's Baltic Provinces in the Latter Half of the Nineteenth Century', *International Politics* (formerly *Coexistence*), vol.33, no.1, March.

Wirth, L. (1945) 'The Problem of Minority Groups', in: R. Linton, ed., *The Science of Men in the World Crisis*. New York: Columbia University Press.

Wischnitzer, M. (1955) *Die Juden in der Welt*. Berlin: Erich Reiss Verlag.

Rapporteur: Mr Worms (1993) 'Explanatory Memorandum', *Human Rights Law Journal*, vol.14, no.3–4 pp.146–8.

Ycikas, S. (1990) 'Introduction to Lithuanian–Jewish Relations in the Shadow of the Holocaust', *Jews and Jewish Topics in the Soviet Union and Eastern Europe*, vol.11, no.1.

Young, I.M. (1990) *Justice and the Politics of Difference*. Princeton: Princeton University Press.

Zaslavsky, V. (1982) *The Neo-Stalinist State*. New York: M.E. Sharpe.

Zaslavsky, V. (1988) 'Ethnic Group Divided: Social Stratification and Nationality Policy in the Soviet Union', in: P.J. Potichnyj, ed., *Soviet Union Party and Society*. Cambridge: Cambridge University Press.

Zinov'ev, A. (1985) *Homo Sovieticus*. London: Gollancz.

Zukier, H. (1996) 'The Essential "Other" and the Jews: from Antisemitism to Genocide', *Social Research*, vol.63, no.4.

Material collected in Lithuania

Basic Documents of the Second Congress of *Sajudis*. Vilnius, 1990.

Documents on the Polish Autonomy compiled by the Lithuanian Parliament. Vilnius, 1992.

Documents on the Jewish Minority Issues in Lithuania compiled by the Office of Emanuelis Zingeris. Vilnius, 1992.

Lietuvos respublikos gyventoju demografine statistika (tautiniu aspektu). Vilnius: Valstybinis nacionaliniu tyrimy centras, 1992.

Lietuvos respublikos pagrindiniu tautybiu gyventojai. Vilnius: Statistikos departamentas prie Lietuvos Respublikos vyriausybes, 1991.

Lietuvos statistikos metrastis, 1993. Vilnius: Metodinis leidybinis centras, 1994.

Lietuvos statistikos metrastis, 1994–1995. Vilnius: Metodinis leidybinis centras, 1996.

Lietuvos statistikos metrastis, 1996. Vilnius: Metodinis leidybinis centras, 1997.

Lithuanian Political Parties, Political Movements and Political Organisations. Vilnius, 1992.

The Lithuanians in Poland – The Poles in Lithuania, 1994. Warsaw-Vilnius.

National Minorities in Lithuania. Vilnius: Department of Nationalities of the Government of the Republic of Lithuania, 1992.

Negotiation with the Russian Federation Concerning the Withdrawal of Russian Military Forces from the Territory of the Republic of Lithuania. Vilnius: Supreme Council of the Republic of Lithuania, 1992.

The Open Letter to the President of the Lithuanian Republic. Vilnius, 15 March 1993.

Parliamentary Record 1/1992. Vilnius: Supreme Council of the Republic of Lithuania.

Parliamentary Record 4/1992. Vilnius: Supreme Council of the Republic of Lithuania.

Parliamentary Record 5/1992. Vilnius: Supreme Council of the Republic of Lithuania.

Parliamentary Record 11/1992. Vilnius: Supreme Council of the Republic of Lithuania.

The Road to Negotiations wih the USSR. Vilnius: State Publishing House, 1991.

Sajudis: Documents. Vilnius, 1989.

Statisticheskii Ezhegodnik Litvi, 1990. Vilnius: Department Statistiki Litvi, 1991.

Statisticheskii Ezhegodnik Litvi, 1991. Vilnius: Department Statistiki Litvi, 1992.

Statisticheskii Ezhegodnik Litvi, 1992. Vilnius: Department Statistiki Litvi, 1993.

Tautiniu mazumu socialines savijautos tyrimai (Lietuvos Rusai). Vilnius: Tautybiu departamentas prie Lietuvos Respublikos vyriausybes, 1991.

Mimeographs collected in Lithuania

Gaidys, V. *Russians in the Baltic States*.

Rapoport, S. *Litovskoe evreistvo v epohu obshchestvenii peremen* (Lithuanian Jews in the Age of Social Changes).

Sipaviciene, A. *Migration Policy in the Baltic States*.

Vilkas, E. *Lithuania – Interlink of West Europe and Russia*.

Vilkas, E. *Economic Reform in Lithuania*.

Newspapers, journals and reports

The Baltic Independent
Baltic News
The Baltic Times
Eho Litvi
FBIS-SOV
Galve
Golos Litvi: Zerkalo Litovskoi Presi
Journal of the Second Assembly of the League of Nations
Lad
League of Nations – Official Journal
Lietuvos rytas
Nasza Gazeta
Opozicija
Respublika
Vechernie novosti
Vilnius

Interviews

Interview with R. Alisauskiene, Vilnius, 24 June 1993.
Interview with S. Alperovich, Vilnius, 14 December 1992.
Interview with I. Arefjeva, Vilnius, 10 December 1992.
Interview with V. Asovskii, Vilnius, 10 December 1992.
Interview with V. Asovskii, Vilnius, 16 December 1992.
Interview with V. Asovskii, Vilnius, 21 June 1993.
Interview with V. Baranovskii, Vilnius, 15 December 1992.

Interview with L. Bielinis, Vilnius, 6 November 1992.
Interview with V. Cepaitis, Vilnius, 1 December 1992.
Interview with M. Cobot(as), Vilnius, 2 December 1992.
Interview with V. Efremov, Vilnius, 9 November 1992.
Interview with A. Eigirdas, Vilnius, 3 December 1992.
Interview with A. Eigirdas, Vilnius, 4 December 1992.
Interview with P. Frolov, Vilnius, 25 June 1993.
Interview with D. Golinsky, Vilnius, 23 June 1993.
Interview with V. Gruzalis, Vilnius, 15 June 1993.
Interview with V. Gruzalis, Vilnius, 18 June 1993.
Interview with V. Gruzalis, Vilnius, 24 June 1993.
Interview with E. Gruzas, Vilnius, 16 June 1993.
Interview with B. Gruzevskis, Vilnius, 25 June 1993.
Interview with T. Iasinskaia, Vilnius, 18 June 1993.
Interview with S. Ietuhov, Vilnius, 27 November 1992.
Interview with M. Jakobas, Vilnius, 4 November 1992.
Interview with V. Jarmolenka, Vilnius, 15 December 1992.
Interview with A. Juozaitis, Vilnius, 11 December 1992.
Interview with G. Kanovich, Vilnius, 5 November 1992.
Interview with J. Karosas, Vilnius, 28 October 1992.
Interview with N. Kasatkina, Vilnius, 24 June 1993.
Interview with Archbishop Khrizostom, Vilnius, 18 June 1993.
Interview with G. Kirkilas, Vilnius, 23 November 1992.
Interview with G. Kirkilas, Vilnius, 22 June 1993.
Interview with H. Kobeckaite, Vilnius, 30 October 1992.
Interview with H. Kobeckaite, Vilnius, 22 June 1993.
Interview with E. Krukauskiene, Vilnius, 3 December 1992.
Interview with A. Kubilius, Vilnius, 23 November 1992.
Interview with A. Kulakauskas, Vilnius, 2 December 1992.
Interview with A. Kulakauskas, Vilnius, 22 June 1993.
Interview with A. Kuliesius, Vilnius, 29 October 1992.
Interview with J. Lakis, Vilnius, 3 November 1992.
Interview with V. Landsbergis, Vilnius, 24 November 1992.
Interview with P. Lavrinec, Vilnius, 8 December 1992.
Interview with P. Lavrinec, Vilnius, 16 June 1993.
Interview with Z. Mackiewicz, Vilnius, 2 December 1992.
Interview with N. Makeeva, Vilnius, 25 June 1993.
Interview with J. Marcinkevicius, Vilnius, 3 December 1992.
Interview with E. Matvekas, Vilnius, 23 June 1993.
Interview with N. Medvedev, Vilnius, 26 November 1992.
Interview with N. Medvedev, Vilnius, 29 November 1992.
Interview with I. Melianas, Vilnius, 30 October 1992.
Interview with T. Muzhnjova, Vilnius, 8 December 1992.
Interview with R. Ozolas, Vilnius, 27 November 1992.
Interview with E. Petrov(as), Vilnius, 11 November 1992.
Interview with E. Petrov(as), Vilnius, 4 December 1992.
Interview with E. Petrov(as), Vilnius, 18 December 1992.
Interview with E. Petrov(as), Vilnius, 25 June 1993.
Interview with A. Plokszto, Vilnius, 5 November 1992.

Interview with A. Plokszto, Vilnius, 15 June 1993.
Interview with T. Pogozhilskaia, Vilnius, 11 December 1992.
Interview with E. Raisuotis, Vilnius, 21 June 1993.
Interview with S. Rapoport, Vilnius, 14 December 1992.
Interview with O. Ruzelyte, Vilnius, 27 November 1992.
Interview with Z. Siemenowicz, Vilnius, 3 December 1992.
Interview with A. Skakowska, Vilnius, 5 December 1992.
Interview with K. Skrebys, Vilnius, 25 November 1992.
Interview with N. Sokolov, Vilnius, 18 June 1993.
Interview with M. Stakvilevicius, Vilnius, 17 June 1993.
Interview with E. Staneika, Vilnius, 2 November 1992.
Interview with E. Sviklas, Vilnius, 2 November 1992.
Interview with S. Temchin, Vilnius, 27 November 1992.
Interview with S. Vaitiekus, Vilnius, 8 December 1992.
Interview with E. Vilkas, Vilnius, 28 October 1992.
Interview with R. Zepkaite, Vilnius, 24 June 1993.

Alperovich, Simon   152, 154
Anderson, Benedict   84
anti-Semitism   21, 31–4, 38, 137,
      138, 140, 141, 146, 149, 151–5,
      162
Arefjeva, Irina   87, 97
Arendt, Hannah   24, 153
Arutiunian, Iurii   47
Asovskii, Vitalii   100

Baranovskii, Vasilii   85
Belorus/ Belorussia   112, 119
Bernhardt, R.   64, 70
Bobbio, Norberto   11
Bobelis, Kazys   65
Brazauskas, Algirdas   52, 54, 55, 58,
      70, 91, 150, 162
Brezhnev, Leonid   19, 45, 46, 52
Britain   33
Brizgys, Bishop Vincentas   39
Brubaker, Rogers   59

Cepaitis, Virgilijus   57, 62, 71, 131
*Chronicle of the Lithuanian Catholic
      Church*   48
Ciser, Lewis   54
citizenship   4–6, 9, 12, 14, 42, 43,
      59, 60, 61, 63–5, 68, 69, 71, 77,
      80, 89–91, 105, 118, 155, 157
   active and passive   6
   defined in inclusive terms   4, 14,
      18, 77
civil rights   6, 74
civil society   5, 9, 10, 12, 46, 74, 102,
      136, 156
Cobot(as) Metard(as)   114, 120, 126
collective rights   5–9, 22, 85, 87,109,
      113, 115, 157
   'polyethnic rights'   7, 8, 95, 113,
      122, 123, 129
   'self-government rights'   7, 20
   'special representation rights'   7, 8,
      95, 116, 122, 123

Communist Party of Lithuania   44,
      49–56, 58, 88, 124, 131, 132, 134
cultural autonomy   5, 7, 29, 31, 62,
      85, 87, 109, 113, 115, 131
Czar Nikolai I   48

Dahrendorf, Ralph   54
democracy   3, 5, 9, 11, 18, 19, 61,
      134, 156, 163
democratic past/ tradition   4, 5, 19, 41
difference   9, 11, 14, 18, 78, 84, 136
dissident movement   19, 49, 50, 58
Dmitriev, Sergei   160

Eastern Europe   9, 10, 12, 14, 16, 24,
      48, 103
Edinstvo   44, 81, 88, 89, 98, 99, 100,
      101, 142
Eigirdas, Arunas   121, 124, 128, 161
Eltsin, Boris   91, 104
emigration   151
equality   12, 13
Estonia   3, 25, 68

fascism   21
Friedman, Bernard   30
Frolov, Piotr   98, 103
Future Forum   57

Gaon Elijah   162
Gazeta Wyborca   116
Gediminas, Grand Duke   33, 137
Gellner, Ernest   46
'Genocide Day of the Jews'   147
Germany   22, 33, 35, 77, 144
glasnost   10, 11, 52
Gorbachev, Mikhail   47, 51, 52, 56,
      86, 87
Gruzalis, Vladimiras   105, 106, 121
Gruzas, Edvardas   91
Gruzevskis, Boguslavas   93, 107
Gudeliai   119
Guinier, Lani   8

heterogeneity   11, 18
Hitler, Adolf   35
Holocaust   15, 19, 21, 37, 39, 137,
    138, 140–2, 144, 145, 147, 148,
    150, 151, 159, 162, 163
Homo Sovieticus   46, 88, 101, 115
Hroch, Miroslav   15

Iasinskaia, Tat'iana   93, 94, 97, 105
Ietuhov, Sergei   92
Ignalina   11
immigration   68, 104
independence   5, 43, 45, 50, 51, 56,
    59, 74, 81, 86, 88, 90, 98, 104,
    124, 133, 137, 140, 142
individual rights   6, 8, 10, 85, 95,
    113, 157
International Covenant of Civil and
    Political Rights   8
international laws   3, 60, 61
Israel   37, 151, 152, 161
Ivanov, Valerii   100, 101, 117

Jakobas, Misha   141
Janowsky, Oscar   32
Jarmolenka, Vladimir   105
Jefremov, Vladimir   43, 84
Jeruzalem of Lithuania   97, 154
'Jews of Lithuania'   144, 145
Jewish Community of Vilnius   141
Jewish national autonomy   20, 26–8,
    30, 31, 42
Juozaitis, Arvydas   57, 58, 104, 133,
    152
Jursenas, Ceslavas   150, 160

Kanovich, Grigorii   140, 152
Karosas, Juozas   49, 73
Kasatkina, Natalija   86, 87, 102, 105
Kaunas (also Kovno)   27, 33, 34, 37,
    39, 40, 56, 77, 100, 112, 138
Keane, John   9
kehilla   28–30
Khrizostom, Archbishop   92, 96, 100
Khushchev, Nikita   19, 44–6
Kirkilas, Gediminas   49, 57, 154
Klaipeda   20, 22, 31, 40, 66, 77, 134,
    138
Konrad, George   10, 46

Krukauskiene, Eugenija   90, 111, 126
Kulakauskas, Antanas   131
Kymlicka, Will   7, 122

Lad   97
Lakis, Juozas   85, 87
Landsbergis, Vytautas   33, 49, 57, 58,
    100, 132, 135, 148, 156, 157
language   4, 12, 13, 45, 55, 59, 66,
    67, 85, 90, 93, 99, 101, 104, 109,
    112, 113, 122, 123, 130–3, 158,
    160
  language *po prostemu*   111, 112,
    126
Latvia   3, 22, 25, 27, 68, 100
Lavrinec, Pavel   97
League of Nations   20, 22–6, 40
Levin, Dov   36, 149
Levin, Nora   151
Lieven, Anatol   117, 147
Lithuanian Democratic Labour Party
    (LDDP)   15, 55, 58, 87, 90, 94,
    99, 119–21, 129, 135, 138, 149,
    150, 154, 158, 159, 163
Lithuanian Freedom League   14
'Lithuanian Jews'   113, 142, 143, 145
Lithuanian Jewish Community   140
Lithuanian national movement,
    Sajudis   3, 4, 8, 11, 13, 14,
    17–19, 43–6, 49, 51, 52, 54–7,
    59, 72, 73, 77, 79, 84–6, 88, 89,
    94, 96, 100, 104, 108, 115, 119,
    123, 128, 130–2, 134, 136–8,
    149, 154, 156, 158
  first congress   52, 147
  second congress   14, 56
  third congress   57, 58
'Lithuanian Poles'   113, 114, 115,
    116, 124, 126, 128, 135, 143
'Lithuanian Russians'   84, 85, 87–90,
    95, 97, 100, 102, 103, 107, 108,
    113, 143

Macartney, C.A.   26, 29
Maciejkaniec, Ryszard   116, 118
Magazyn Wilenski   127
Makeeva, Nina   94
Makelis, Edvardas   161
Maley, William   83

Marcinkevicius, Justinas   43, 45
Matvekas, Evaldas   97
Mazeikiai   105
Medvedev, Nikolai   41, 56, 73, 86, 89
Melucci, Alberto   9
memory   12, 20, 45, 79, 85, 118,
     127, 128, 138, 150
migration   81, 103, 105, 106
Mikniskes (Michnovo) Orthodox
     Community   41
Ministry for Jewish Affairs   28–30
Minority Declaration   20, 25, 26,
     28–30, 40, 41
Minority Treaties   18, 24–6, 30,
     40, 41
Mouffe, Chantal   9
Mussolini, Benedito   35

Nasza Gazeta   127
'national communists'   45
national identity   5, 14, 43, 45, 48,
     54, 62, 77, 79, 81, 84, 89, 103,
     107, 109, 111, 118, 120, 127,
     140, 156, 162
National Jewish Council   28–30, 40
national movements   5, 13, 14, 19,
     31, 79
nationalism   3, 4, 12, 15, 18, 42, 47,
     77, 81, 91, 103, 107, 156–8
   defined in exclusive terms   4, 14,
     18, 42
Nationalist Union   32, 33

Obertishev, Nikolai   94
Okinczyc, Czeslaw   114, 127
Old Believers   41, 83, 85
Oleszczuk, Thomas   47, 48
opposition movements   17, 43, 47,
     50, 51
Ozolas, Romualdas   51, 58, 71, 125,
     131, 132

Palauskas, Arturas   150
Peace Conference   18, 22, 24, 26, 40
Peace Treaties   22, 24
perestroika   51, 86, 137, 144, 152
Petro(as), Eugenij(us)   90, 97, 131,
     133, 134
Ploksto, Artur   40, 115, 119, 121, 123

pluralism   9
plurality   11, 18
Pogozhlskaia Tat'iana   100
Poland   4, 22, 24, 25, 27, 40, 88, 111,
     112, 114–20, 123, 128, 129,
     132
'Poles of Lithuania'   115, 116, 122,
     124, 126, 128, 135
Polish Electoral Action   161
Polish University   72, 114, 119, 120,
     121
Polisudski, Jozef   117
political autonomy   5, 109, 115
political rights   6, 74, 99, 131
Polonisation   15, 111, 112, 122
Prunskiene, Kazimiera   57

Raisuotis, Erevistas   68, 119
Rapoport, Sergei   141
Roman Catholic Church in Lithuania
     48
Rose, Richard   78, 83
Russia   27, 43, 88, 94
Russian Community   92, 101
Russian Cultural Centre   16, 81,
     98–101
Russian Society   101
'Russians of Lithuania'   86–90, 92,
     94–7, 100, 101, 103, 105, 108
Russification   15, 46, 50, 51, 112,
     117, 159

Sakharov, Andrei   48
Salcininkai (Soleczniki) region   109,
     117, 118, 123, 125, 126, 128,
     130–3, 135, 161
Schermers, H.   64, 70
Sedaitis, Judith   71
Senkewicz, Jan   161
Shinkariova, Ana   93
Shtromas, Aleksandras   49, 53
Siauliai   37
Siemenowicz, Zbigniew   120
Sipaviciene, Audra   105
Skakowska, Apolonia   119, 121, 126
Skubiszewski, Krzystof   133
Slezevicius, Adolfas   162
Smetona, Antanas   33
Smith, Theresa   47

Snieckus, Antanas   53
social movements   10
social rights   6, 74
Sokolov, Nikolai   72
Soloveichik, Max   28
Soviet era/ period   6, 18, 19, 45, 48,
     49, 51–3, 56, 71, 72, 88, 99, 104,
     113, 142, 144, 152, 156, 158,
     159
'Soviet Jews'   142
'Soviet Poles'   117, 128, 135, 142
'Soviet Russians'   88, 89, 103, 126
Soviet Socialist Republic of Lithuania
     4, 14, 19, 22, 35, 36, 150, 158
Soviet Union   22, 39, 43–54, 57, 74,
     79, 85–9, 100, 103, 104, 107,
     109, 111, 117, 130, 134, 142,
     144, 145, 152
Sovietisation   15, 46, 50, 58, 117,
     134, 157
Stakvilevicius, Mindaugas   72, 90, 91,
     121
Suslov, Mikhail   151
Svencionys   37
Sviklas, Eduardas   105

Temchin, Sergei   94
'territorial bureaucracy' model   53,
     54
Terliackas, Antanas   153
Touraine, Alan   13
Truska, Liudas   146
Turska, Halina   112
tutejszy   111, 112, 128

Union of Poles   109, 112, 114, 115,
     119, 120, 123, 134

Valancius, Bishop Motiejus   48
van der Stoel, Max   70
Vardys, V. Stanley   50, 71
Venclova, Tomas   54, 128
Versaite, Irene   147
Verslininkaj   32
Vilkas, Eduardas   108, 130
Vilnija   128
Vilnius (also Wilno/Vilna)   15, 27,
     33, 35, 37, 41, 56, 66, 101, 105,
     115, 116, 118–22, 127, 137, 138,
     150, 162, 163
Vilnius   97
Vilnius Question   25, 117, 122, 127,
     128
Vilnius region   25, 31, 40, 109, 112,
     117–19, 123, 125, 126, 128,
     130–5, 161, 162
Visaginas   105
Voldemaras, Augustinas   33
Vytautas the Great   38

Warsaw   27, 115
Wilson, Woodrow   22

Young, Iris Marion   7, 122

Zarasai   112
Zeligowski, General Lucijan   22, 31,
     117, 129
Zemyna club   11
Zepkaite, Regina   41
Zhirinovski, Vladimir   91
Zingeris, E.   16, 162
Zingeris, Markas   162
Ziukas, Povilis-Vytautas   107
Znad Willie   97